◆ WOODWORK PROJECTS ◆

DOLLS' HOUSES

Geoffrey West

◆

The Crowood Press

First Published in 1996 by
The Crowood Press Ltd
Ramsbury, Marlborough
Wiltshire SN8 2HR

British Library Cataloguing-in-Publication Data

A catalogue reference for this book is available from the British Library

ISBN 1 85223 957 3

Line illustrations by Bob Constant.
Photographs by the author except for those on pages 25, 54 and 108 by Tony Cooper.

Acknowledgements
With thanks to Bostick Ltd for giving me detailed technical information about their comprehensive range of adhesives. I would like to acknowledge the help of Kristin Baybar, Gospel Oak Village, London and The Dolls House at Bromley, Kent – two specialist shops that also stock a wide range of accessories.

Typefaces used: text, New Baskerville and Garamond; headings, Optima Bold.

Typeset and designed by
D & N Publishing, Ramsbury, Wiltshire SN8 2HR

Printed in Great Britain.

CONTENTS

CHAPTER one

Concept to Completion

Thomas Chippendale and other leading eighteenth-century furniture designers made dolls' houses that were exact copies of real buildings, filled with furniture that replicated their own full-sized creations. Those gifted with patience and tenacity sometimes like to approach the dolls'-house maker's craft with the same attention to detail, but more often a less rigid approach is chosen, so that projects originally envisaged for a full-sized house can be realized in miniature within a reasonable time-scale. Consequently, dolls'-house makers (or miniaturists) range from those who like to work to a high level of precision and accuracy to artists and craftspeople who wish to express their own ideas in a flexible way. Alternatively, a dolls' house may be designed for a young child, who simply wants to use it for play. This book contains detailed plans and instructions for making three complete houses, of varying complexity but each of a totally different type.

Over two centuries ago dolls' houses were made principally for adults. During the intervening years, most people's perception of a dolls' house was that of a child's toy, but now there is a growing trend towards adult ownership again, where perfect reproductions or interesting styles are becoming collectors' items. This is particularly apparent in the USA. where dolls' houses are referred to as 'doll houses'.

There are miniaturists' craft fairs held regularly all over the country where craftsmen and women display their work, and museums, such as the Bethnal Green Museum of Childhood, have a range of houses on view; there are also several thriving dolls'-house collectors' magazines.

While smaller children may not appreciate the intricacies of a perfectly crafted house, older, more discerning youngsters may take a deep interest in detail, and will probably want to make additions and contribute ideas at the planning stage. The house will become a valued item, often shared between parents and children who will treat its decoration and furnishing as a continuing hobby, passing it down from generation to generation until eventually it becomes a family heirloom.

Taking trouble over internal architectural features such as staircases and banister rails, fireplaces and hearths is time well spent, since these are the things that can make the difference between a bland, impersonal interior and one that is interesting and looks 'lived in'. The internationally recognized scale is 1:12, which corresponds to currently available accessories.

Once the dolls' house has been constructed, furnishings and furniture can be added. Wallpaper with small-scale designs is available, as are tiny items such as miniature paintings for the walls, and kitchen and bathroom fittings.

Every style of house has clearly defined characteristics pertaining to the architectural era being copied. Dolls' houses built in the Georgian style are always popular as the belief in the importance of perfect mathematical proportion between different room measurements and external features was intrinsic to the early eighteenth-century builders' philosophy.

Andreas Palladio and Inigo Jones, the sixteenth-century architects whose work inspired the early Georgian architects, believed that true perfection of form could be attained in everyday life; they considered that realization of mathematical ideals would allow architects to mirror the true perfection of nature itself.

Palladian principles of proportion influenced the majority of Georgian house exteriors until the late eighteenth century, when technological advances gave rise to larger windows, simpler door-cases and stuccoed brickwork. Door patterns of the period varied enormously, but most characteristic was the six-panelled design. Door-cases were normally arranged in the Palladian 'temple front' manner: two pilasters or columns supporting an entablature, perhaps topped by a segmental or triangular pediment. This pediment was later dominated by ever-increasing sizes of fanlight. Interiors of Georgian houses are also characterized by strict symmetry, as well as elaborate cornices, friezes, pilasters and ornate mouldings. Fireplaces and ceiling decorations were typified by the work of Robert Adam, and furniture by Chippendale, Hepplewhite and Sheraton.

In stark contrast, Tudor dwellings are anything but disciplined in design. Irregularly positioned external beams, roofs and gables may sometimes slope at surprising angles, the whole structure occasionally resembling a Tudor galleon – which, since the builders were often originally shipwrights, is hardly surprising. Derived from the very crude 'cruck' design, in which adjacent living trees were bent horizontally and lashed together so as to provide the semblance of a roof to build from, Tudor homes still evoke the charm and shadow-ridden mystery of a lost age. The black ceiling beams, brick fireplaces, and oak-timbered and uneven flagstoned floors of their interiors can all be created in miniature.

Cottages vary according to the prevailing vernacular style, and are often defined by colours of roofing tiles, whether external timbering is used, differing hues of stone or brick and many other seemingly random factors. Some, of course, have thatched roofs.

When designing a house, it is a good idea to decide first on an external style and then work from the inside out. Decide on the number and position of rooms first, then accommodate these within the chosen shell.

The three dolls' houses detailed in this book are envisaged as complete projects, with methodical attention to detail and accuracy. Therefore, if for any reason the reader decides to alter any of the measurements, he or she should think through the whole job before starting and, in the light of the alterations, recalculate sizes as necessary.

Floorboards can be reproduced by carving grooves in good-quality plywood. Flagstones can be made from air-hardening clay, and mosaic tiles can be imitated by cutting vinyl floor tiles to size. Walls are normally plain, sometimes with skirting boards (thin moulding) and possibly a picture rail. For certain periods of house, wainscoting (wooden panelling) from floor level to half-way up the wall may be appropriate; wood veneer would give best results for this, with the top rail made from decorative moulding.

Various types of ceiling can be reproduced. The joists and cross-beams of Tudor dwellings can be copied using standard mouldings carved at the edges to produce an age-worn effect. Black beams against white ceilings are remarkably effective, lending mystique and authenticity to a Tudor interior. For Georgian and Victorian houses, central ceiling roses can be purchased from specialist dolls'-house shops. Decorative wooden mouldings may be used for cornices and friezes.

For fireplaces, hearths and mantlepieces, straightforward designs can be made relatively easily. Air-hardening clay can be used to make brick fireplaces, these then painted for authenticity.

Staircases and banister rails are usually made from wood, and can have piano wire for the rails. Good wooden banister rails are available from dolls'-house shops. Tudor houses might have straightforward oak staircases, or spiral stairs which wind around a central pillar.

Doors can be constructed from 9mm (⅜in) plywood or MDF (medium-density fibreboard), and architraving (the door surround) from timber moulding. An advantage of using MDF for doors is that it can be carved so as to reproduce panels.

Construction normally follows the same basic pattern for any house. First there is the planning stage, where dimensions can be judged from paper or cardboard cutouts, or by 'scaling up' from photographs. Next, mark out the main components and cut them from plywood and/or MDF. Then assemble the structure using screws only, and no adhesive (first fix).

The next stage should be the construction and hanging of the opening front section, and the cutting and assembly of windows and frames. The roof and any chimney(s) should be fitted afterwards. The house is then dismantled.

Parts of the assembly that will be internal panels are then surface-finished, and all doors and architraves are decorated and fitted. The structure is then reassembled and final adjustments made, and the walls and floors are fixed permanently in position.

Finally, the various internal fittings (staircase, banisters, fireplaces and so on) are made and fixed in place, and the exterior is then surface-finished.

This book contains detailed instructions for the construction of three quite different houses. First there is the country cottage, where the design is simple, the house is relatively inexpensive to make, and it is attractive to children and adults alike. The prototype for this house was finished in white-painted stipplecast, with shuttered windows and a tiled roof. Internally, there are four rooms, with boarded floors.

The Tudor house is a more intricate project for those who like a type of architecture that is rich in atmosphere. It has a front double-door opening, and a removable tiled roof. The outside is timber-beam construction; the inside has flagstone floors, a brick fireplace, Tudor-style boarded doors, ceiling beams and dark oak floorboarding. There are seven rooms.

Finally, there is the large Georgian house, with eight rooms. This project requires time and patience as there is plenty of internal detail. The outside features quoins (corner stones), elaborate finials and a portico, and realistic glazed windows; inside there are panelled doors, floorboards, metal banister rails and plain fireplaces.

CHAPTER 

Materials and Tools

MATERIALS

Until a few years ago, plywood was chosen for the construction of craftsman-made dolls' houses, while cheaper, mass-produced products were made from hardboard, plastic or stiff card. Nowadays, however, medium-density fibreboard (MDF), is frequently used to very good effect, especially for the main shell of a house. A typical dolls' house is likely to contain MDF, plywood, various timber mouldings and acetate for windows. Other materials used will include all adhesives, paints and physical fixing devices such as screws, nails, hinges etc. Model shops, of the kind used by model-railway and aircraft constructors, are valuable sources for the more unusual materials, but timber merchants and DIY stores stock most of the items detailed below.

(M) in the following text indicates that a model shop is the most likely place to find a particular material. Specialist dolls'-house shops may also sell useful items such as fire grates and carved newel posts for stairs, although some of these specialist items can be very expensive. These shops also sell such things as tiny hinges and screws for internal doors, which may be difficult to find anywhere else.

SHEET MATERIALS FOR MAIN STRUCTURE AND INTERNAL WALLS

Medium-density fibreboard (MDF)

This material is brown and has a dense cross-section. Made from softwood forest thinnings, it is stable in sheet form, with no splits or knots, and is suitable for routing (cutting a groove) and carving.

Advantages: MDF has a perfect surface finish, little tendency to warp, is easy to cut and drill, and is reasonably priced. It bonds readily to itself and other timbers with conventional wood glue (PVA adhesive). It can be carved to make realistic window shutters, panelled doors and so on because the material is of equal density throughout, unlike plywood.

Disadvantages: MDF lacks intrinsic strength. The lack of fibrous grain means that nails will not hold; chipboard-thread screws have to be used instead, with a correctly sized pilot hole made first so that the screw does not split the material.

Thickness: 6mm (¼in), 9mm (⅜in), 12mm (½in) and upwards.

Safety precautions when working with MDF: When cutting MDF with a jigsaw or when power sanding, always wear a face mask with a filter designed for use with wood dust, and keep the working area ventilated (open a window); MDF dust is especially fine and could possibly cause irritation.

Plywood

Plywood is manufactured from a number of thin sheets of timber that have been bonded together. This material varies in quality and price, the best (birch) being light in colour with a very close-grained surface finish; in cross-section it is firm and non-friable. The cheaper varieties tend to be darker in colour, the cross-section of less dense, more crumbly material and the surface finish of a looser grain altogether.

Advantages: Plywood is strong and robust. It will hold panel pins and screws reasonably well, even in edges (except when these fixing devices need to be load-bearing). The grained surface lends itself to the replication of floorboards or wainscoting panels. Plywood is easily stained to a darker colour, and gives a good finish when sealed with polyurethane varnish. It bonds easily to itself and to other timbers.

Disadvantages: The surface of plywood needs to be grain-filled if a good paint finish is required. The cross-section is sometimes noticeably coarse and uneven, and there is occasional warping over large areas. On purchase, the timber surface must be checked for flaws such as woodworm exit holes and knots.

Thickness: 3mm (⅛in), 6mm (¼in), 9mm (⅜in), 12mm (½in) and upwards in standard size sheets, as well as smaller sheet sizes of 0.8mm (1⁄32in) and 1.5mm (1⁄16in) available from model shops.

Acetate sheet

Acetate sheet is used for windows. It is very thin, and is normally available in small sheets (300 × 210mm/11¾ × 8¼in). It is safer and easier to cut than glass. (M).

SUNDRY TIMBER AND METAL ITEMS

Timber mouldings

Normally made of ramin (a hardwood) or softwood, these come in a variety of cross-sectional profiles: round dowelling, quadrant (quarter of a circle), picture-frame type (various profiles), square, rectangle, plus many more. These mouldings are used widely for internal/external additions for strength or decoration.

Balsa wood

Balsa is an extremely soft, light timber with a spongy grain, useful for external or internal decoration where carving is required. It has no structural strength whatsoever and can be cut with a craft knife. It is obtainable in a wide variety of profiles and sizes. (M).

Piano wire

Useful for banister rails. It is very hard and non-elastic, and cannot be cut with a hacksaw. In fact, it can only be cut using the slot on the side of the jaws of pliers and considerable force is required (M).

MALLEABLE MATERIALS

Filling compounds

Typically white or grey pastes, these compounds are normally ready mixed and are basically inert filler powders suspended in a water-soluble solvent. The difference between ordinary filler and fine filler is that smaller particles are used in the latter, producing a smoother paste that sands easily and fills the tiniest crevices (hence it is often called 'surface-finish filler'). Fillers can be smoothed with a knife whilst wet to produce a good finish.

Polyester-resin fillers

These compounds are intended for use with metal or glass fibre, and are unnecessarily expensive to use with wood or wood compounds. They cure by chemical reaction, not by evaporation of solvent, and therefore cannot be smoothed whilst wet but must be left slightly proud of the surface and sanded level afterwards. They are useful when gap-filling in metal, or when making good gap-filling joints between metal and wood. Available from car-accessory shops.

Wood fillers

Suitable wood fillers are air-drying pastes, available in a range of timber colours. They are ideal for filling holes invisibly in timber that is to be sealed with polyurethane varnish.

Modelling clay

There are two types of air-hardening clay generally available. One type dries fairly quickly on exposure to the atmosphere (it is wrapped tightly in foil or plastic), and is useful for large-scale projects such as modelling bricks on fireplaces, making paving slabs and other similar applications. This is the type used for the projects in this book. The other type requires oven heat to dry and may well be suited to particular projects, especially small-scale ones. Both types are obtainable from model shops or art materials suppliers.

FIXING DEVICES

Panel pins

These are thin nails specially designed to minimize damage to the grain of host timber; their small heads are easily punched below the wood surface and the subsequent depression can be filled invisibly.

Screws

Screws are used for pulling two surfaces together, or for where nailing is inappropriate (hinges, doors and so on). Screws that are to be load-bearing – for instance those intended to bear the weight of a house front – will not grip adequately in the end grain of plywood or MDF because the grain is not as tightly packed as in timber. In this situation a fillet of timber should be bonded into the edge of the panel to receive the screws. Screws have a cross-head (Pozidriv or Phillips) or slots, and for most purposes are countersunk. The diameter is measured in the UK by figures: 1 (smallest) to 14 (huge), and in length from 6mm (¼in) upwards. For constructional work, as opposed to fastening hinges, a usual diameter size for miniaturist purposes would be 4. Bright finish (rust-proofed) steel is normally adequate, but brass screws are used for fastening brass hinges; these are softer and pilot holes may need to be made with steel screws first. For applications where screws must hold in plywood or MDF, always use chipboard-type screws, whose particularly close thread continues along the complete length.

Hinges

Hinges are normally made of brass. The largest likely to be used (for hanging opening house fronts) is 50mm (2in). Larger rectangular hinges with an opening inner panel are sometimes used on bigger houses, as are piano hinges. The latter are long strips of continuously hinged metal, drilled for screws at intervals and usually made of light steel; plastic piano hinges are unsuitable.

Tiny hinges (9mm/⅜in) made of very thin brass-finish steel are useful for internal and external doors; these hinges are available from good hardware or model shops or places specializing in dolls'-house fittings, as are the necessary miniature screws.

ADHESIVES

Wood adhesive, or 'white glue'

'White glue' is the most useful adhesive of all, ideal for all woods including plywood

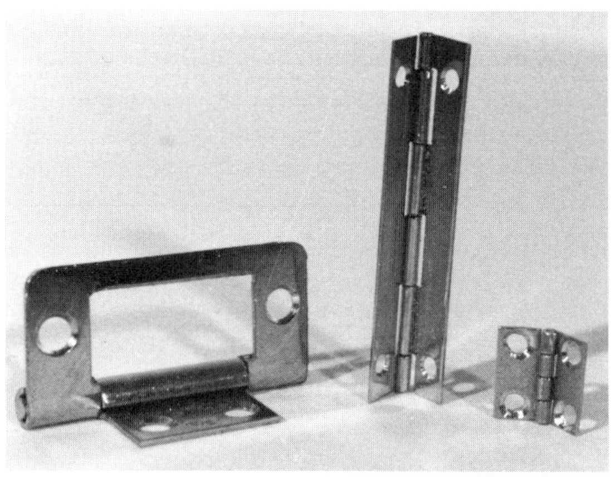

Various types of hinge.

and MDF, and is a white, non-flammable, water-borne adhesive based on polyvinyl acetate (PVA). Most manufacturers produce a special rapid-hardening type which is more viscous than the standard PVA glue and is specifically formulated for wood. The standard PVA is less glutinous and thus more suitable for bonding paper, cardboard and other porous materials, while still remaining an excellent wood glue.

After an even layer is applied to both clean surfaces, the joint is pressed together so that an immediate suction bond is formed. When one or both of the pieces to be joined is relatively light and there are no external forces (such as from warping) that may pull the joint apart, clamping is unnecessary. If, however, weight or other factors pull the two surfaces apart so that no suction bond can form, clamping or screwing is vital until the adhesive is dry. Drying time is dependent on the volume of applied adhesive, ambient temperature and so on. Where the joint pulls apart and it is impractical to apply pressure, another adhesive should be used.

White glue works well because the liquid penetrates and is absorbed into the top layers of grain, ultimately forming a joint that is normally stronger than the material itself.

Advantages: This adhesive is clean, neat, non-toxic, non-flammable and easy to use. It is inexpensive, and spills are easily removed with a damp cloth. It is the best and most widely used general woodworking adhesive.

Disadvantages: White glue is only suitable for porous materials (and possibly some plastics, according to the manufacturer's recommendations). Joints sometimes have to be pressed (clamped).

Typical applications: Used for making the main shell of a house; also for all general woodworking where a suction bond will form or where pressing the joint is an option. Generally speaking, PVAs are unsuitable for non-porous materials such as metals; however, some manufacturers claim that standard PVA will bond certain plastics (check the manufacturer's recommendations).

Contact adhesive: solvent-borne neoprene

A fawn-coloured gel adhesive based on polychloroprene rubber, suitable for bonding most materials, both porous and non-porous. As with other solvent-borne adhesives, both cleaned surfaces are coated, allowed to dry and then brought together; and the joint will instantly 'grab' to make a powerful bond. These products are available as a thick gel, or a liquid.

Advantages: A very strong instant bond is formed without the need for clamping. This adhesive will work with a wide variety of materials, and will even bond painted articles without the need for cleaning surfaces.

Disadvantages: Contact is a difficult adhesive glue to use neatly; spills are hard to remove and only acetone or nail polish remover will work. It is flammable and also has a strong chemical odour in use. Because this adhesive does not penetrate the material surface the bond is less permanent, yet even so it is adequate for most purposes.

Typical application: Fixing a painted staircase to a wall, where strength is required and screws are inappropriate.

Clear adhesive: solvent-borne, based on nitrile rubber

This will stick most materials and in many ways is similar to neoprene, except that it is cleaner to use and has a less powerful odour. Clear adhesive is used in the same way as neoprene. The dried film is virtually colourless and non-staining.

Advantages: As neoprene, but it is lighter, cleaner and quicker in use. The initial drying time is faster, so that surfaces can be brought together sooner.

Disadvantages: Not quite such a powerful bond as neoprene, therefore less suitable where a high bond-strength is required. It is relatively expensive when used over large areas. It is flammable, and although it has an odour this is not so strong as that of neoprene.

Typical application: Fixing painted window frames to a painted house frontage; there is no need to strip to bare wood.

Epoxy resin

A two-part thick viscous paste that has to be mixed; it cures by chemical reaction. It will bond most materials, porous or non-porous. It has the added advantage that it is gap-filling – in essence it behaves like an extraordinarily adhesive liquid plastic. One type takes hours to dry, but there is a newer, quick-drying kind. It is ideal for metal-to-metal or metal-to-wood bonds where gap-filling is required, and is one of the most powerful adhesives known.

Advantages: It has a gap-filling capacity, dries clear, and has an excellent bond. Clamping is not required. It has a wide range of applications.

Disadvantages: The joint has to be supported (not clamped) in position until it is set – there is no 'grab', as with contacts. The drying time is slow, even for the specially accelerated formulation. It is expensive.

Typical application: Fixing metal banister rails to wooden stairs, especially where the rails fit too loosely in the receptor holes.

Super Glue: cyanoacrylate

Cleanliness is essential for this colourless liquid to work successfully, but an instant permanent bond is formed with only momentary pressure required. Super Glue dries by reaction with atmospheric moisture. It was principally designed for non-porous surfaces such as metals, but it will also bond wood (hard, tightly grained wood preferably) and many other materials, with the exception of fabric, paper and card. Various formulations have been developed for different materials (glass, metal, plastics), but the standard type is useful for most applications. A gel (non-drip) Super Glue is now available, which is easier to apply and has a marginally slower drying time, thus allowing for repositioning mistakes.

Advantages: It dries rapidly and bonds strongly. It is perfect for small-scale work, and is clean and neat.

Disadvantages: Not the ideal glue for softwood or other porous materials, and nor is it any use for gap-filling – it will only work on close-fitting joints. It is expensive, and is therefore only viable for specific, limited applications. It is potentially dangerous as it bonds to the skin in seconds.

Typical application: Constructing delicate small-scale wooden furniture or mitre-jointed window frames where screws and nails are inappropriate and clamps cannot be used.

PAINTS AND OTHER SURFACE FINISHES

Primer (oil-based)

A primer must be applied to bare woods that are to be painted subsequently.

Emulsion paint

A water-based paint that dries to a matt or silk (slight sheen) finish. Emulsion is the usual paint of choice for the exterior walls of a house.

Gloss paint

An oil-based paint that requires an oil-based undercoat. It is used for interior mouldings, and exterior window and door frames.

Woodstain/varnish

Woodstain is a spirit-based chemical that penetrates wood grain to darken it. It is never possible to make a wooden surface lighter by staining. Once stained, the surface needs to be sealed by a polyurethane varnish (clear yellowy liquid) to give a gloss finish. A range of stain colours is readily available, as are combination stainers/sealers. Clear polyurethane varnish alone will bring out the beauty in any timber, whether stained or left plain. Although it always darkens wood slightly, the resultant sheen is impressive and the cheapest plywood can be made to look like beautiful Scandinavian pine.

Textured coating material

A plaster-based finish developed for decorating plaster surfaces within the home. Used for replicating stipplecast finish on exterior house surfaces.

TOOLS

Most of the tools required are standard DIY hand tools. An electric drill is necessary and so is a jigsaw. If these are not available, then hiring might be a worthwhile option, particularly as the work can be planned to make optimum use of hire time.

STANDARD TOOLS REQUIRED

Saws A handsaw will be needed for general cutting of larger battens. Also, a fine-toothed tenon saw is necessary for mitre cutting and general cutting-to-size of fine mouldings. A hacksaw (large) is required for cutting steel screws, nails or metal generally, and a junior hacksaw is useful for small-scale metal and woodwork; the blades are cheap and easily replaceable.

Jack plane For removing the bulk of waste material from a timber surface before final smoothing, and also to establish a straight edge along a board.

Smoothing plane This is shorter than the jack plane; it is useful for trimming edges and for small-scale work.

Spokeshave Can be useful for carving,

especially irregular shapes such as curves. It is not vital.

Chisels Both 6mm (¼in) and 38mm (1½in) straight chisels with bevelled edges are essential; it is useful, but not vital, to have sizes 9mm (⅜in) and 25mm (1in) in addition. A chisel should be sufficiently sharp to cut timber by hand pressure, or by knocking with the bony part of the palm; it should never be struck with a mallet unless it is a specially designed chisel, made for the purpose. The use of such a chisel is not recommended for dolls'-house manufacture.

Oilstone For sharpening chisels and plane-irons.

G-clamps Two 150mm (6in) and two 254mm (10in) clamps for compressing newly-glued joints.

Electric hand drill Plus a selection of bits (including countersink).

Vice Timber jaws are required as metal ones may mark timber.

Screwdrivers Large, medium and small. A Phillips/Pozidriv headed screwdriver will also be needed.

Try-square This is for marking lines perpendicular to the edge of a piece or sheet of timber, or for checking that adjacent faces of a batten are at right angles to each other.

Bevel square This is similar to the try-square, but the position of the blade relative to the stock can be adjusted to any angle, allowing lines to be marked at a predetermined angle to an edge.

Marking gauge This tool is useful for scribing lines a measured distance from, and parallel to, the edge of a piece of timber.

Rules A retractable tape rule will be required, plus a flat steel rule or a woodworker's wooden rule (the four-section type that folds up). A small (150mm/6in) metal rule is also very useful.

Bradawl The sharp pointed type has a variety of uses: marking, grooving floorboards, beginning screw holes and so on. The point should be fine, sharp and hard.

Pencils A 2H pencil is needed for accurate measurement marking and an HB pencil for general freehand work.

Sundry items You will need a mitre block, or ideally a precision mitre saw (*see* box), a hammer, metal file, pliers and pincers (for removing wrongly positioned pins), and a sharp craft knife with replaceable blades. Also necessary are assorted paint brushes; sandpaper (coarse, medium and fine), and a jigsaw with fine wood-cutting blades.

Useful but not vital are an electric orbital sander (for sanding flat panels), and sash clamps for clamping wide sections of timber (possibly required for the Georgian house).

A precision mitre saw is an extremely useful and accurate device that is not very expensive and worth acquiring if much mitre work is envisaged (for example, as in the Georgian house). The saw and runner mechanism is incorporated in the metal cutting box, and can be adjusted precisely for all required angles. In addition to this, an end stop is included so that precisely similar lengths can be cut repeatedly (this is useful for making stair treads, for example, which have to be of identical length and cut to 90°).

CHAPTER 

Techniques

SHARPENING TOOLS

Chisels and plane-irons soon blunt, and it is vital that they should be sharpened regularly on an oilstone. If the tool is badly worn or has been previously sharpened incorrectly, it may be necessary first to grind the cutting edge to an angle of 25°, using a mechanical grinder. If you do not have access to one, then have the tool ground in this way at a blacksmith's works or hardware shop. Once the tool is ground correctly it should not be necessary to repeat the process for a long time.

PROCEDURE

1. Soak the oilstone liberally with ordinary household lubricating oil. Never try to remove this oil, for its purpose is to float the metal fragments away from the stone after the sharpening process.
2. Hold the tool against the stone so that the blade's angle is tight up against the abrasive face. For blades that are wider than the stone (e.g. plane-irons) it is necessary to hold the metal at an oblique angle so that the complete width is in contact simultaneously.
3. Lift the back of the blade so that the reverse edge of the metal is slightly raised from the stone. The tool is now being held at a 30° angle to the stone, or fractionally wider than 25°.
4. While pressing hard on the back of the front edge of the blade, pull and push the metal along the stone's length a number of times, keeping it held at the same angle. Use all the stone's length. The film of oil will turn black, and it is important to add more oil when needed; never use the stone dry.
5. Inspect the blade and notice the swarf of steel curving behind the edge. Place the blade flat side down on the stone and drag it along sideways (at right angles to the previous movement) two or three times to remove the metal swarf. Take care to keep all the metal flat on the stone; if the back of the blade is raised, the freshly sharpened edge will be destroyed. No particular pressure is required.
6. Check for sharpness by slicing along the edge of a piece of waste wood: the blade should slide through easily.

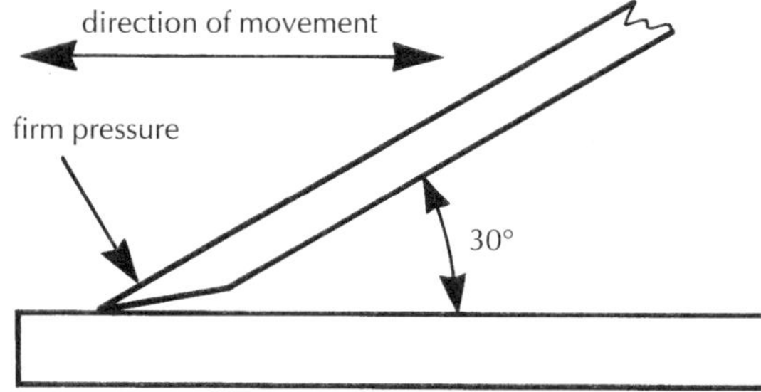

Sharpening a chisel.

MARKING AND MEASUREMENT

Measurements for the projects are given in metric and imperial units, and it is important to choose one system and then stick to it throughout: because of fractional discrepancies due to conversion, mixing the two would cause problems.

A 2H pencil is required, sharpened to a chisel point so as to produce the thinnest possible line in order to reduce the scope for inaccuracy. Expose approximately 9mm (⅜in) of lead, then rub each side of this on sandpaper to produce a chisel-type edge (not pointed). The pencil is used with the flat edge against the ruler or marking line.

POINTS TO REMEMBER

1. When marking sheet materials, always allow 9mm (⅜in) for waste between cutting lines. This is because the thickness of the saw must not impinge on the finished dimension: you should always be careful to cut with the saw blade to the waste side of the line. Mark and cut batten or moulding piece by piece so as to avoid having to mark for waste.
2. A retractable steel measure can be laid flat on a panel, and measurement is therefore accurate. When using a wooden rule, turn it on its edge so that the gradation mark can be matched precisely to the wood surface: used flat, the gradation mark is distanced from the surface, and inaccuracies may occur due to this parallax error.
3. When using a wooden or flat metal rule it can sometimes be helpful to touch its

USING A MARKING GAUGE

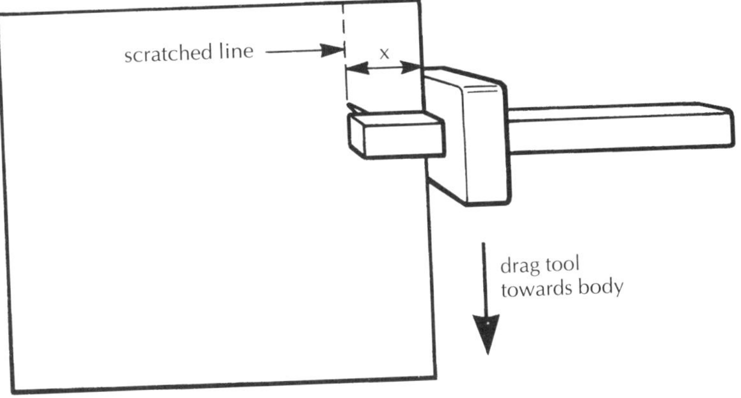

x = distance from edge to be marked

A marking gauge is extremely useful for measuring a precise distance from an edge, for instance when marking a line for nail or screw clearance holes.

After adjusting the gauge's head the correct distance from its point, and keeping the head of the tool hard up against the timber edge, drag the scribing point across the timber surface towards the body; the resultant scribed line will be parallel with the edge and the desired distance from it.

end and the juxtaposing timber edge with a fingertip so as to ensure that the two are in line.
4. When measuring from an edge, always make sure that the rule or tape is at right angles to it, if necessary using a try-square as a guide.

CUTTING

CUTTING WITH A JIGSAW

1. Slice up a large piece of MDF or plywood into sections first, rather than cutting each piece individually. These sections can usually be held in the vice to divide into the final component parts.
2. Keep the heel of the tool firmly on the work and exert slight pressure downwards and forwards.
3. A jigsaw blade makes a cut approximately 2mm ($\frac{5}{64}$in) wide, therefore it is vital to make sure that the blade's edge is precisely *adjacent* to the line, with the thickness of the blade positioned wholly in the waste area. This principle also applies to all other saws.
4. Keep your fingers away from the blade. Intricate work should be held in a vice or clamped to a bench, leaving both hands free to control the tool.
5. To cut out square or rectangular holes (e.g. for stairwells or windows), drill a 6mm ($\frac{1}{4}$in) hole in two diagonally opposite corners so that the jigsaw blade can be inserted. Complete the four cuts, finishing off by removing the unwanted material from the two rounded (previously drilled) corners.

CUTTING MITRES

Mitres will need to be cut for window frames and sills, door frames and so on. (*See* Tools Chapter 2 for a description of a precision mitre saw.)

1. Place the length of moulding in the mitre box as shown opposite, and make the first cut: the mitred end of piece A.
2. Measure and mark length y, and cut the moulding at right angles (piece A).
3. Use piece A to measure and mark the exact size of piece C on the outer edge of the length of moulding.
4. Position the length of moulding in the mitre box so that the other 45° saw slots correspond with the proposed saw line. Cut. This is piece C.
5. To cut piece B, repeat stage 1, measure and mark length x along the mould-

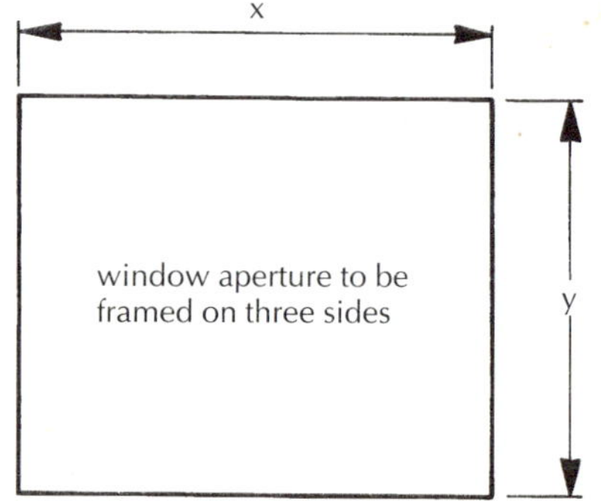

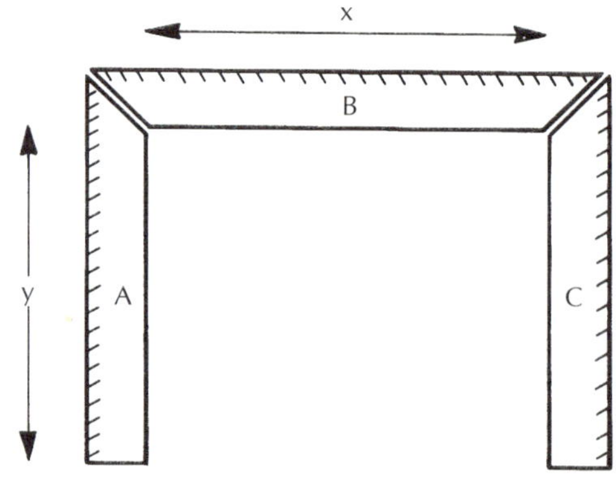

indicates outside edge of moulding

Cutting mitres.

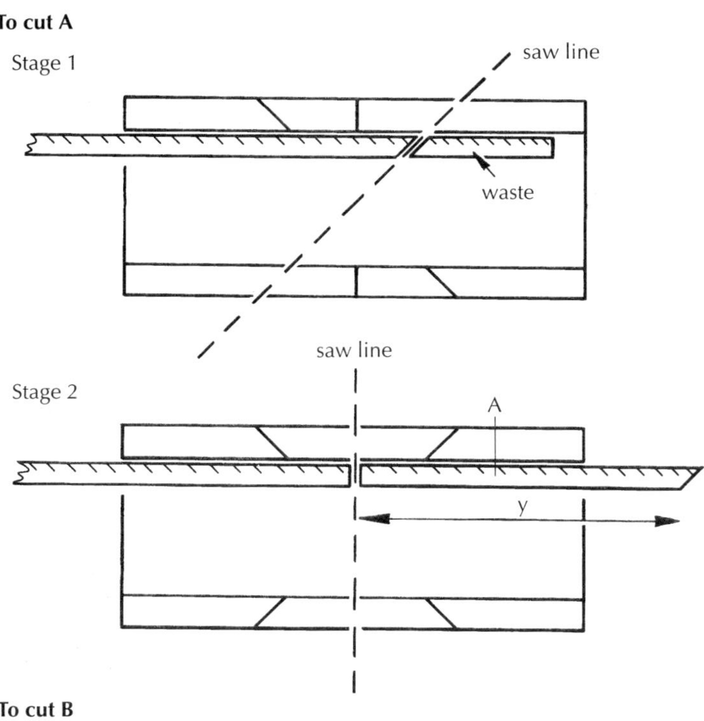

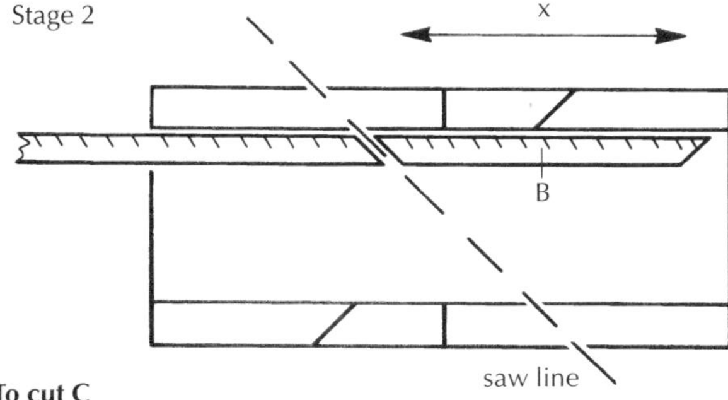

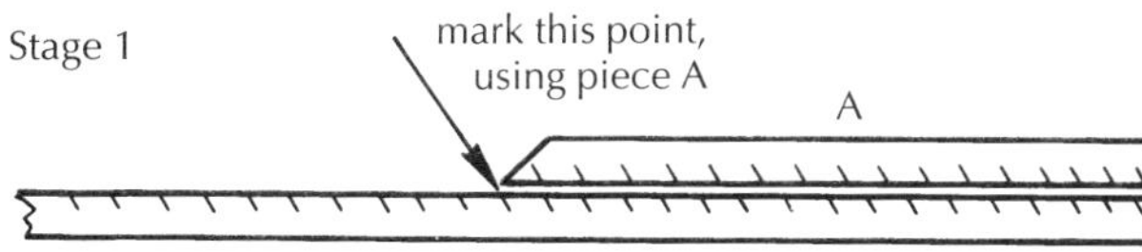

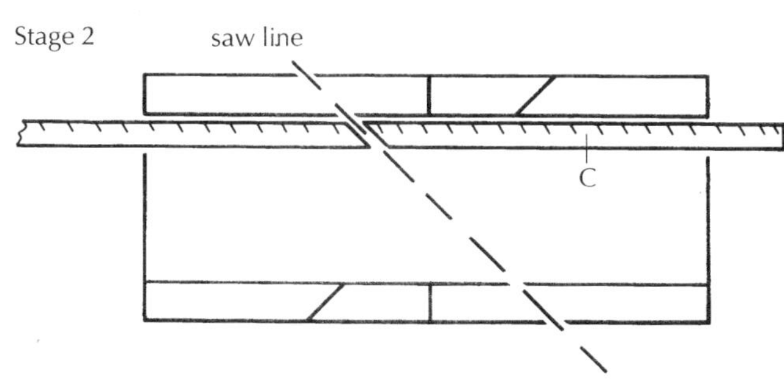

ing's inner edge, then cut along the other 45° saw slots.

POINTS TO REMEMBER

1. Ensure that the saw is sharp.
2. Check that the proposed saw line accurately intersects your marked point on the outermost edge of the timber.
3. Always keep the batten or moulding held firmly against the relevant surface of the mitre box.
4. To begin a cut, pull the saw backwards across the line two or three times until it slides forwards with ease.
5. Clean up torn grain with sandpaper before fixing.
6. Wherever possible, cut mitred pieces in opposing pairs, so that one may be marked from the other for accuracy.
7. It is often difficult to achieve a perfect mitre joint. Small holes and discrepancies can be filled invisibly afterwards.
8. If a great deal of mitre work is planned, for instance for the Georgian house, it may be worthwhile buying a precision mitre saw (*see* box on page 13).

Cutting mitres.

JIGS

These are useful for assembling several component parts into a complete unit, so that structures which should be identical (such as window frames) are always the same size. A jig is also useful as a convenient way of keeping parts in the correct position whilst adhesive sets. Normally a three-sided MDF or plywood box with a base, a jig can be tailor-made as required.

METHODS OF ASSEMBLY

There are two methods of assembling the carcass of a house:

1. The main carcass of a house (the shell) is screwed and glued along the edges and base, with surfaces meeting edges. The inner walls are assembled and inserted as a whole after the interior of the carcass is decorated. Sometimes it is possible to make reciprocally matching slots in internal party walls and floors, so that these components can be assembled as a unit.
2. The house is assembled piece by piece, then dismantled. The component parts are decorated, then the structure is reassembled permanently.

MAKING THE SHELL

Set the marking gauge to exactly half the thickness of the plywood or MDF used, then scribe a line along the inner edge of panel A. For screwing, use 19mm (¾in) or 25mm (1in), size 4 (UK) countersunk chipboard-thread screws (rustproofed). For bonding MDF to MDF, MDF to plywood, or plywood to plywood.

1. Drill 2mm ($\frac{5}{64}$in) pilot holes at 76mm (3in) intervals along the scribed line on panel A.
2. Holding the panels in the correct position for fixing, use a sharp-pointed bradawl to make a mark through one

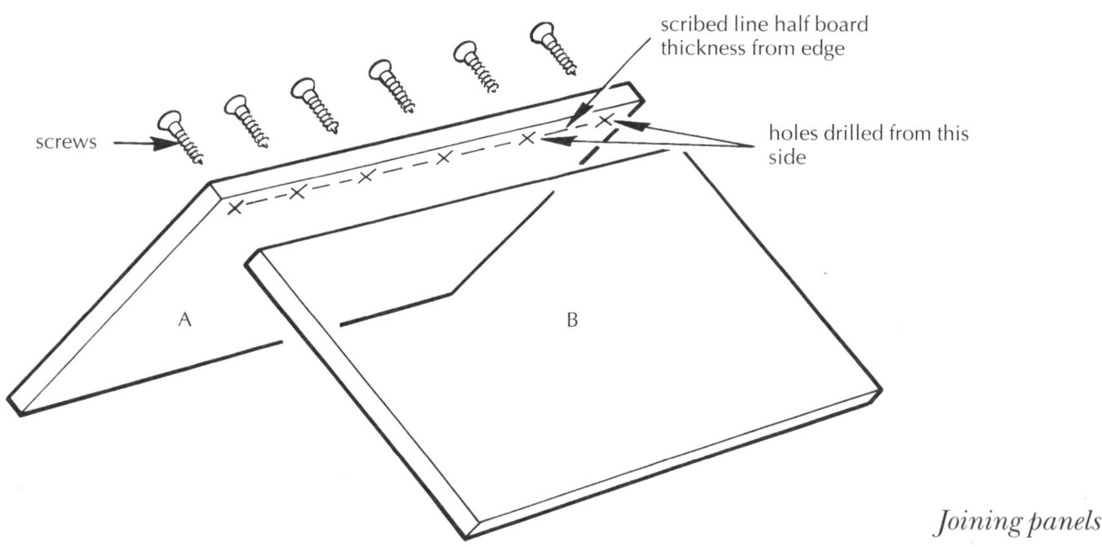

Joining panels.

of the holes in panel A into the edge of panel B.
3. Take the panels apart, and using a 2mm (5⁄64in) drill, bore this marked screw reception hole to a depth of 12mm (½in) or 15mm (⅝in), according to screw length. **Note**: Ensure that this hole is in the centre of the thickness of the panel, even if the mark is slightly off-centre.
4. Enlarge the corresponding hole in panel A with a 3mm (⅛in) drill.
5. Screw panel A to panel B.
6. Mark the positions for the other screw reception holes as in stage 2.
7. Take the panels apart and repeat stage 3 for the other reception holes in panel B.
8. Repeat stage 4 for all the clearance holes in panel A.
9. Countersink the clearance holes in panel A (the outside face of the panel).
10. Apply PVA adhesive to both joint surfaces, and screw panel A to panel B.
11. Clean off excess adhesive with a damp rag.

FRONT HINGEING

Screws will not hold satisfactorily for load-bearing purposes in the end grain (thickness) of either plywood or MDF, therefore it is necessary to bond sections of timber (ramin or other hardwood) along the edge which is to accept hinge screws for potentially heavy opening front sections. Pieces of timber slightly thicker than the panel should be used and the excess material removed afterwards. PVA adhesive will bond hardwood pieces to plywood, provided they are a reasonably tight fit and are clamped in position (sash clamps are ideal). Epoxy resin must be used for bonding timber to MDF. When the adhesive is fully cured, cut out some of the timber to the depth of the thickness of the closed hinge, using the method described for internal doors; the same procedure is used whether for miniature hinges for internal doors or larger hinges for front panels.

For the country cottage and the Tudor house described later, the front sections have chamfered edges where they meet, thus eliminating the possibility of gaps. The Georgian house has an overlapping section to cover any possible gap.

HANGING INTERNAL DOORS

The following procedure can be used for either plywood or MDF doors:

1. Ensure that the hinges close properly when the screws are in the holes; if not, countersink the holes further so that the plates close reasonably flat.

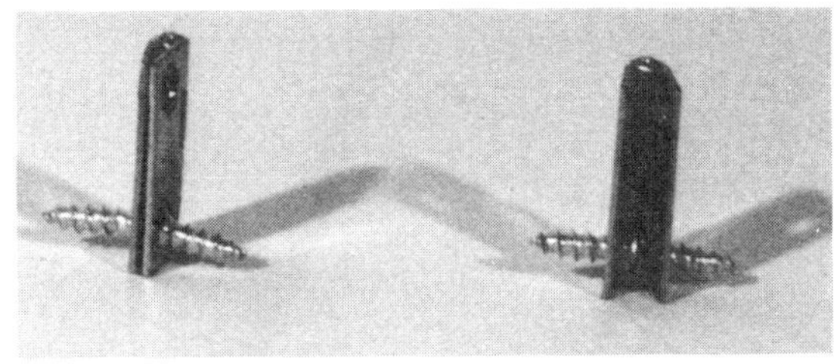

Closed hinges, to show how screw heads can prevent correct closing if the holes are not countersunk: countersunk holes on the left, not countersunk on the right.

As above, showing hinges open.

2. Mark the hinge positions on the door's edge.
3. Remove material from the edge of the door that is the size of the hinges and the same depth as their thickness. Rebate the hinges (*see* right and below).
4. Fit hinges according to left- or right-hand opening. Fix screws so that the hinge pivot line is aligned to the edge of the door, normally in the exact centre of the thickness of the door material.
5. With the wall panel held in the vice, hold the door in its correct opened position with the hinges opened out. Mark the position of one screw hole for each hinge and fix, beginning the screw hole with the point of a sharp-pointed bradawl. After any necessary final adjustments, fit the last two screws.

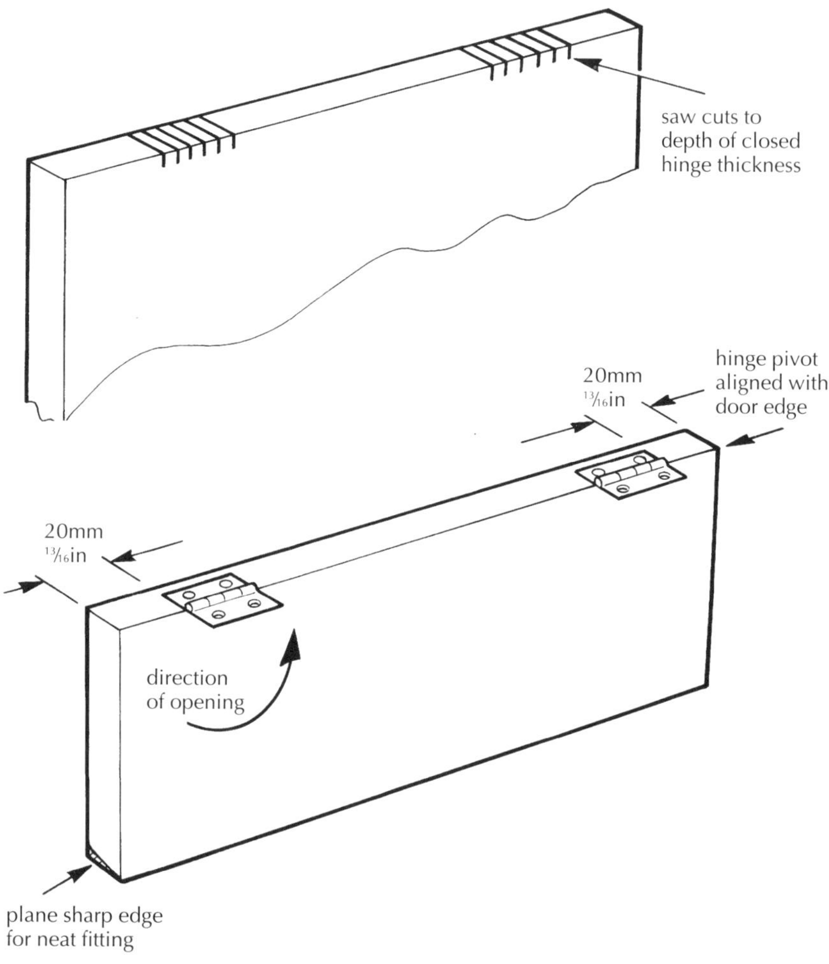

Recessing and fixing hinges on internal doors.

REBATING HINGES

Rebating in the strict sense means cutting away a section of timber that is the exact size of the hinge (i.e. not cutting across the complete width of panel). In this instance, and when hanging opening front sections, cutting right across the panel is acceptable.

There are three stages, which are as follows:

1. Holding the door in a vice, make shallow saw cuts (1.5mm/1/16in) with a tenon or junior hacksaw on the marked lines, keeping to the waste side of the lines.
2. Make several similar saw cuts between these lines for each hinge, as above, so as to divide up the waste material to be removed.
3. Remove waste with a small chisel. Always chisel towards the centre of the wood grain, angling slightly upwards if necessary, then turn the work round and start from the other side. Chiselling across the complete width is likely to tear the grain from the face of the panel.

POINTS TO REMEMBER

1. Miniature hinges are intended to be fixed in position with tiny pins. This is impractical when hanging a door, therefore it may be necessary to drill the holes fractionally larger to facilitate tiny screws, cautiously using a 5mm (5⁄16in) drill to countersink the hole afterwards. It can sometimes be helpful to hold the body of the drill in a vice for these processes, bringing the hinge, *held in pliers*, against the drill tip.
2. Hinges should be recessed into the edge of the door.
3. It is better to make the door slightly oversize, so that it can be planed to fit afterwards.

MAKING STAIRS

In the houses detailed later, all measurements for making the staircases are already calculated. For those wishing to adapt these designs or make their own entirely, the general strategy is outlined below.

GENERAL CALCULATIONS

Width The average stairs are 762–914mm (30–36in) wide, so scaling this down means they should be 64–76mm (2½–3in) in width. For most interiors, the wider measurement would take up a disproportionate amount of room, therefore 51mm (2in) for a small cottage, ranging to 64mm (2½in) for a larger dwelling is a good compromise.

Length available This is the overall distance measured horizontally from the beginning of the bottom tread to the end of the top. Always remember to allow room at the bottom and the top for reasonable access, and decide if opening doors will need to be taken into consideration.

Height From the floor of the lower room to the floor above, excluding the thickness of the upper floor material.

Fitting Decide whether the stairs are to be positioned against a wall to the left or the right, with a view to banisters.

Type and height of banisters You will also need to decide whether you will use, for example, metal rods or a continuous wooden banister panel.

PROCEDURE

The procedure which follows is for a staircase fitting against a left-hand wall, with a continuous wooden banister panel. This is as for the country cottage. For the Tudor house and the Georgian house the treads are longer, as it is unnecessary to stick a plywood panel on both sides for these houses. For all the projects in this book, the exact sizes for all the stair parts are specified.

1. From a rectangular piece of 6mm (¼in) plywood, mark the distances for the length and height, as below. Draw the position of the front edge of the bottom and top stairs. Rule along the diagonal line: this is the stair-line.
2. Cut treads from square-section ramin or softwood timber, 19 × 19mm (¾ × ¾in), using a mitre block or precision mitre saw to ensure a 90° cutting angle (which is vital). Their length should be the overall staircase width, minus two times the thickness of plywood used: the overall width minus 12mm (½in). Either use a marking gauge to mark these measurements and mark and cut separately, or set the end stop on the precision mitre saw so that pieces of identical length can be produced.
3. Using PVA or contact adhesive, stick the treads in position, overlapping each other as shown and ensuring that the edge meets the stair-line and that the blocks are laid parallel with the base

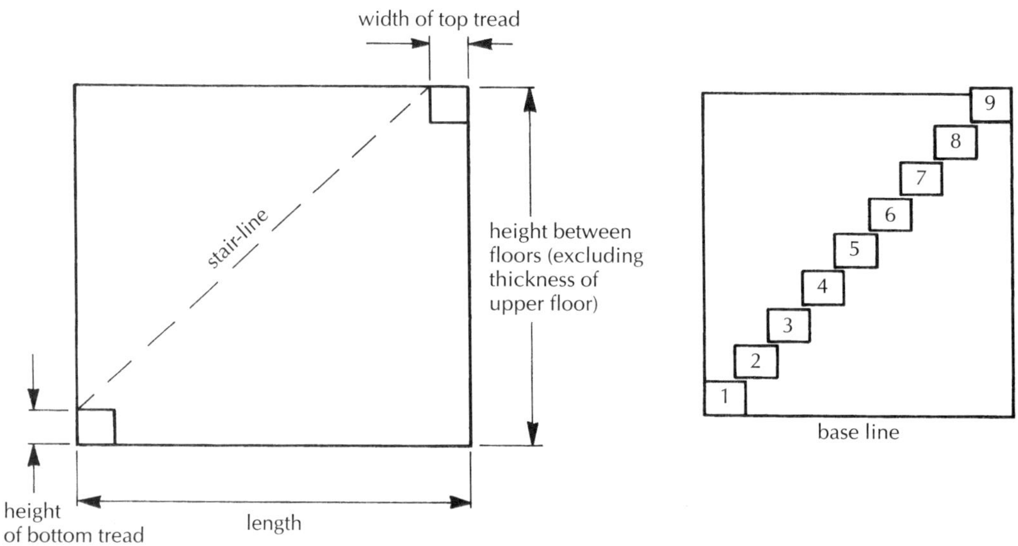

Stairs: marking the end panel.

Positioning treads.

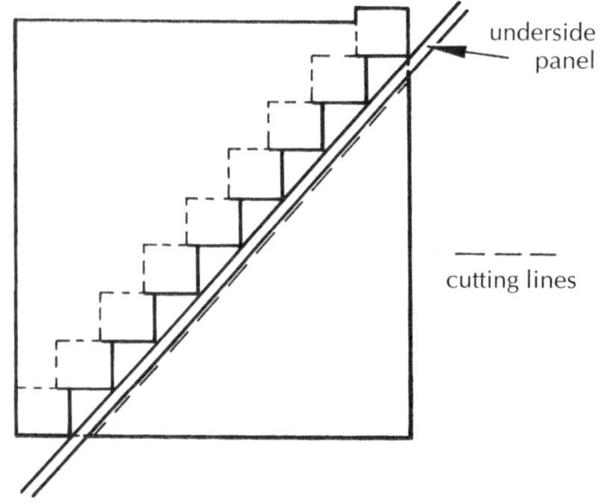

Positioning the underside panel line, and cutting lines to remove waste.

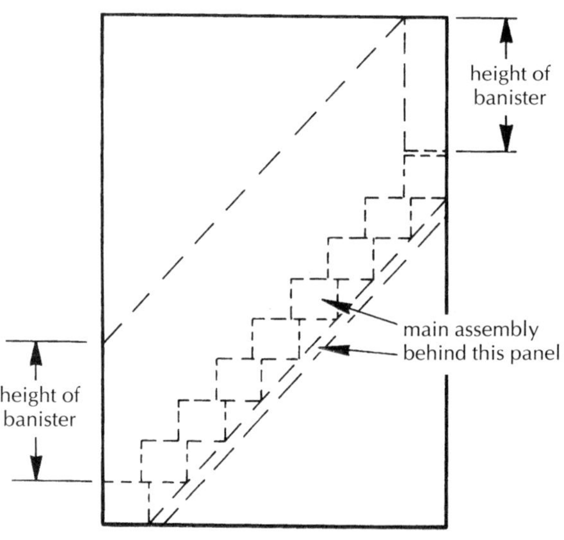

Fitting the banister panel.

line. Sometimes it may be necessary to go over the stair-line slightly, and this is permissible; but the treads must be parallel with the base line at all costs. No clamping should be necessary.

4. Cut a piece of plywood the same width as the treads, but slightly longer than the stair-line. Stick it edgeways against the panel and to the underside of the treads.
5. Cut away plywood as shown in the diagram. It is easier to cut an initial long

diagonal line from the end panel and then trim close to the treads and risers. If, as is likely, the top step projects above the panel, trim this overlapping timber off.

6. Glue the resultant assembly to a piece of 6mm (¼in) plywood that is large enough to allow for banister rail height (*see* diagram).
7. Mark the height of the banister rail at the top and bottom, and join these marks. Cut as shown, trimming in line with the top stair so that this will fit against the underside of the upper floor.
8. Fill, then sand any surface defects and rough edges; then finish the banister rail according to taste.

CREATING FLOORBOARDS IN PLYWOOD

This should be done before the house is finally assembled. Real floorboards are normally between 100–150mm (4–6in) in width, therefore a true scaled-down size would be 13mm (½in). For practical purposes, a 15mm (⅝in) width looks authentic, is less time-consuming and is a good compromise size.

PROCEDURE

Marking

1. Make sure that the grain of the plywood runs from side to side of the house, as seen from the front. Establish the true front edge of the floor; if planed after assembly, it will effectively shorten the width of the most noticeable board.
2. Mark off at 15mm (⅝in) intervals at each side from this edge. Use a relatively soft (HB), sharp pencil and mark very lightly. Draw the floorboard width lines by joining these points. These are the parallel-grain lines.
3. Decide upon a convenient length of board (between 152mm/6in and 305mm/12in) and mark the lengths as shown, ensuring that the simulated board joints are staggered. These are the cross-grain lines. Always bear in mind the position of internal dividing walls, which may affect the choice of board length – a row of joint lines may be covered up.

Cutting

For each parallel-grain line:

1. Using a sharp craft knife and a metal ruler, cut a shallow groove along the line.

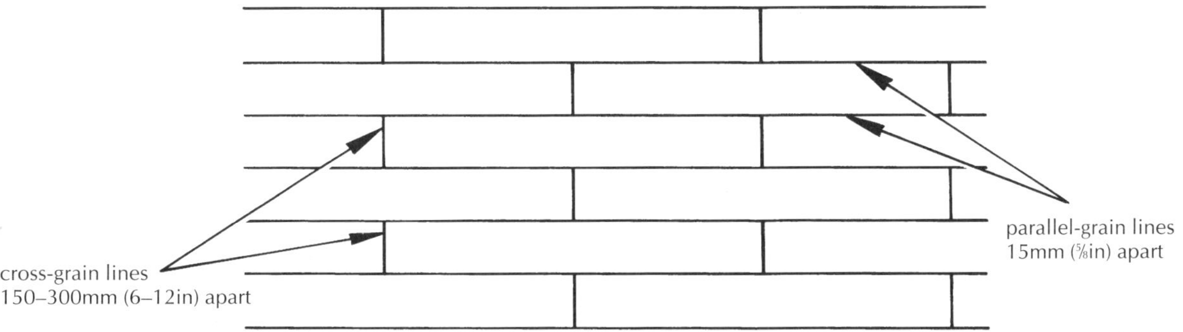

Floorboarding.

2. Move the cutting guide rule fractionally to one side of the cut line and make another cut at a slight angle so that it joins the first incision.
3. Using the point of a sharp bradawl, start at one end to prize up the sliver of timber that has been liberated. Push the bradawl so as to lift the tiny strip of material from the veneer layer, leaving behind a shallow groove.

For each cross-grain line:

1. Cut a shallow groove as for the parallel-grain lines, and similarly cut a second one adjacent to it, this time *not* angling the second cut.
2. Using a sharp bradawl, drag the point between the two groove lines: tiny chunks of timber will come away instead of a continuous strand of wood (as happens when the parallel-grain lines are made).

Finishing Off

1. Sand thoroughly to remove pencil marks.
2. Stain to a darker colour if required (for instance, dark oak if creating a Tudor interior) or leave plain, and then finish with several coats of polyurethane varnish, following the manufacturer's instructions.

CHAPTER four

The Country Cottage

Quintessentially British, the archetypal cottage is small, detached and situated deep in the heart of the countryside. Of course, some cottages are not small by any means, some are in terraces and there are a number in cities. A dictionary definition of a cottage is: 'a small, simple house, especially in the country', with a second definition being 'a dwelling forming part of a farm establishment, used by a worker'.

It seems to be the link with Britain's past that is attractive: a harking back to a time when the country was principally an agricultural economy. A century ago the majority of rural buildings, including most country cottages, were at one time small farms in their own right. Thus the words 'farmhouse' and 'cottage' can sometimes be synonymous, except that the generally recognized concept of a farmhouse is that of a larger building altogether.

The farmhouse derived from the fifteenth-century longhouse, where the farming family sheltered with their animals and produce under one roof. The longhouse was a building with cramped living quarters at one end, room for the animals and fodder at the other, and a joint entrance in the middle. In the early sixteenth century, people began to live separately from their livestock, but still most farmhouses were humble, single-width dwellings. However, rising affluence in the south-east of England at around this time meant that the buildings could be enlarged and improved, with lowland farmhouses doubling in depth and incorporating many new features such as cross wings and gable wings, all of which were designed to improve the farmer's working conditions.

Vernacular styles varied tremendously, dependent upon the local building materials. The Cotswolds were known for their multi-gabled manor-like farmhouses of yellow stone, whilst timber-rich areas such as Suffolk and Essex produced half-timbered farmhouses. In Norfolk there was a Dutch influence, where brick and flint farmhouses had vaulted Dutch gables at either end. Thatch-roofed cob houses – those made of clay mixed with straw or rubble, and cast on a stone base – are a vernacular style typical of Devon, some of which are still in existence, dating from medieval times. Cornwall has more granite buildings than anywhere in England. The Yorkshire Dales are famous for the local grey stone that dominates the landscape in dry stone walls, cottages and farmhouses.

The following country cottage design is not based on any particular vernacular style or period. The front opening with easy access provides good play value.

DESCRIPTION AND DIMENSIONS

Shape: Rectangular (apart from the gabled roof).

Size: Width 559mm (22in); depth 304mm (12$\frac{11}{16}$in); height 500mm (19$\frac{5}{8}$in).

Rooms:

Ground floor right:	Width	205mm (8$\frac{1}{16}$in)
	Depth	287mm (11$\frac{5}{16}$in)
	Height	165mm (6½in)
Ground floor left :	Width	177mm (7in)
	Depth	287mm (11$\frac{5}{16}$in
	Height	165mm (6½in)
First floor right:	Width	220mm (8$\frac{5}{8}$in)
	Depth	287mm (11$\frac{5}{16}$in)
	Height	300mm (11$\frac{13}{16}$in at highest point)
First floor left:	Width	177mm (7in)
	Depth	287mm (11$\frac{5}{16}$in)
	Height	300mm (11$\frac{13}{16}$in at highest point)

Hall with stairs and landing area.

Floors: Floorboards, top surface of plywood veneer layer carved to simulate these. Varnished.

Walls: Emulsion-painted, colour according to taste.

Roof: Tiles, replicated from 0.8mm ($\frac{1}{32}$in) plywood.

Access to interior: Front-opening, double doors, split to the left of central tiled porch section.

Exterior finish: Textured plaster-based finish, treated to simulate stipplecast.

Windows: Latticed, painted black, with square frames. Mock shutters (optional).

Front: Five windows, front door enclosed within tiled-roof porch.

Interior details: Straight-run staircase with solid banister. Opening doors to all rooms.

MATERIALS

All the materials used are shown with metric and imperial sizes: whichever is chosen, it is vital to stick to it throughout. If the constructor wishes to use plywood throughout in preference to MDF, this is perfectly acceptable as long as the following points are borne in mind:

1. Fill the grain with fine filler before priming/painting internal walls and ceilings.
2. Shutters cannot be carved in plywood – either make plain shutters, or do without.
3. Make the window frames for the cottage from hardboard.

SHEET MATERIALS

6mm (¼in) MDF

Left side, right side	2 @ 477 × 293mm 18¾ × 11½in

TOOLS

- Jigsaw with small, fine wood-cutting blades
- Electric hand drill with high-speed steel twist bits: 2mm(5/64in), 3mm (1/8in) and 4.5mm (3/16in) plus a countersink bit
- Tenon saw (fine teeth)
- Junior hacksaw
- Mitre block or precision mitre saw
- Small Phillips or Pozidriv screwdriver
- Small and very small conventional blade screwdrivers
- Chisels: 6mm (1/4in) and 13mm (1/2in)
- Tin snips
- Large plane (460mm/18in)
- Smaller plane (255mm/10in)
- Paintbrushes: 50mm (2in), 25mm (1in), 13mm (1/2in) and 6mm (1/4in)
- Tiny artist's paintbrush for finishing edges
- Small craft knife with blades
- Oilstone for sharpening plane-irons, chisels and craft-knife blades; oil
- Vice with wooden jaw inserts
- Workbench (any old table will do)
- Marking gauge
- Try-square
- 2H pencil and HB pencil
- Sandpaper: medium, fine and very fine
- Large (1m/39in) metal measuring rule that can also act as a straight edge
- Medium (300mm/12in) metal rule
- Small (150mm/6in) metal rule
- Retracting metal tape-measure
- Bradawl with sharp point
- Two G-clamps: 150mm (6in) or larger

Back		547 x 330mm	21½ × 13in
Roof 1, roof 2	2 @	610 × 250mm	24 × 9⅞in
Porch side 1, porch side 2	2 @	155 × 45mm	6⅛ × 1¾in
Porch roof 1, porch roof 2	2 @	90 × 56mm	3 9/16 × 2 3/16in
Window frames	5 @	82 × 82mm	3¼ × 3¼in
Shutters (if required)	10 @	82 × 35mm	3¼ × 1⅜in

9mm (⅜in) MDF

Left side upper/ lower wall unit	477 × 293mm	18¾ × 11½in
Right lower wall	287 × 165mm	11¼ × 6½in
Right upper wall	306 × 293mm	12 × 11½in
Front left section	310 × 230mm	12¼ × 9⅛in
Front right section	360 × 310mm	14¼ × 12¼in
Eaves strip	570 × 15mm	22½ × ⅝in
Front door	155 × 75mm	6⅛ × 3in
Interior doors	4 @ 150 × 65mm	5⅞ × 2 9/16in

6mm (¼in) plywood

First floor	547 × 287mm	21½ × 11¼in
Ground floor	559 × 320mm	22 × 12⅝in
For making stairs and banisters	175 × 175mm	6⅞ × 6⅞in
	and 250 × 175mm	9⅞ × 6⅞in

0.8mm (1/32in) plywood

For making roof tiles.

4 sheets 900 × 305mm 36 × 12in

or equivalent if only smaller size sheets available

TIMBER MOULDINGS

13mm (½in) triangular section	570mm (22½in)
19mm (¾in) square section for stair treads	350mm (14in)
6mm (¼in) dowel for doorknobs	150mm (6in)
50mm (2in) square section for chimney support	60mm (2½in)
25mm (1in) dowel for chimney	50mm (2in)
12mm (½in) side L-shaped for ridge tiles	670mm (26½in)
9mm (⅜in) square-section hardwood for porch roof support and inserts for hinge screws	300mm (12in)
12 × 6mm (½ × ¼in) for window-sills and top of window section if shutters required	1,100mm (45in)

HARDWARE

- 200 25mm (1in) No 4 chipboard-thread countersunk galvanized steel screws, with Pozidriv/Phillips heads
- 50 19mm (¾in) No 4 screws as above
- 4 brass hinges, 25mm (1in) long, 6mm (¼in) flanges
- Screws for above
- 10 13mm (½in) miniature hinges for internal doors
- Miniature brass screws for above
- Miniature screw/eye and ring for front door knocker
- Approximately 500 × 500mm (20 × 20in) of wire mesh (6mm/¼in holes) for lattice over windows; obtainable from garden centres in sheet form

SUNDRIES

- PVA (white) wood adhesive
- Epoxy resin adhesive
- Clear contact adhesive (nitrile, 'all purpose')
- Cyanoacrylate adhesive for doorknobs; gel type preferably
- Textured-surface finish material
- Filler, ready-mixed type preferably
- Especially fine filler, for filling surface blemishes and wood grain
- Emulsion paint for interior
- Emulsion paint for exterior (white used in prototype)

THE MAIN STAGES IN CONSTRUCTION

There are fourteen stages in construction:

1. Cutting all major components from the sheet materials.
2. Making shell without final fixing.
3. Making the inner walls and floor assembly (W/F assembly).
4. Fitting W/F assembly into shell.
5. Making and hanging internal doors.
6. Decorating interior: internal face of side walls, back and all of internal walls. Carving floorboards and varnishing floors. Decorating internal doors.
7. Permanent assembly of house.
8. Roof and front-opening sections.
9. Roof tiling and chimney.
10. Front section cut-outs and porch.
11. Window frames, mock shutters and front door.
12. Stairs.
13. Exterior decoration.
14. Finishing off.

- Emulsion paint for roof and porch tiles (grey used in prototype)
- Black emulsion paint for window lattice
- Primer
- Undercoat and gloss for interior doors
- Undercoat and gloss for exterior window frames, shutters and front door (blue gloss used in prototype)
- Polyurethane timber varnish (clear)
- Sandpaper; medium and fine

CONSTRUCTION

This design, relies solely on screwed and glued construction rather than pinning, because panel pins grip less securely in MDF than in plywood. Another advantage of screwing is that the structure may be assembled completely and the component parts adjusted and then decorated before permanent bonding.

Following the instructions in Chapter 3, Techniques, cut the major component parts from 6mm (¼in) MDF, 9mm (⅜in) MDF and 6mm (¼in) plywood. Although some wastage is unavoidable, panels are sold in various sizes and offcuts are useful to save for future projects. Aim for accuracy, if necessary completing a cut oversize and finishing off by cautious planing. Right angles are also important. When each part is judged correct, write the measurement in a corner of the panel as a time-saving way of identifying it later.

SHELL

Parts involved:
Side walls, left and right; ground floor; back.

CUTTING

Mark and cut the side walls with a jigsaw as in diagram: two diagonal roof lines, and three sides of a square for two hinge

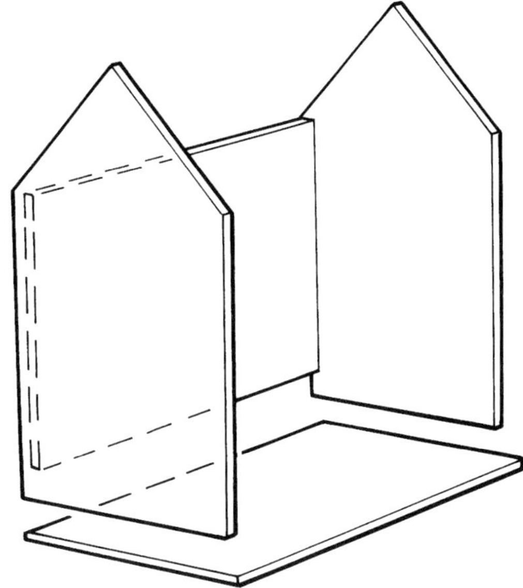

Component parts of the shell.

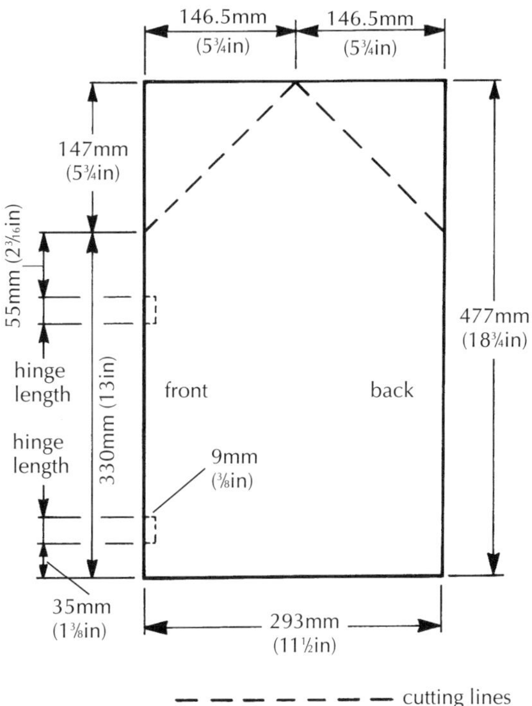

Side walls: cutting plan.

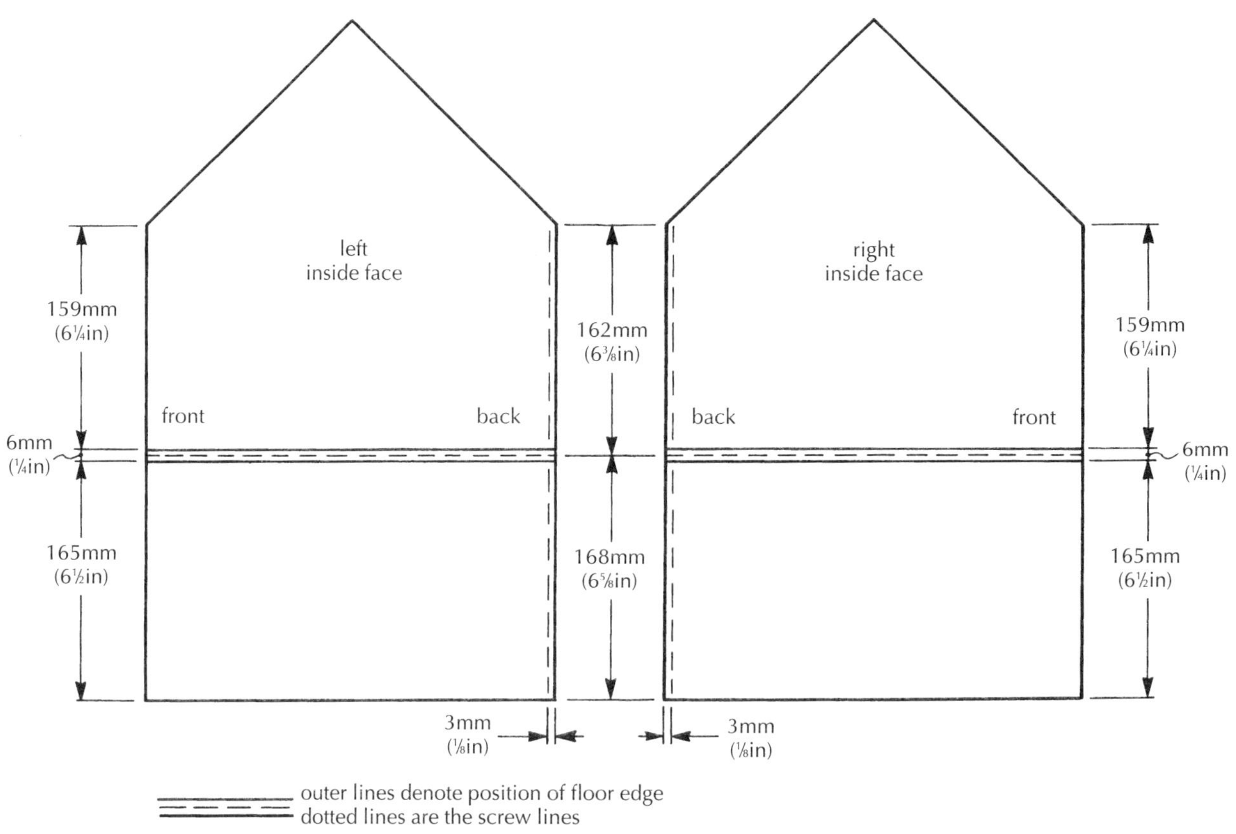

Screw lines for the side walls (inside faces).

timber inserts (these will act as hinge screw receptors). It is important to achieve a straight line for the longer cuts; the horizontal cuts are not so crucial. When these cuts are completed, hold the panels against each other so as to check that the roof slope on both sides is identical.

HINGE ATTACHMENT

1. Cut suitable lengths of 9mm (⅜in) square-section ramin (or other hardwood) batten, using a mitre block or machine to ensure a 90° angle. These fillets will receive the hinge screws, as these will not grip adequately in MDF.
2. Fit the fillets in position. The most important mating faces are the long edges, so ensure that the timber surfaces and the MDF cut edges meet snugly when the fillets are in place, if necessary planing the pieces of timber to fit. The fillets will be proud of the panel on both sides and should be flush with the edge (to be later recessed so as to make allowance for the thickness of a closed hinge).
3. Bond these fillets in place with epoxy resin (no other adhesive is suitable). Put the panels aside to dry for several hours, meanwhile continuing with later stages if time is short. Curing time is

variable as some epoxy resins are specially formulated for speed, but make sure that the cure is complete before continuing to stage 4.

4. Plane the excess timber so that the timber fillets are flush with the panel surfaces on both sides.
5. Using a chisel and tenon saw (or junior hacksaw), accurately remove enough timber to allow room for the closed hinge on all four hinge sites – if in doubt about the method, refer to Chapter 3, Techniques, for the correct method of cutting a slot for a door hinge.
6. Mark the positions of the hinge screws, then drill small pilot holes before screwing the hinges in position, making sure the holes are dead centre in the thickness of the timber infill pieces.

SCREW LINES

For each side panel:

1. With the marking gauge set to half the thickness of the panel (3mm/⅛in), scribe the screw line as shown.
2. Measure and mark the eventual position of the first floor as above, then measure and mark a line midway between these floor edge lines: this is the screw line, which corresponds to the centre of the thickness of the floor panel.
3. Drill 2mm (5/64in) holes at approximately 75mm (3in) centres along the screw lines.

For the ground floor:

1. Some plywood panels have a good and a bad side, therefore choose the best for the top surface of the ground floor.

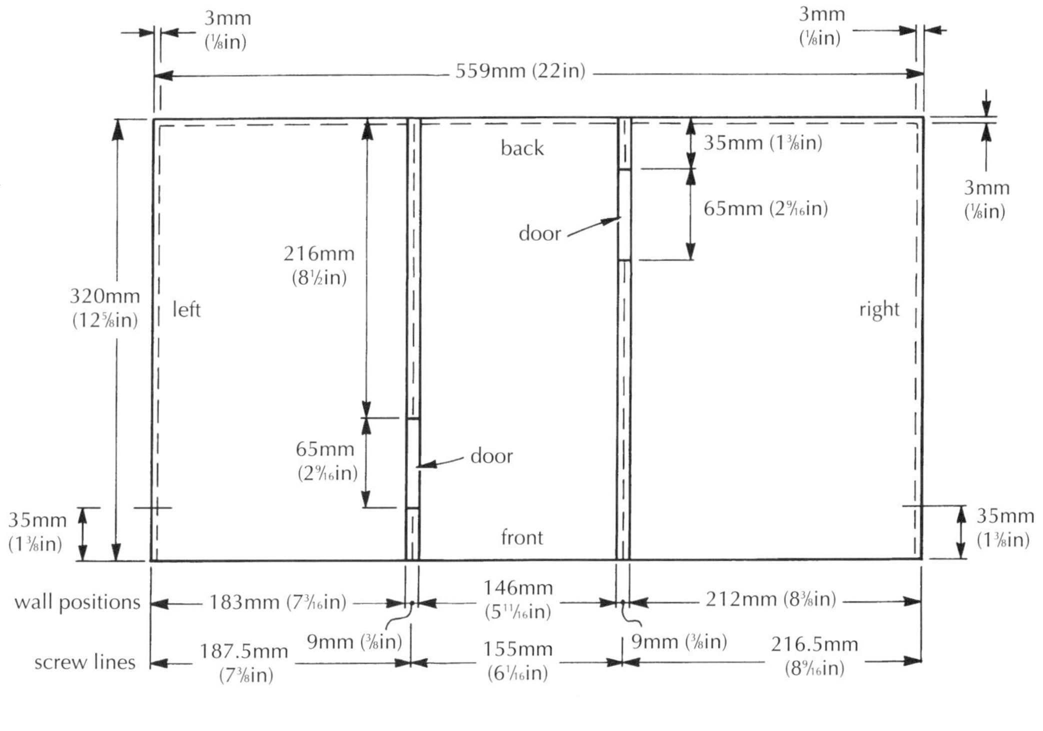

Screw lines for the ground floor, top surface uppermost.

With this best timber surface uppermost, scribe with the marking gauge along one long side and both short sides, using the same setting as that used for the side walls.

2. Mark the parameters of the lower left and lower right internal wall edges. Draw a line midway between and parallel to these lines: this is the screw line.
3. Drill 2mm (5/64in) holes at 75mm (3in) centres along the outer screw lines, ensuring that the first holes on the two widthways lines are no less than 35mm (1⅜in) from the front edge; this is to avoid the possibility of splitting the MDF panel when the screw is driven home. Do not drill screw holes in the other two screw lines at this stage.

For the back:
Mark the wall and the first-floor edge-parameter lines and screw lines as shown, then drill all the screw holes as in stage 3 above.

BACK AND SIDES ASSEMBLY

1. Holding the back and one side in the correct relative position, mark the side edge of the back panel through the bottom hole in the side panel with a sharp-pointed bradawl.
2. Remove the side panel and drill a 2mm (5/64in) pilot hole to a depth of 15mm (⅝in) at the marked site, ensuring that the hole is centred exactly in the thickness of the MDF edge. Begin the hole with the bradawl, so as to make it easier

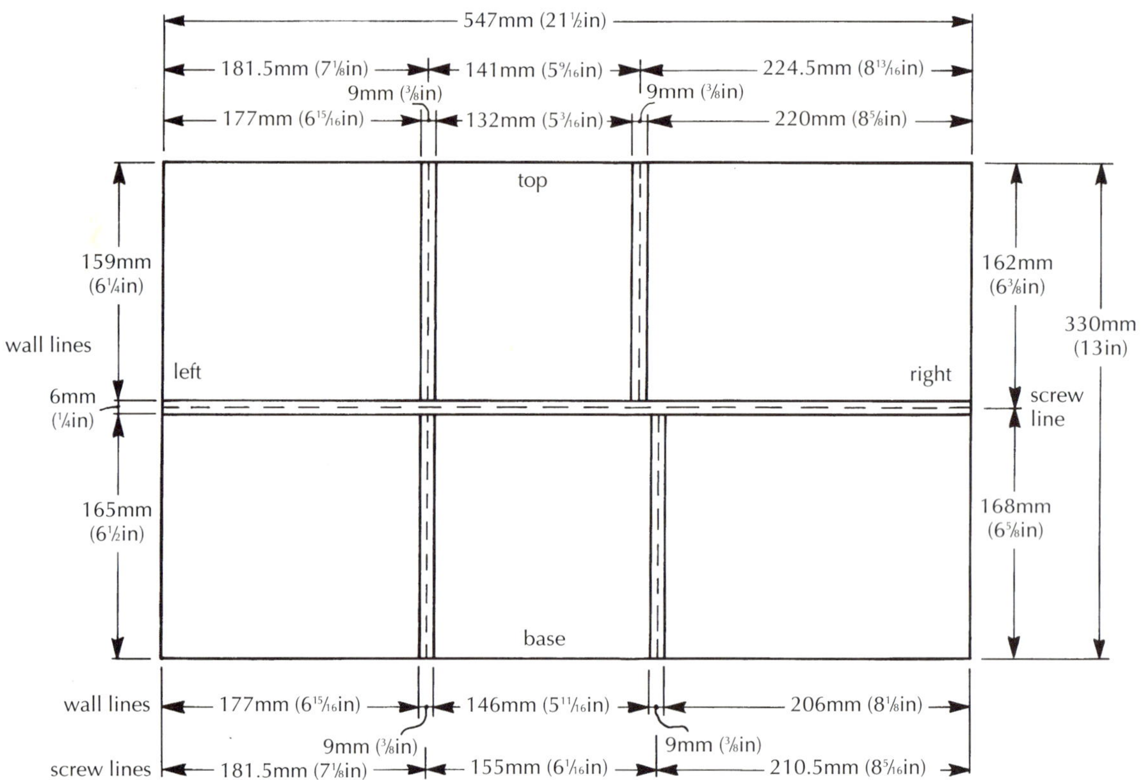

Screw lines for the back, inside face shown.

DRILLING PROBLEMS

Potential snag

If a screw pilot hole is not central in an MDF panel edge, the panel may bulge to one side when the screw is driven home. In this event, remove the screw and abandon this screw site, drilling another hole near by.

Advice

Using a thin twist bit to drill accurately into an MDF or plywood edge can be difficult as it is easy to snap the drill bit if the angle is altered while drilling; always maintain a right angle and use a slow speed if the drill speed can be adjusted. It can be easier to begin the hole after releasing the trigger; the slow-down in revolutions allows the operator's hand to be steadier and thus better attuned to selecting a target. Once the hole is established, and before drill chuck motion has ceased, press the trigger again to complete the task.

to direct the drill accurately. **Note**: Centralize this hole even if the marked depression is slightly off-centre.

3. Enlarge the corresponding side panel hole to 3mm (⅛in) for clearance of the screw shank.
4. Screw the side panel and back together, using a 19mm (¾in) No 4 chipboard-thread screw with countersunk Pozidriv or Phillips head.
5. Again using a bradawl, mark through all other potential screw holes into the edge of the back panel.
6. Unscrew the components and repeat stages 2 and 3 for all the holes.
7. Screw the components together.
8. Repeat the procedure for the other side panel.

Empty shell.

GROUND FLOOR TO BACK AND SIDES

1. Lay the back and sides assembly on its back.
2. Position the ground floor against it.
3. Using the same procedure as with the back and side-panel assembly, mark first one screw hole, then repeat for all the others and assemble.

INNER WALLS AND FLOOR ASSEMBLY (W/F ASSEMBLY)

Parts involved:
Left side upper/lower wall unit; right lower wall; right upper wall; first floor.

CUTTING

Mark and cut the four panels as shown, ensuring that the first-floor plywood surface has a good grain finish, just as you did with the ground floor. Using an HB pencil, mark location destinations on the panels: left, right, back and front, as in the diagram. Avoid marking the plywood unduly, as all pencil marks will have to be sanded off later.

Slide the left upper and lower wall unit onto the floor panel so that the front edges are aligned. If assembly is very tight or impossible, cautiously widen one or both of the relevant slots until a correct sliding fit is facilitated. Dismantle.

ASSEMBLING FIRST-FLOOR INNER WALLS AND FLOOR

1. Mark the position of the upper right-hand wall base edge on the first-floor surface. As usual, mark a central screw-hole line between these edge parameter lines.
2. Drill just two 2mm (5/64in) holes along this line, front and back, avoiding the door cut-out area.
3. Turning the first-floor panel upside-down, mark the underside as shown, repeating stage 2 for this new screw line, again using only two screws.
4. Positioning the right upper wall on the floor in its correct position, aligning the two front edges, mark through one of the screw holes and drill the pilot in the right upper wall base in the usual way.

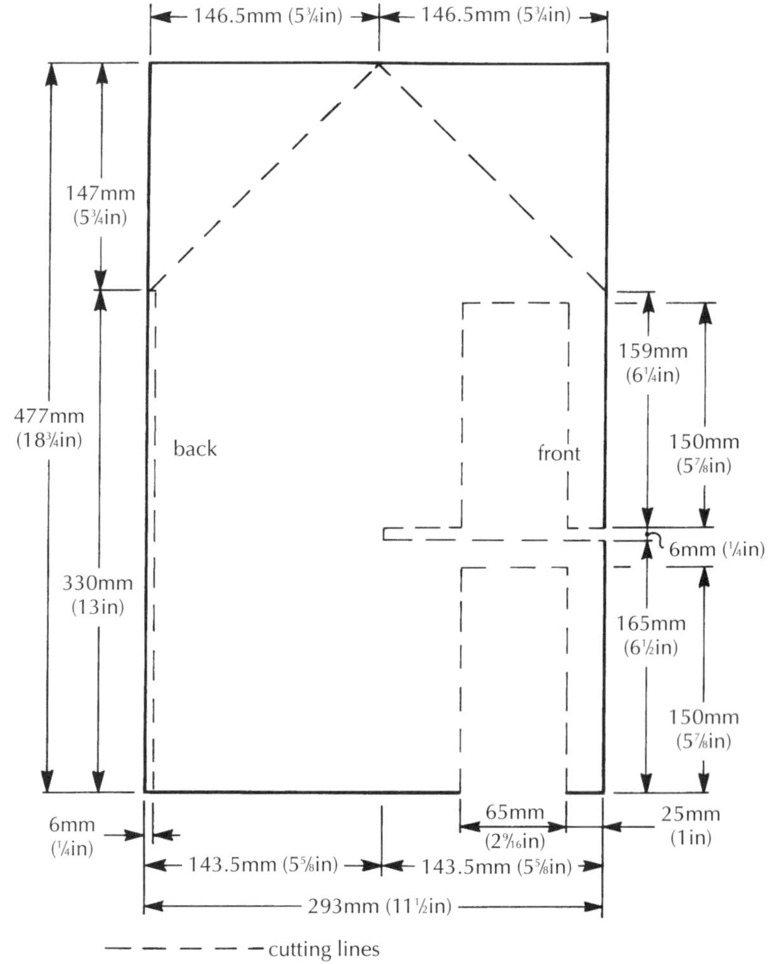

Left upper and lower walls: cutting lines.

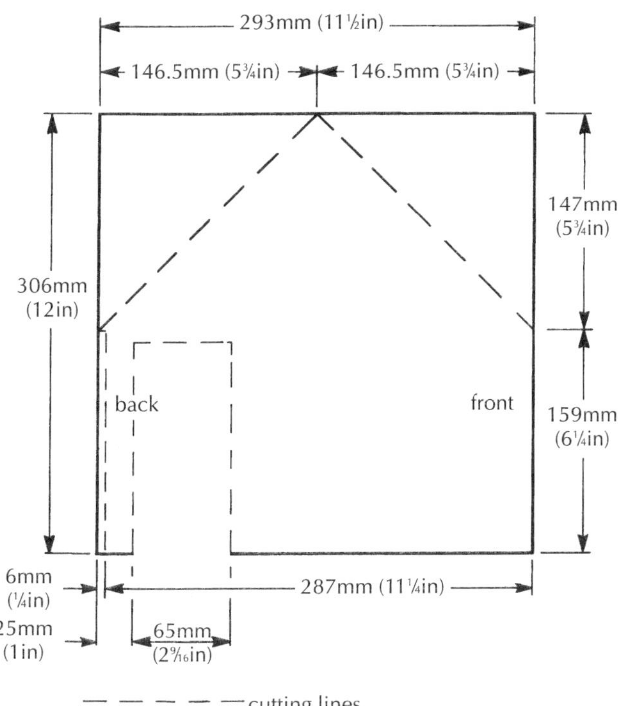

Right upper wall: cutting lines.

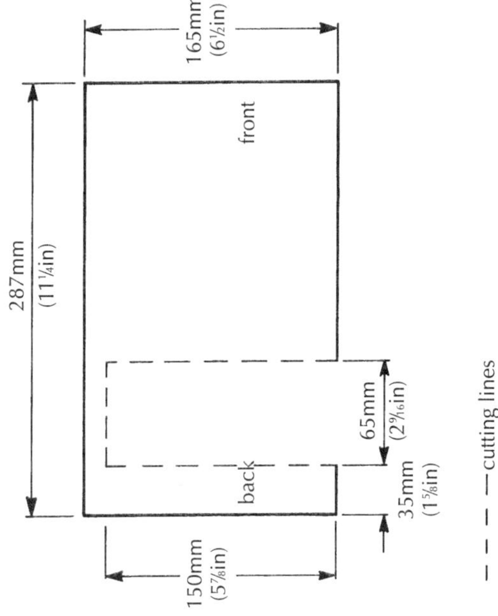

Right lower wall: cutting lines.

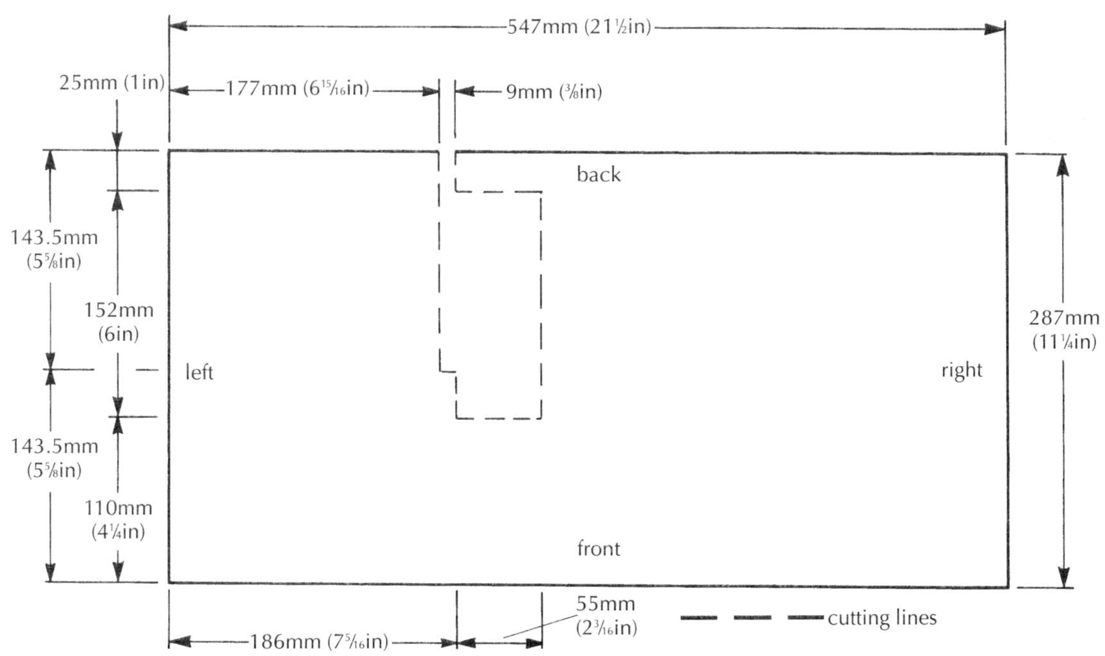

First floor: cutting lines (top surface).

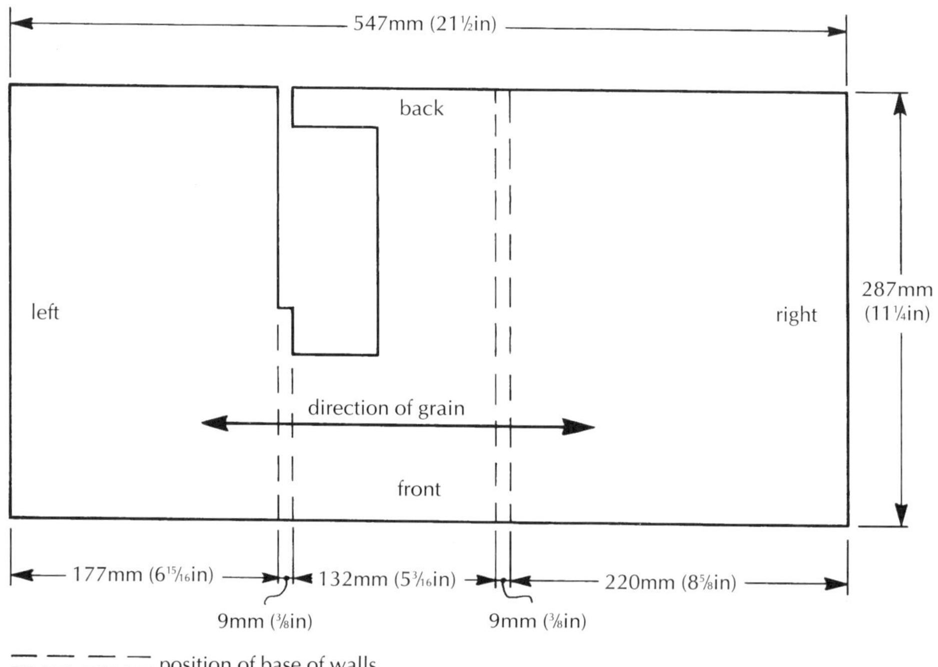

First-floor top surface, to show the position of the upper-storey walls.

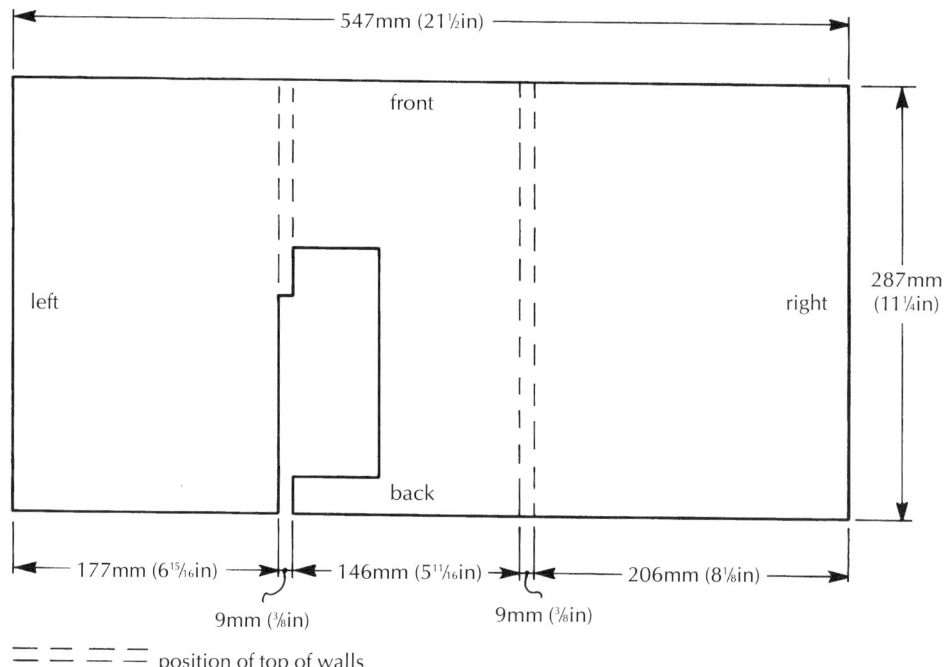

Underside of the first floor to show the position of the lower-storey walls against the ceiling.

Enlarge the clearance hole in the floor to 3mm (⅛in) and screw the panels together, this time using 25mm (1in) No 4 chipboard-thread screws. The 9mm (⅜in) MDF is less prone to splitting, therefore a longer screw is desirable for the resultant extra strength of bond.

5. Repeat for the other screw hole.
6. Dismantle the assembled unit.
7. Repeat steps 4 and 5 for the lower right-hand wall.
8. Assemble the complete unit.

PLANING TIPS

1. Always use a plane to remove unwanted timber: this ensures a straight edge. When planing plywood across the grain, work from an edge to the middle when possible as working towards an edge can tear the end grain.
2. Be careful not to plane away too much material. The sides of the empty shell are unsupported and may be presenting at an angle greater or less than 90°. If the first floor is the correct size and its corners are true, it should serve to correct any angle faults in the structure and solidify the house as a whole, even if it does not appear to fit perfectly at first.

FITTING THE WALL AND FLOOR ASSEMBLY INTO THE SHELL

Slide the W/F assembly into the shell and check that it fits correctly, if necessary making minor adjustments.

Wall and floor assembly.

1. Using an HB pencil, lightly mark suitable positions on the ground floor for screw fixings for the lower walls, avoiding door positions (holes at 75mm/3in centres).
2. Remove the W/F assembly from the shell.
3. Drill 2mm (5/64in) holes as marked in stage 1.
4. Replace the W/F assembly in the shell, and use a bradawl to mark a couple of prospective screw destination holes from the back panel into the rear of the first floor, one at each end.

5. Remove the W/F assembly and drill pilot holes in these two marked spots; enlarge the screw clearance holes to 3mm (⅛in).
6. Replace the W/F assembly and drive two 25mm (1in) No 4 screws into the holes and tighten so that the unit is pulled into position.
7. Mark all the other holes in the usual way.
8. Remove the W/F assembly from the shell. Drill all the pilot holes and enlarge all the clearance holes.
9. Reassemble and drive all the screws home. Use 25mm (1in) screws.
10. Using a try-square, check that the walls stand at 90° to the floors. A slight disparity is acceptable and may be unavoidable.
11. Cut a length of triangular-section ramin or softwood (12mm/½in wide) to 548mm (21⅝in).

MARKING FOR SCREW DESTINATION HOLES: TIP

When marking for screw destination pilot holes, ensure that the edges of panels are within the marked lines on the panels to which they are to bond. If they are not, the bradawl may miss the wall altogether.

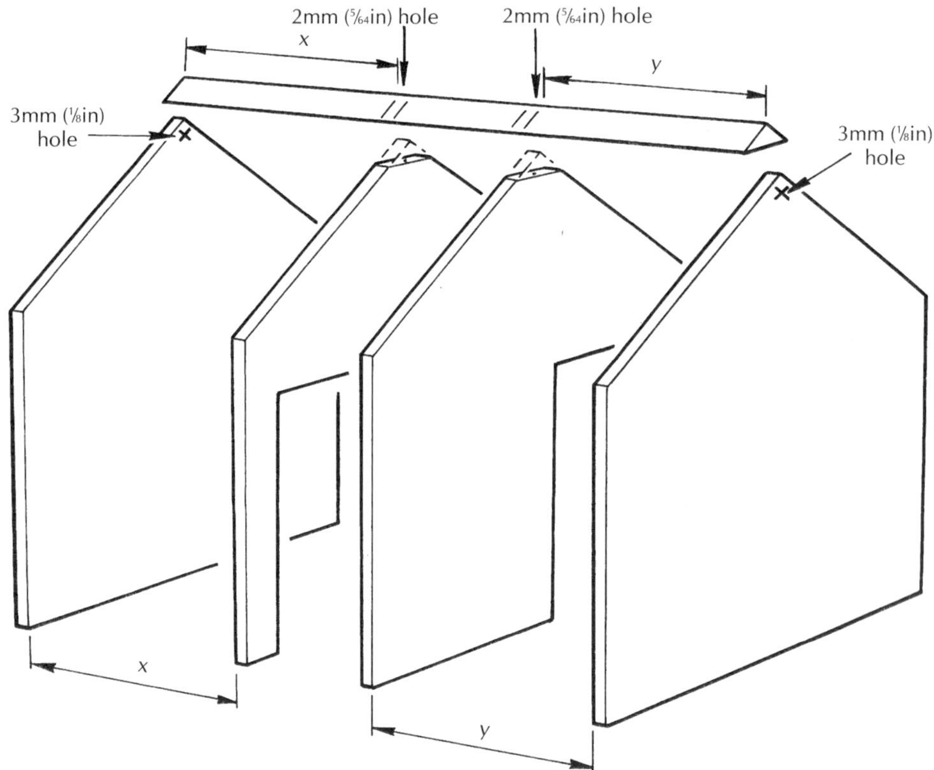

The fitting of the apex roof joint.

12. Drill 3mm (⅛in) holes at the top of the end walls, near to the apex of the triangle, as in the diagram opposite.
13. Mark the correct position along the length of the triangular batten for the apex of the upper walls 1 and 2 on all three sides. Drill 3mm (⅛in) holes midway between these lines through one flat face, so that the drill bit emerges at or close to the opposing apex of the triangular profile.
14. Cut the two upper walls as shown: remove enough of the material to allow for the cross sectional profile of the triangular batten. (Be careful not to cut off too much material. If this happens, use thin slivers of plywood as packing pieces so that the batten fits correctly.)

Constructed house.

15. Fit the batten and mark the positions of the screw destination pilot holes, then drill these and screw the batten in position. The addition of this batten ensures that the top-storey inner walls stand upright.
16. Run a long metal rule or straight-edge along both sides of the roof slope. If it is found that any of the walls stand proud of the rest, plane their top edge cautiously until the straight-edge shows no humps or gaps along the four surfaces. Normally it is only the inner walls that may require attention, particularly as minor discrepancies are permissible.

Wall and floor assembly in position.

17. As in stage 16, run a straight-edge along the front of the house. Plane off any projecting wall or floor edges, apart from that of the ground floor, which should project in front of the rest (see next stage) so as to form a base for the opening front sections.
18. The front edge of the ground floor should project beyond the rest by 9mm (⅜in). Measure this distance and mark a cutting line for later, when the house is dismantled.

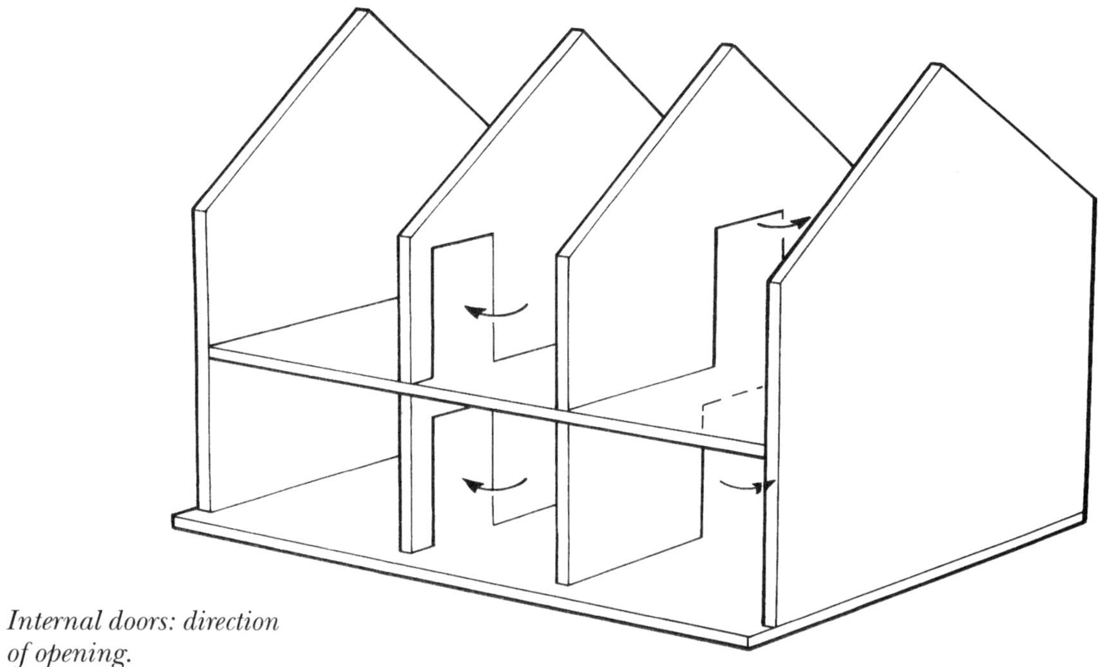

Internal doors: direction of opening.

INTERNAL DOORS

Parts involved:
Four interior doors.

1. The diagram above shows the direction of opening of the internal doors, and which of the two long edges of each door frame houses the hinges. Mark the internal wall door frames accordingly for reference when the house is dismantled.
2. Dismantle the complete assembly.
3. Cut off the ground floor overlap at the cutting line in stage 18 on page 39.
4. Cut four rectangles from 9mm ($\frac{3}{8}$in) MDF, size 150 × 65mm ($5\frac{15}{16} \times 2\frac{9}{16}$in).
5. Fit hinges to the doors (*see* Chapter 3, Techniques).
6. Hang the doors (*see* Chapter 3, Techniques). It is virtually impossible to see if a door is too short if the shortfall is at the base, and allowing for an approximately 2mm ($\frac{5}{64}$in) gap between floor and base can make things quicker and simpler. Similarly, there is no point in painting the base of the doors: these edges will never be seen and are useful areas for making identification marks, as required in the next stage.
7. Identify corresponding doors and their frames by numbering them on their bases and the base of the relevant wall.
8. Remove doors.
9. For door handles, use cyanoacrylate glue to bond 5mm ($\frac{3}{16}$in) lengths of 6mm-diameter ($\frac{1}{4}$in-diameter), round dowelling onto each side, 100mm ($3\frac{15}{16}$in) from the bottom of the door, and inset slightly. A few moments of hand pressure are all that is required to make a good bond.

DECORATING THE INTERIOR

1. Apply primer and undercoat, and then gloss paint to the doors.
2. Apply primer, then emulsion paint to the internal faces of the side walls, the back and all the internal walls. Before treating

the ground-floor ceiling (plywood) in the same way, fill the grain with fine surface wood filler and sand smooth.

3. Rehang the internal doors and make sure that they close properly. Sometimes the thickness of the coats of paint may cause a door to jam; trimming and repainting is then required.
4. Mark and carve the long-grain and cross-grain grooves on the top surface of both floors (refer to Chapter 3, Techniques), measuring the floorboard widths from the front edge so that any partial widths occur at the rear. Floorboard width is 15mm (⅝in), and length is 305mm (12in).
5. Seal the carved surfaces with polyurethane varnish, following the manufacturer's instructions. Normally two or three coats are required, sanding with fine sandpaper between coats and allowing each to dry out thoroughly.

PERMANENT ASSEMBLY

1. Countersink all 3mm (⅛in) screw holes, taking care at the panel edges not to cut through the material entirely.
2. For the two sides, the back and the ground floor, use a 6mm (¼in) chisel to scrape all the paint/varnish from where the sheet edges will join the panels, along the screw lines. Similarly, drag a chisel along the edges to be bonded removing any paint.
3. Screw the first floor to the lower right-hand wall (use no adhesive).
4. Apply PVA wood glue to the cavity around the screw head and the base of the timber infill piece, then push the piece of veneer into position. Repeat for the other screw heads. Sand smooth with medium paper until the infill pieces match the rest and varnish.
5. Screw the upper right wall in position (again, no adhesive).
6. Slide the left W/F assembly onto the first floor.
7. Apply PVA adhesive to all edges and surfaces that are to be joined, and assemble the back, sides and ground floor, driving home all the screws.
8. Applying adhesive as above, push the W/F assembly into position and drive home all the screws.
9. Remove excess adhesive with a damp cloth before it dries.

DISGUISING SCREW HEADS

Use infill plywood veneer pieces to disguise screw heads in the first-floor boards: remove a piece of the top layer of veneer from a scrap piece of plywood of the same type as used for the first floor. Cut a small square or rhomboid shape from it: this piece must be slightly larger than one of the countersunk screw holes in the floor. Sand the edges of this piece slightly so that they slope downwards from the top (in other words, the base area is fractionally smaller than the top). Place this piece over the screw-head hole area in the first floor, and draw round it. Cut a groove along these lines and remove material within the cut shape with a suitable chisel, to just the depth of the top layer of veneer. Check that the infill piece fits snugly in the cavity, preferably proud of the surface so that it can be sanded smooth later. Repeat the process for the other countersunk screw hole in the first floor.

10. Remove paint from the areas which are to bond to the triangular roof joist, apply the adhesive, and screw this in position.

ROOF AND FRONT OPENING SECTIONS

Parts involved:
Roof 1; roof 2; front left and right sections; eaves strip; 13mm (½in) triangular-section timber; L-shaped profile 12mm (½in) timber.

THE ROOF

1. Using a plane, chamfer the top long sides of each roof panel to a 45° angle (approximately), then position them on the roof slopes to make sure that there is little or no gap where they meet at the top edge.
2. Ensure that the roof overhang is equal at each side, then fix the two panels in the correct position, using a couple of 19mm (¾in) screws driven into the side walls, near to the ridge of the roof. Pilot drill the destination holes, and enlarge the clearance holes in the usual way.
3. Measure and mark a line at gutter level that allows a 22mm (⅞in) overhang beyond the front of the house. Remove the roof panel and cut along this line. Repeat for the other panel.
4. Prime and emulsion paint the inside – (the ceiling area) – of the panels.
5. Refit panels, this time marking for screw lines accurately along the slope of the four walls that will be in contact with the surface. Drill screw holes at approximately 75mm (3in) centres, and countersink.
6. Remove the panels, scrape off the paint where the wall edges are to join them. Apply adhesive to the areas to be bonded, refit and drive all the screws home.
7. Cut an L-shaped 12mm (½in) wide moulding to the correct length for fitting on the ridge of the roof. Bond this to the ridge using only PVA adhesive. Initial firm pressure is all that is necessary in these circumstances, since the glue will bond by suction (*see* Chapter 2, Materials).

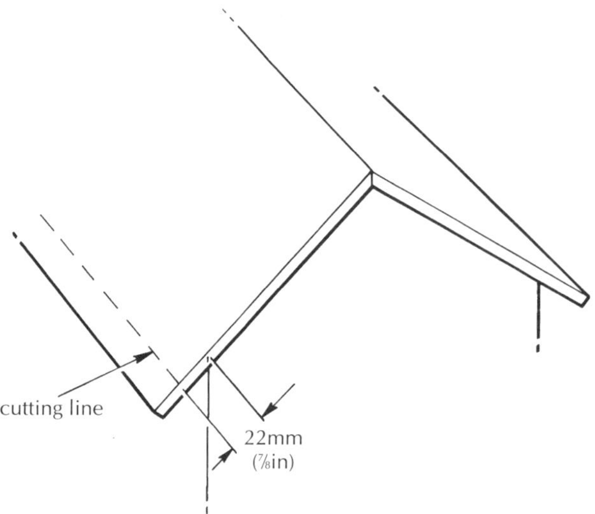

Roof panel fixing.

Front view of house without fronts.

THE FRONT OPENING SECTIONS

1. Chamfer one long edge of the 15mm (⅝in) wide eaves strip of 9mm (⅜in) MDF so that it will fit against the front of the house and under the front eaves, allowing approximately 8mm (5⁄16in) to project below the roof overhang. Adjust the position of this strip until the distance from its bottom edge to the ground floor is the same on both sides: approximately 307mm (12 1⁄16in). Drill suitable holes and screw this strip in position into the top of the front of the four walls of the house, as below.
2. Mark along this strip 207mm (8 3⁄16in) from the left side of the house and the same distance along the ground floor, so that these two marks are correctly above one another. Joining these marks forms the front break line, along which the front of the house divides to open.
3. Take the left-hand front section and trim it to fit between the ground floor and the eaves strip.
4. Use a try-square to ensure that the *right*-hand edge of the panel is square to the top and bottom, planing if necessary.
5. Scribe a line with the marking gauge, 9mm (⅜in) in from the right-hand edge along the *front* of panel.
6. Clamp the panel to the workbench and plane the MDF edge to a 45° angle, so that a wedge-shaped edge is produced. Aim to complete the planing at the marked line, thus ensuring the correct angle of 45°, gradating from 9mm (⅜in) at the marked line and sloping down to zero.

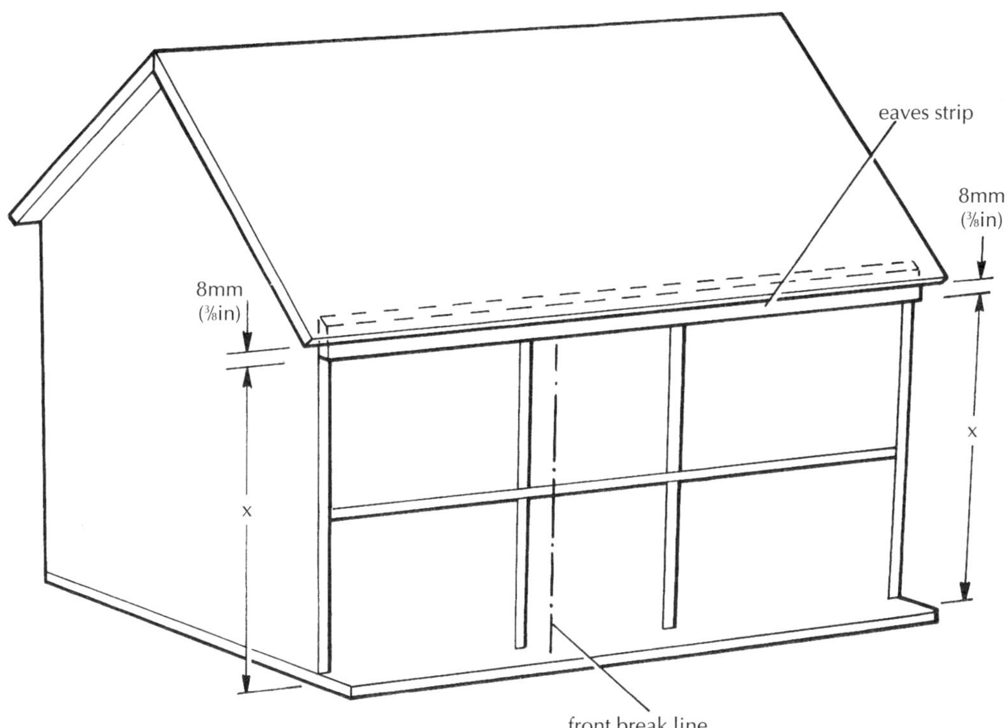

Eaves strip fixing position and the front break line.

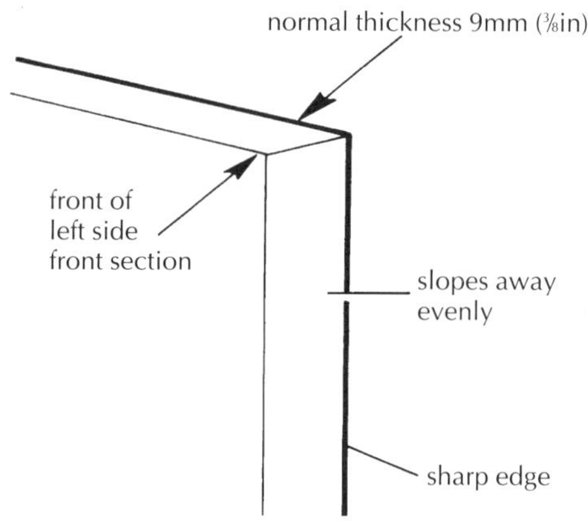

Left-hand section of front to show mating-edge chamfer.

View of front opening section.

7. Repeat stages 3 and 4 for the right-hand front section, but this time ensure that the *left*-hand edge is square to the top and bottom.
8. Scribe a line 9mm (⅜in) in from the left-hand edge, but this time scribe on the *back* of the panel, not the front as before.
9. Repeat stage 6 for this panel, but remove the material from the back of the panel edge, not the front. The left and right sections are to overlap, as in the photograph.
10. Placing the two front sections on the front of the house, move them together so that they overlap as they should. Plane each until they overlap correctly, and the blade of the right-hand edge meets the thickness of the left at the front break line.
11. With the left and right fronts meeting correctly as above, draw a line on each panel to denote the overlap at the right and left of the house. Trim off this overlap for both panels.
12. Fix the panels to the left and right wall hinges: mark the hinge positions accu-

SCREW HOLES FOR HINGES

In the unlikely event of using up two screw-hole positions on a hinge, neither of which is correct, the best option is to drill another screw hole in the hinge flange. Hinges are normally soft brass and present no particular problems. Countersink the hole with a much larger drill in a similar way to when countersinking miniature hinge flanges.

Front view of house with fronts open.

rately when the doors are in the closed position, using this level to ascertain the correct height for the screw positioning. Lateral screw positioning is necessarily a matter of careful judgement, but if one screw in one hinge is done at a time, mistakes can be rectified.

ROOF TILING AND CHIMNEY

Parts involved:
0.8mm (1/32in) plywood; 50mm (2in) square-section timber; 25mm (1in) dowel.

TILING

1. Cut a 0.8mm (1/32in) plywood sheet to a length of 630mm (24¾in), with the grain running lengthways.
2. Cut this lengthways into strips, 23mm (15/16in) wide. Use a marking gauge to scribe a line from a marked straight edge, then cut along this line with a sharp craft knife against a metal rule: after two deep cuts, the strip can be folded upwards and will snap off. Plane the remaining sheet edge to ensure that the next strip will have one straight edge, which should then be marked. Repeat the procedure for as many strips as will be necessary.

TILING TIP

If 0.8mm (1/32in) plywood sheet is unavailable in the required length (630mm/24¾in, with the grain running lengthways), the requisite length may be obtained by joining two strips at the juncture of two complete tiles. The join will be invisible, as the upper portion of the row will be concealed by the tiles above. Match the joint gap to the gaps between the other tiles (see stage 5).

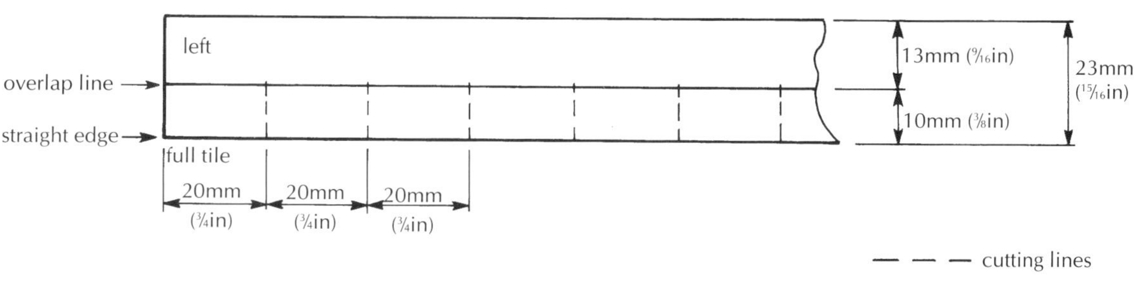

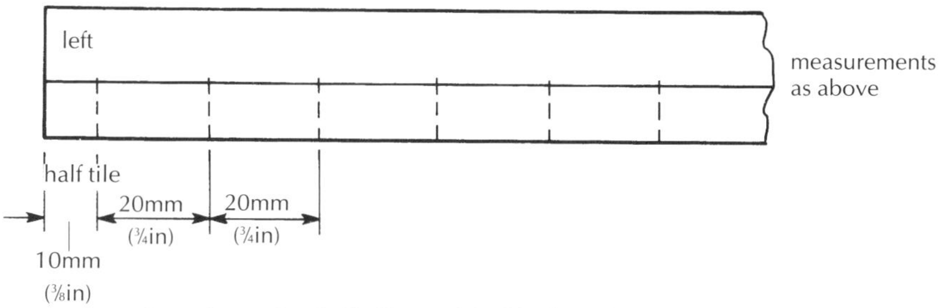

Roof-tile rows; cutting plans for full tile and half tile at left.

3. Again using the marking gauge, scribe a line 10mm (⅜in) away from the marked (i.e. straight) edge for each strip. This is the overlap line.

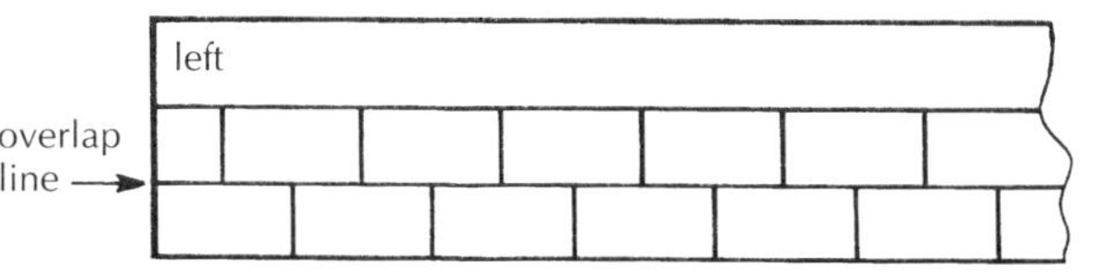

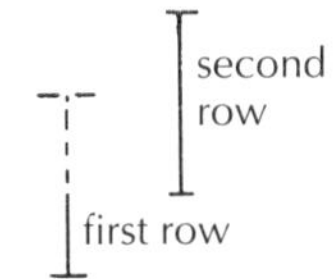

Method of fixing roof-tile rows.

4. Holding the strip against a long rule, mark along it at 20mm (¾in) intervals with an HB pencil, beginning from the left (delineate this end for later). Mark half of the cut strips in this way. Mark the other half of the strips beginning with an initial left-end measurement of 10mm (⅜in), as shown above; this latter measurement indicates a half tile.
5. Cut along these lines, extending the cut approximately 2mm (1⁄16in) beyond the overlap line. An electric fretsaw or bandsaw would be the tool of choice for cutting, but a jigsaw can be used, with the work held securely in a vice. Make sure that the panel is adequately supported, for jigsaw cutting may be tricky; pliers, or mechanics' adjustable grips could be used for this. **Note**: always keep fingers *behind* and *well away* from the jigsaw blade, however tempting it may be to support the work in this way.

   Alternatively, these slots may be cut easily using a junior or standard-size hacksaw while holding the strip in a vice. When cutting with a hacksaw, no more than 6mm (¼in) must project above the jaws of the vice, or the thin panel may bend and snap. Cutting with a knife across the grain is not advised.
6. Draw lines along the slope of the roof panels at 25mm (1in) intervals from the bottom to the top. Check that the length from ridge to gutter is constant from left to right.
7. Apply PVA adhesive to the bottom 25mm (1in)of one of the roof panels and to one side of a strip of tiles that begins with a full tile width, then stick the tiles in position, aligning the left-hand (marked) end with the roof's left edge, and the base line with that of the panel, allowing the overhang to project over the right-hand side. Push firmly along the complete length of the row so that suction develops between the adhesive-covered surfaces. There is no need to maintain pressure to achieve a bond under these circumstances.

AVOIDING A SIDEWAYS SLANT WHEN GLUING TILES

Use the lines marked on the roof at 25mm (1in) intervals as a way of visually checking that the rows of tiles are running parallel with the gutter and ridge line, and are not slanting sideways. If a sideways slant becomes apparent, a small disparity can be corrected by fractionally sloping the rows above to compensate. Correct this kind of fault early on, as it is important that the lines are completely parallel near the ridge; any slanting here will be immediately obvious.

8. Repeat the procedure, this time selecting a strip of tiles that begins with a 10mm (⅜in) tile on the left (marked) end, so that the bottom edge of this second row meets the overlap line of the first. The tile joints will appear staggered, as in the diagram opposite.
9. Repeat this procedure, alternating a full width of tile on the left with a half width, all the way up the roof.
10. Keep adding rows of tiles until no more can be applied; the top row is likely to need trimming along its length (at the top) to fit. If the distance between the highest overlap line and the edge of the L-shaped moulding is greater than 12mm (½in), move the row down slightly so as to make room for another. The final row will then be too wide and must be trimmed. When no more rows of tiles can be applied, measure the gap between the L-shaped moulding edge and the overlap line on the top row of tiles, and cut individual tiles from the thin plywood accordingly. Stick these in position one by one, matching the gaps to those below.
11. After tiling both roof planes, mark the L-shaped ridge moulding at 20mm (¾in) intervals along the front, staggering the joints according to the row of individually cut tiles immediately below. Cut shallow lines on the front of the moulding with a tenon saw, continuing these cuts across the other plane of the moulding so as to simulate ridge tiles. If these lines happen to coincide with the joint lines in the row of tiles below on the rear plane of the roof, it does not matter.
12. Trim off the overlap on the right-hand side of the roof panels.

THE CHIMNEY

1. Cut a length of 50 × 50mm (2 × 2in) batten, 50mm (2in) long. This forms the block of the chimney.
2. Mark as below for cutting a roof-mating angle.
3. Cut out the V-shaped section, using a tenon or cross-cut saw and holding the block of wood in the vice.

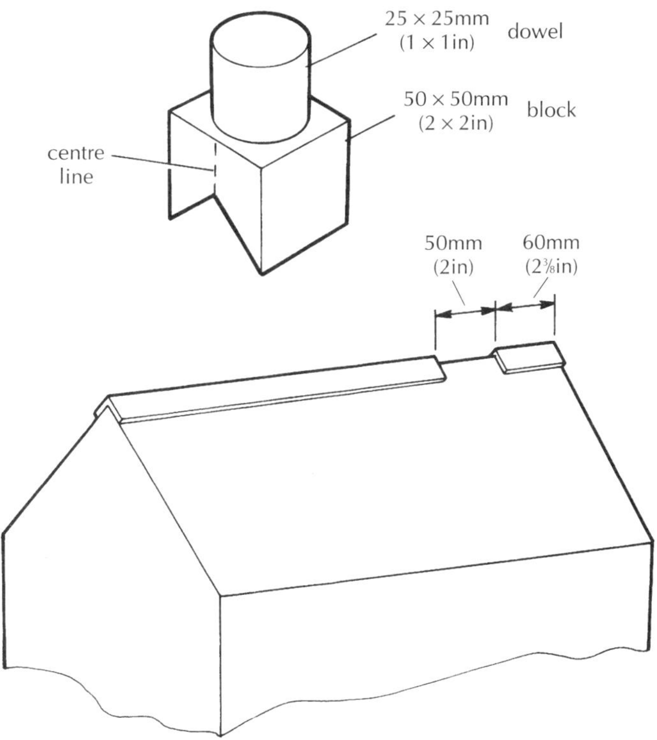

Chimney: component parts, plus cutting of V-shaped moulding to facilitate chimney reception.

4. Clean up the interior planes of this V-shaped area with a chisel.
5. Measure 60mm (2⅜in) in from the right-hand edge of the roof, and mark two lines on the ridge moulding to denote the position of the chimney, as above.
6. Using a tenon saw, cut through the moulding within these lines and remove the pieces with a chisel.
7. Trim the block so that it sits on the roof with as few gaps as possible.
8. Cut a 25mm (1in) length of 25 × 25mm (1 × 1in) dowel, and stick this onto the top surface of the block using epoxy resin adhesive.
9. Stick the chimney in position on the roof, using epoxy resin adhesive.

FRONT SECTION CUT-OUTS AND PORCH

Parts involved:
Porch sides 1 and 2; porch roofs 1 and 2; 9mm (⅜in) square timber; wire mesh; 0.8mm (1/32in) plywood.

CUTTING THE FRONT-SECTION APERTURES

1. Cut out the window and front door apertures as below, measuring accurately from the left and right-hand edges of the left and right front panels.

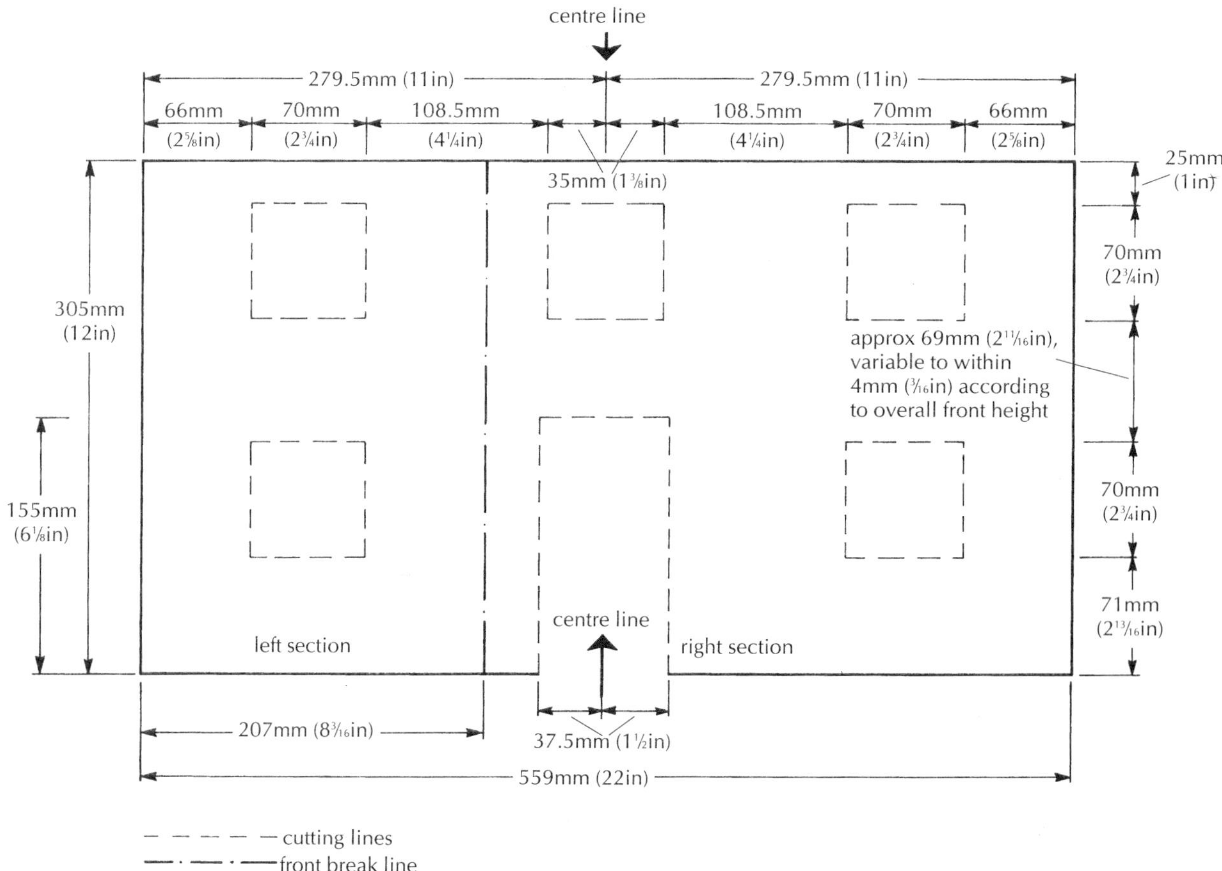

Front sections: window and door cutting lines.

Front view of house with fronts shut.

For all windows:

2. Working from the front of the panel (exterior face), draw a box surrounding the window aperture, 3mm (⅛in) away from the edges of the hole. Cut grooves along these marked lines, then remove the material (i.e. make a rebate) from between the window aperture edge and this line to a depth of approximately 1.5mm (1/16in).
3. Cut squares of garden mesh of the same size as the enlarged area: 76 × 76mm (3 × 3in). Cut these squares at an angle to the edges of the sheet so that the mesh cells present diamonds rather than squares.
4. Stick these squares of mesh into the rebated window cavities, trimming to fit as necessary. Use nitrile (clear, all-purpose) contact adhesive.

PORCH

1. Chamfer with a plane the top (narrow) edge of both porch side panels. Fix in position as shown in the diagram below, by screwing through the door surround into the edge of the porch panel (do not use adhesive at this stage).
2. Chamfer with a plane the top narrow edge of both porch roof panels, so that the panels meet reasonably well when in

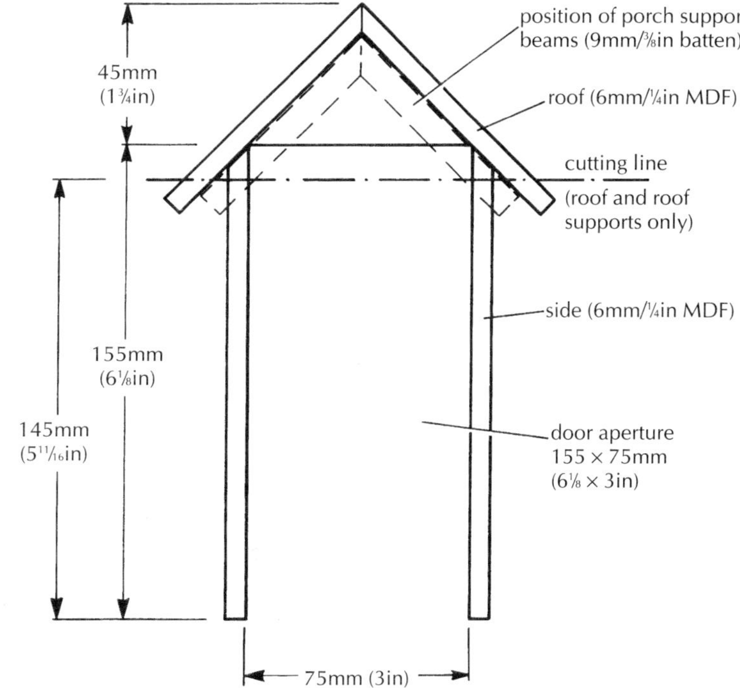

Porch.

the correct position; the join will be concealed, so imperfect fitting is acceptable.
3. Fix these porch roof panels in the same way as the sides.
4. Holding a ruler parallel with the base of the house, mark along the front edge of the porch roof panels to delineate the correct angle, as in the diagram on the previous page.
5. Remove the porch roof panels and plane, or cut and plane the lower edges to the correct, marked angle.
6. Remove the porch side panels and replace permanently, screwing and gluing.
7. Screw and glue the porch roof panels in position.
8. Cutting the angles to match the porch roof angles, use 9mm (⅜in) square batten to make the porch support beams, as in the diagram on the previous page.
9. Glue a suitable length of ridge tile moulding (12mm/½in L-shaped) along the apex of the porch roof.
10. Tile the porch roof using the same method as for the main roof.

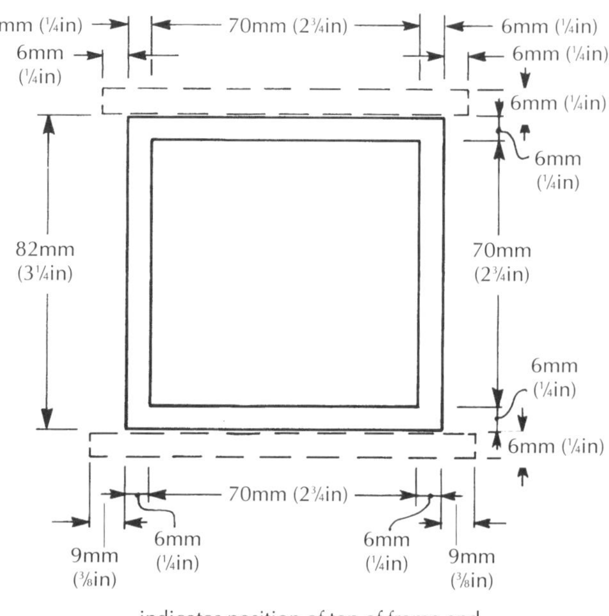

Window frames and shutter fixing mouldings.

WINDOW FRAMES, MOCK SHUTTERS AND FRONT DOOR

Parts involved:
5 window frames; 10 shutters; front door; 12 × 6mm (½ × ¼in) timber.

WINDOW FRAMES

For each window frame:
1. Cut a frame from 6mm (¼in) MDF, as in the diagram. Cut the outer lines first, then the inner. Either an electric fretsaw, or a jigsaw may be used. Alternatively, a hand-held fretsaw or keyhole saw may be used.
2. Cut two lengths of 12 × 6mm (½ × ¼in) timber moulding: 93mm (3 11/16in) for the top and 102mm (4in) for the window-sill. Use a mitre block or machine to ensure square ends.
3. Using contact adhesive, glue these lengths on edge to the top and the bottom of the frame, so that the mouldings are flush with the back of the unit and project equally on either side.

SHUTTERS

Whether or not to add mock shutters is a matter of personal taste. Their addition improves the overall appearance of the finished house, but it may be decided they are not worth the extra time and trouble involved in their construction, in which case ignore the following stages 1 to 8.

There is also the option of adding shutters at a later date if required.

For each shutter:

1. Prepare ten panels of 6mm (¼in) MDF at 82 × 35mm (3¼ × 1⅜in) for making the mock shutters.
2. Using the marking gauge, scribe a border 6mm (¼in) in from the sides and the same distance from the top. Mark the top.
3. Measure 6mm (¼in) down from this top line, and draw a line parallel to it. Repeat, drawing lines below this between the two side scribe lines at 6mm (¼in) intervals until approximately 8mm (5/16in) from the base (twelve lines in total, including the top scribed line).
4. Measure and mark lines 2mm (5/64in) below these lines, and parallel to them.
5. Score a deep line with a craft knife along each of the original (upper) lines.
6. Using a sharp 19mm (¾in) or 12mm (½in) chisel positioned on the lower line, slice material at an angle to meet the upper line. The resultant carvings should have a straight-cut upper edge and the lower edge sloping towards it should be at an angle of approximately 45°.
7. Stick the shutters in place with contact adhesive, as in the photograph of house exterior. Allow approximately 3mm (⅛in) of the window frame to be visible each side.
8. Prime, undercoat and gloss paint the shutters and frame as a unit. It may be preferred to paint the shutters a different colour from the window frames, in which case they should be painted before fixing.

THE FRONT DOOR

The front door is made from 9mm (⅜in) MDF, and its size is 153 × 75mm (6 1/16 × 3in). Cut this, fix and rebate the hinges in the usual way, and hang in the frame. A handle or knocker may be fixed as required; a suitable screw eye and ring is obtainable from ironmongers and/or hardware shops (*see* photograph of house exterior).

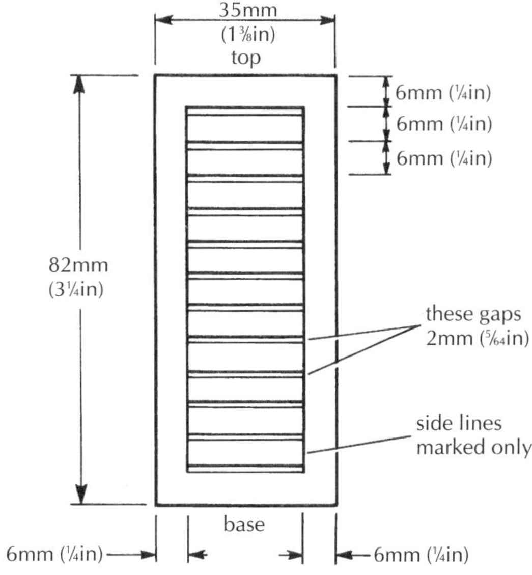

Making mock shutters.

FASTENING THE FRONT SECTIONS

A small hook and eye is the method used in the prototype, but a strong magnetic catch would be equally effective. If using the hook and eye, mark through the open front door the position of the ground-floor ceiling on the inside of the right front panel, when the front is closed. Open the front and fix the eye just underneath this mark. Close the front panel again, this time with the hook attached to the eye. Mark the position on the ceiling to fix the hook. Open the front and fix the hook in place. If a magnetic fastening is decided upon, this should be fixed in the same location.

STAIRS

Parts involved: 6mm (¼in) plywood panels; 19mm (¾in) square-section timber for treads.

The stairs are for hanging on a left-hand wall; the banister is a solid panel. See the instructions in Chapter 3, Techniques, to augment the specific points detailed below.

1. The length of run is 175mm (6⅞in), and the height between floors is 165mm (6½in). The banister rail height is 75mm (3in). Mark the left-hand plywood panel accordingly for the stair line.
2. Cut nine treads, each 38mm (1½in) long, using a mitre block or precision mitre saw. It is very important to have 90° cuts and equal lengths or the stairs will not assemble correctly. Use the end stop on the precision mitre saw for accurate tread cutting, or screw a piece of scrap timber onto the mitre block to perform the same function.
3. Continue as in Chapter 3, Techniques, to assemble the structure.
4. Mark the top of the banister rail by measuring the banister height (75mm/3in) from the top of the bottom stair, and from the top of the penultimate stair. Join these marks to make the banister rail line. Cut off the surplus timber.
5. Mark and measure the correct height from the base (165mm/6½in) to part of the height (riser) of the top stair. Cut away the upper portion of the stair and the plywood attached to it. Do not cut the banister rail panel.
6. Cut off the banister rail at the top as in the diagram, so that the rail finishes at the beginning of the final step. This allows the stairs to be inserted under the first floor, so that the thickness of the floor makes up the full stair thickness.
7. Check that the stairs fit correctly in position, trimming to fit if necessary.
8. Fill all the gaps and cavities with filler and sand when dry, then fill all open grain with fine surface filler and sand. Do not fill the grain on the left side

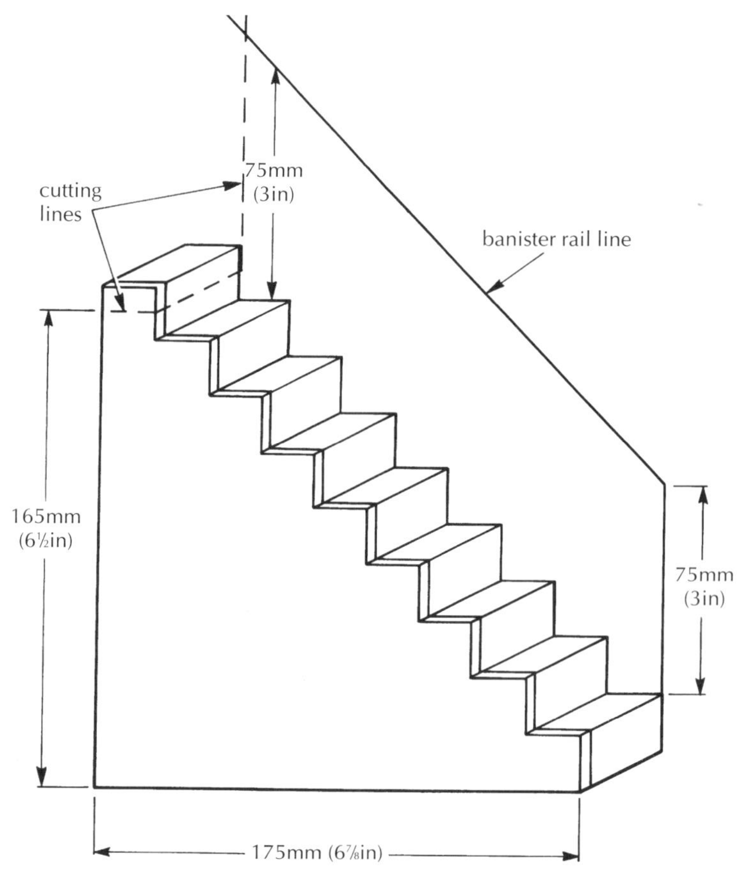

Staircase construction and banister rail cutting.

CHOICE

Stairs can be left as a box (as the prototype), or the underneath part of the triangle can be removed as depicted in Chapter 3, Techniques. Since the hall in the country cottage is narrow, it is unnecessary to remove these parts as no extra room area would be attained. It also means an under-stairs cupboard can be created if required.

wall of the stairs since this will abut the lower left wall and will not be seen.

9. Prime, undercoat and gloss paint the assembly.
10. Stick the stairs in position using contact adhesive.

EXTERNAL DECORATION

1. Fill all the screw-hole cavities and blemishes with a surface filler, and finish off so the panels are smooth.
2. Use texture coating material to cover the external walls and front of the house. Before this material is dry, dab the surface with a 50mm (2in) or smaller brush a number of times until a realistic stipplecast-type finish is created. It is best to do a small area at a time.
3. Prime all bare wood areas and then paint the walls and front with emulsion.
4. Prime the roof tiles and porch roof tiles, and emulsion paint them a suitable colour.
5. Paint the metal window mesh black on both sides.
6. When painting is completed, stick on the window frame/mock shutter assemblies using clear contact adhesive. The one above the porch is likely to foul the ridge beam on the porch, so trim part of the top of this with a chisel.

FINISHING OFF

1. Inside the house there will inevitably be damaged and flawed areas of paintwork which must be made good with filler and paint, particularly where walls and floors have been fixed to flat panels and the paint has been scraped off.
2. Extras such as skirting boards may be added if required. These should be cut, marked for identification and painted before cutting and fixing in place with contact adhesive. They can be used to cover up badly finished paint areas.

EXPERIMENTING WITH TEXTURE COATING MATERIAL

Experiment with texture material on scrap timber to develop the surface texture required. The brush should be soft, such as a toothbrush with splayed bristles if possible.

On the front area, do not apply the texture material within 10mm (⅜in) of the windows. This is so as to present a flat surface on which to glue the window frame/mock shutter assemblies.

CHAPTER 

The Tudor House

Timber-framed houses were developed from the old longhouses, or cruck construction homes, where people lived alongside their animals in a single room that had a hole in the roof to take away the smoke from their fires. Originally built by shipwrights, these structures were incredibly weatherproof, and many are still standing today. The structural timber moves substantially over the course of time, as may be witnessed in the examples of Tudor houses still standing. However, these buildings were constructed in such a way as to withstand such movements, the rest of the materials used being equally flexible.

The timber frame was erected first, then wattle and daub was used to infill the resultant square or rectangular panels. Wattle varied according to local materials, but normally consisted of oak laths, jammed in vertically between the horizontal timber members to make a framework to accept the daub. Where larger panels were to be covered, a smaller number of vertically positioned oak laths were sprung into holes in the timbers, and hazel twigs or 'withies' were woven horizontally around these uprights and sprung into the vertical studs on each side. Chestnut, alder and holly were sometimes used for these vertical staves or rods, hazel was the most common wood used for interweaving because of its pliability.

Daub was a kind of primitive concrete made from earth, clay, sand, cow manure, chopped straw, flax or animal hair and water. Amazingly, this material can still be re-used when dismantling old buildings, and is extremely weatherproof and serviceable. The cow manure acts as a binder for the mix, and also strengthens and waterproofs it. The daub was thrown at the wattle from both sides, then smoothed and allowed to dry. Shrinkage caused inevitable cracks which were afterwards infilled once more, the final surface sometimes being covered with lime plaster.

In spite of all the major building innovations since that time, it is recommended that these original materials are used when renovating such buildings, and daub is being manufactured by specialist producers today.

Very often the upper storey projects over the lower at the front, this outcrop being referred to as a jetty. It is assumed that one reason for this is that the craftsmen discovered that the floor joists for the upper floor could be supported more effectively by the front lower wall if this wall was stepped back from the outermost edge. Surprisingly, these floor joists were normally laid flat, builders in those days not realizing that far greater tensile strength could have been achieved by laying them on edge. Another possible reason for having a jetty in town houses might have been that it was intended as a measure of protection for pedestrians, in the days before piped drainage systems, who had to pass by houses where foul water was constantly being thrown from upper windows. The Shambles, in York, has some good examples of Tudor houses where the upper storeys project on both sides of the street.

Many surviving timber-framed houses have markedly sloping timbers and sagging roofs, which is probably a result of natural movement; the flexibility of the materials allows the structure to adapt rather than crack and collapse. On a full-sized house these idiosyncratic features add to the charm and mystery; on a dolls' house, however, they tend to look unreal. The right approach therefore is to aim for a properly measured, accurately proportioned house, while adding finishing touches to remove the 'smooth' neatness that can mar the appearance of some Tudor dolls' houses. Outside, wooden mouldings that are to simulate exterior timbers can be chiselled and sanded so that their edges are rounded rather than square. Inside, timber ceiling joists are treated similarly, and doors are made so as to simulate boarded construction.

DESCRIPTION AND DIMENSIONS

Shape: Rectangular (apart from the gabled roof). Chimney projects approximately 200mm (8in) above the rest.

Size: Width 690mm ($27\frac{3}{16}$); depth 380mm (15in); height 735mm ($28\frac{15}{16}$in), or 905mm ($35\frac{13}{16}$in) to top of chimney.

Rooms:

Ground floor left:	Width	370mm ($14\frac{9}{16}$in)
	Height	195mm ($7\frac{11}{16}$in)
	Depth	300mm ($11\frac{13}{16}$in)
Ground floor right:	Width	230mm ($9\frac{1}{16}$in)
	Height	195mm ($7\frac{11}{16}$in)
	Depth	300mm ($11\frac{13}{16}$in)
First floor left:	Width	250mm ($9\frac{7}{8}$in)
	Height	195mm ($7\frac{11}{16}$in)
	Depth	300mm ($11\frac{13}{16}$in)
First floor middle:	Width	158mm ($6\frac{1}{4}$in)
	Height	195mm ($7\frac{11}{16}$in)
	Depth	300mm ($11\frac{13}{16}$in)
First floor right:	Width	180mm ($7\frac{1}{8}$in)
	Height	195mm ($7\frac{11}{16}$in)
	Depth	300mm ($11\frac{13}{16}$in)
Top floor left:	Width	394mm ($15\frac{1}{2}$in)
	Height	293mm ($11\frac{9}{16}$in)
	Depth	350mm ($13\frac{13}{16}$in)
Top floor right:	Width	205mm ($8\frac{1}{8}$in)
	Height	293mm ($11\frac{9}{16}$in)
	Depth	350mm ($13\frac{13}{16}$in)

Floors: First and top floors are carved, made of dark-oak-stained plywood to simulate oak floorboards. The ground floor is surfaced with paving stones made from air-hardening clay.

Roof: Tiles, replicated from 0.8mm ($\frac{1}{32}$in) plywood.

Chimney and stack: Surface covered with air-hardening clay to simulate brick.

Exterior finish: MDF panels with various timber mouldings affixed in a pre-arranged formation.

Frontage: Intricate pattern of timber mouldings, incorporating a jetty overlooking the lower storey, supported by individually shaped timbers. Five large windows and a front door.

Windows: Latticed, painted black with frames incorporated into frontage timber patterning. Square-pattern lattice in the main house windows, diamond pattern in the roof gable windows.

Access to interior: Front-opening double doors, split to the left of the central front door. Removable roof.

Interior: Straight-run staircases, Tudor style, with single handrails. Individually made doors are crafted to simulate plank construction, held together by cross battens on one side, and lengthwise battens on the other. Fireplace with brick interior (made from air-hardening clay) and large mantelpiece. Ceilings timbered with small and larger intersecting beams.

MATERIALS

SHEET MATERIALS

9mm (⅜in) MDF

Sides S1, S2	2 @	710 × 355mm	28 × 14in
Back		608 × 417mm	24 × 16½in
Rectangular walls	3 @	300 × 195mm	11¹³⁄₁₆ × 7¹¹⁄₁₆in
Triangular wall		355 × 293mm	14 × 11½in
Base		626 × 330mm	24¾ × 13in
Right front section (FSR)		390 × 370mm	15⅜ × 14⅝in
Left front section (FSL)		390 × 290mm	15⅜ × 11⁷⁄₁₆in

Strips for making top (jetty) part of front sections:			
23mm (⅞in) wide	2 @	370mm	14⅝in
	4 @	190mm	7½in
	2 @	280mm	11⅛in
Strips for making chimney stack and chimney:			
44mm (1¾in) wide		700mm	27⅝in
		560mm	22⅛in
		340mm	13⅜in
		90mm	3⅝in
		180mm	7⅛in
		130mm	5⅛in
		134mm	5⅜in
37mm (1½in) wide		270mm	10⅝in
Chimney top		90 × 90mm	3½ × 3½in
Roof bracing pieces	4 @	90 × 90mm	3½ × 3½in

6mm (¼in) MDF

Roof:			
Main front panel		666 × 361mm	26¼ × 14¼in
Back panel fixed panel		666 × 290mm	26¼ × 11⁷⁄₁₆in
Back panel upper strip		666 × 83mm	26¼ × 3¼in
Gable side sections	4 @	210 × 120mm	8¼ × 4¾in
Gable front panels	2 @	180 × 180mm	7⅛ × 7⅛in
Chimney:			
Stack side panel		910 × 160mm	35⅞ × 6⁵⁄₁₆in
Lower tray		90 × 90mm	3½ × 3½in
FSR top section panel		370 × 200mm	14⅝ × 7⅞in
FSL top section panel		275 × 200mm	10⅞ × 7⅞in

TOOLS

The same tools are used as for the country cottage, plus a bevel gauge, and a bodkin or knitting needle for marking lines on air-hardening clay.

6mm (¼in) plywood

Fireplace:

Sides	2 @	111 × 50mm	4⅜ × 2in
Back		111 × 102mm	4⅜ × 4in
Base		102 × 43mm	4 × 1¾in
Staircase sides	2 @	220 × 200mm	8¾ × 7⅞in

9mm (⅜in) plywood

Top floor (grain lengthways)		608 × 340mm	24 × 13⅜in
First floor (grain lengthways)		608 × 300mm	24 × 11¹³⁄₁₆in
Doors (grain widthways)	4 @	150 × 65mm	6 × 2⁹⁄₁₆in
Front door (grain widthways)		135 × 75mm	5⁵⁄₁₆ × 3in
FSR and FSL window cavity spacer pieces:			
23mm (⅞in) wide	4 @	140mm	5½in
	4 @	100mm	4in
	2 @	160mm	6⅜in
	2 @	90mm	3⅝in

0.8mm (1⁄32in) plywood

For roof tiles:

5 sheets of 915 × 305mm (36 × 12in) or equivalent if only smaller size sheets available. From these to be cut 2 pieces 111 × 30mm (4⅜ × 1³⁄₁₆in) to be used for the sides of the fireplace.

TIMBER MOULDINGS (PLAIN)

12 × 12mm (½ × ½in)	3m (10ft)
34 × 6mm (1⁵⁄₁₆ × ¼in)	7.5m (25ft)
12 × 6mm (½ × ¼in)	20m (67ft)
12mm (½in) dowel	1m (4ft)
6mm (¼in) dowel	0.5m (2ft)
15 × 9mm (⅝ × ⅜in)	1m (4ft)
9 × 9mm (⅜ × ⅜in)	1m (4ft)
6 × 6mm (¼ × ¼in)	4m (14ft)
21 × 9mm (¹³⁄₁₆ × ⅜in)	0.5m (2ft)
19 × 9mm (¾ × ⅜in)	4m (14ft)
21 × 21mm (¹³⁄₁₆ × ¹³⁄₁₆in)	1.5m (5ft)
L-shaped 34 × 34mm (1⁵⁄₁₆ × 1⁵⁄₁₆in)	1m (4ft)
4 × 4mm (³⁄₁₆ × ³⁄₁₆in)	1m (4ft)

Balsa:

13 × 6mm (½ × ¼in)	2m (7ft)
6 × 6mm (¼ × ¼in)	5m (17ft)

HARDWARE

- 200 25mm (1in) No 4 chipboard-thread countersunk galvanized steel screws, with Pozidriv/Phillips heads
- 100 19mm (¾in) No 4 chipboard-thread countersunk galvanized steel screws with Pozidriv/Phillips heads
- 4 38mm (1½in) length brass hinges plus screws
- 10 13mm (½in) miniature hinges plus screws for doors
- Brass pins: 13mm (½in), 16mm (⅝in) and 19mm (¾in); one packet of each
- Metal garden mesh for windows, 6mm (¼in) cell size. One sheet, minimum size 610 × 610mm (24 × 24in)

SUNDRIES

- PVA wood glue
- Clear contact adhesive
- Epoxy resin adhesive
- Cyanoacrylate adhesive
- Air-hardening clay
- Wood primer
- Metal primer
- Black emulsion paint for exterior and interior timbers
- Emulsion paint for interior and exterior
- Dark-oak wood stain
- Polyurethane wood sealer
- Sandpaper: coarse, medium and fine

CONSTRUCTION

As with the cottage, the components are screwed and glued together, allowing the structure to be assembled completely (first fix) without glue, and then taken apart for internal decorations prior to final glued assembly. Unlike the cottage, this house is

THE MAIN STAGES IN CONSTRUCTION

There are eighteen stages of construction, in this order:

1. Cutting all the major components from the sheet materials.
2. Cutting holes, marking/drilling screw lines, marking panel positions.
3. Assembling main structure: first fix (screws only).
4. Construction of roof and gables.
5. Fitting windows and beams to gable fronts.
6. Tiling main roof panels and gables.
7. Front sections: construction and hanging.
8. Timber framing decoration on front sections.
9. Making and hanging internal doors.
10. Floorboards (carving plywood surfaces).
11. Chimney stack and chimney: making basic structure.
12. Decorating internal structure (separate panels).
13. Final assembly.
14. Chimney and chimney stack brickwork.
15. Fitting timber beams to sides and back of house.
16. Interior, final tasks: fireplace, paving slabs, staircases and banisters.
17. Exterior painting.
18. Finishing off.

not made up as a separate shell with an internal structure; it is made up as a whole, the separate sections decorated individually.

CUTTING HOLES, MARKING/DRILLING SCREW LINES, MARKING UNIT POSITIONS

Parts involved:
Left side (S1); right side (S2); back; base; 3 rectangular wall panels (W1, W2 and W3); triangular wall panel (W4); first floor (floor 1); top floor (floor 2); 12mm (½in) square-section hardwood moulding.

Important Note: some procedures outlined below are identical in principle to those used for making the country cottage, therefore these are not set down in detail again. Where this is the case, a C appears in brackets before the relevant section, in which case the constructor may wish to refer to the previous chapter.

THE SIDE WALLS LEFT AND RIGHT (S1 AND S2)

1. Mark and cut the panels, as shown.
2. (C) Using 12 × 12mm (½ × ½in) hardwood moulding, fit the hinge fillets where marked, and glue with epoxy resin adhesive; then trim the excess materials at the sides and front.

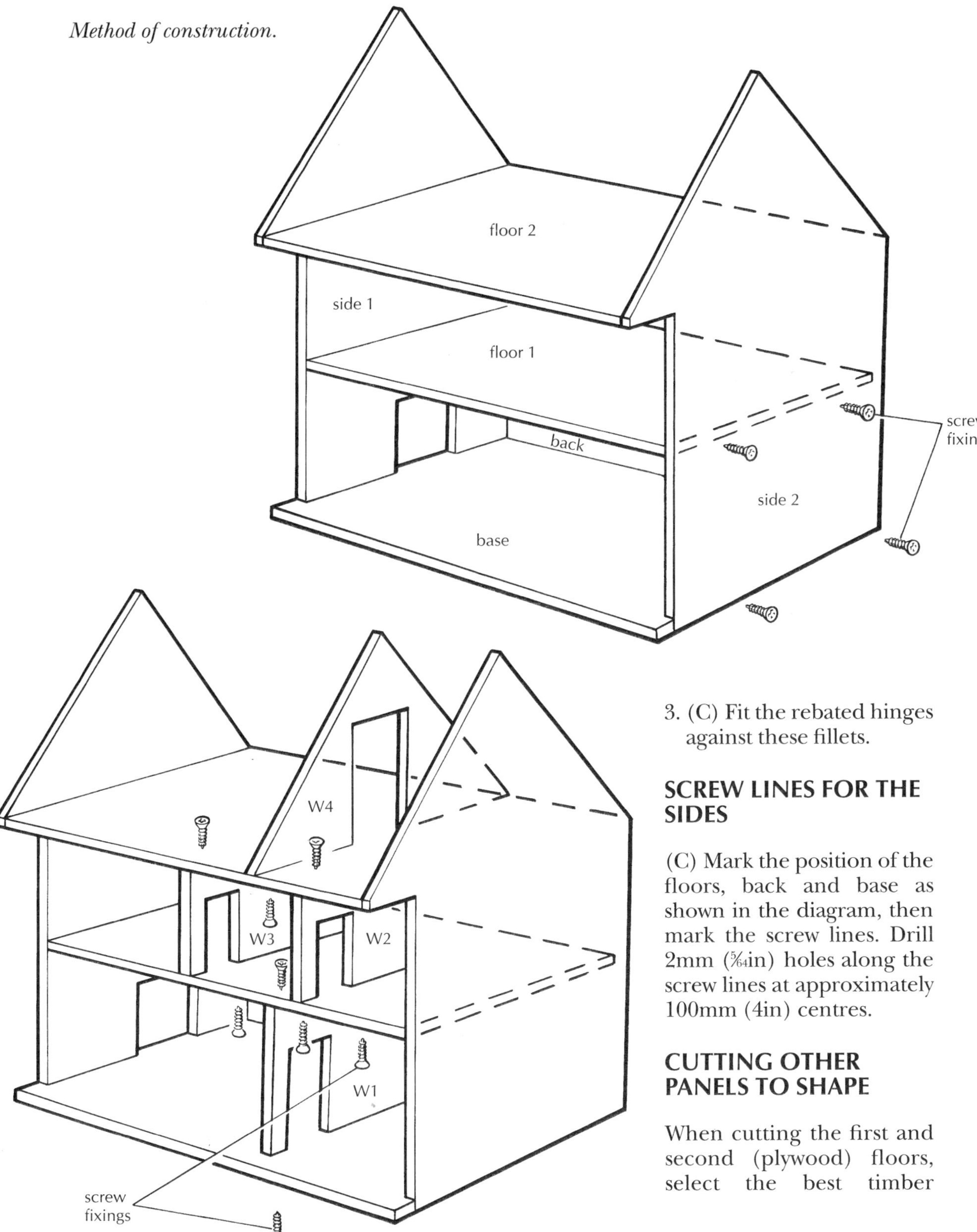

Method of construction.

3. (C) Fit the rebated hinges against these fillets.

SCREW LINES FOR THE SIDES

(C) Mark the position of the floors, back and base as shown in the diagram, then mark the screw lines. Drill 2mm (5⁄64in) holes along the screw lines at approximately 100mm (4in) centres.

CUTTING OTHER PANELS TO SHAPE

When cutting the first and second (plywood) floors, select the best timber

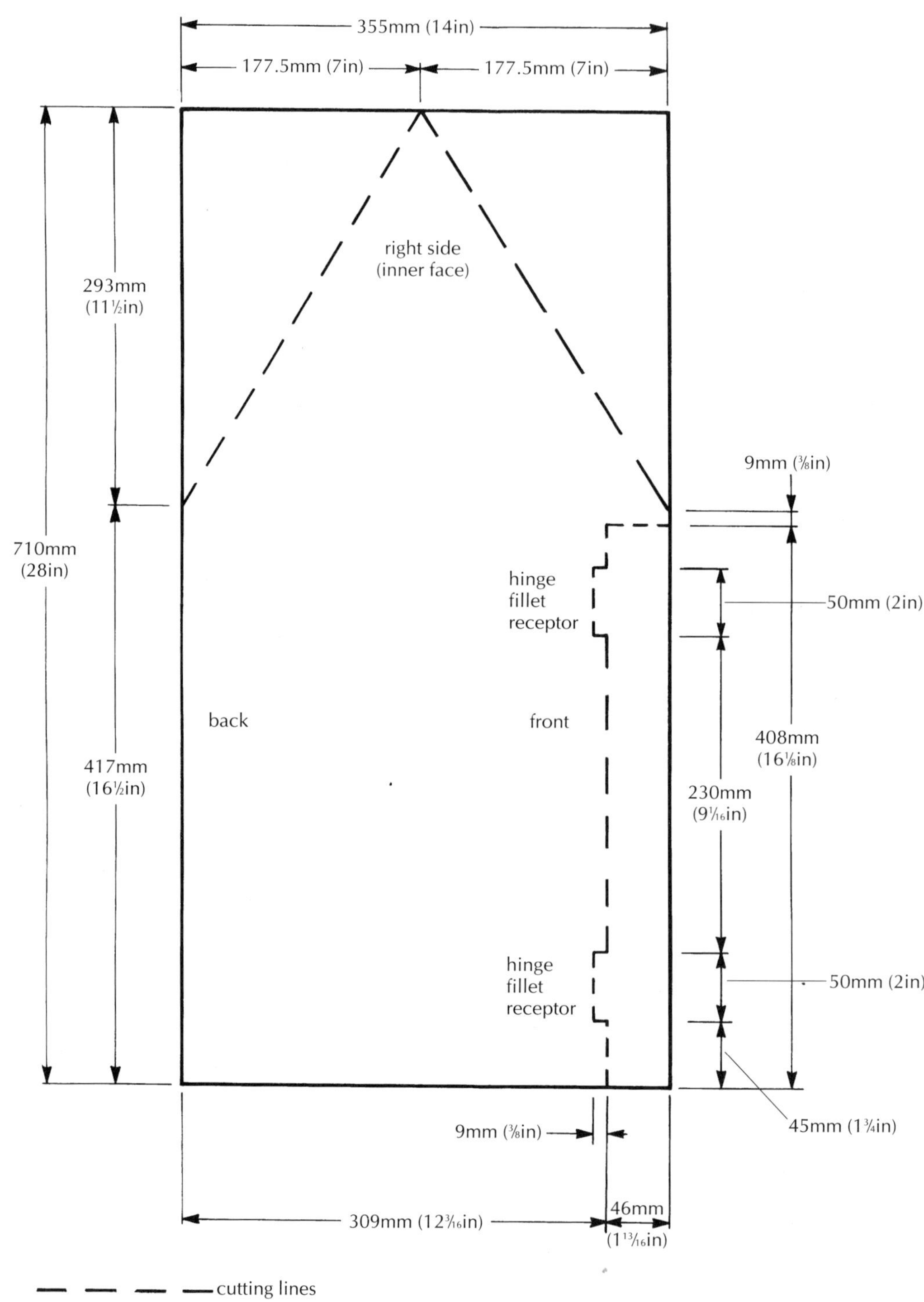

Side wall right – cutting lines.

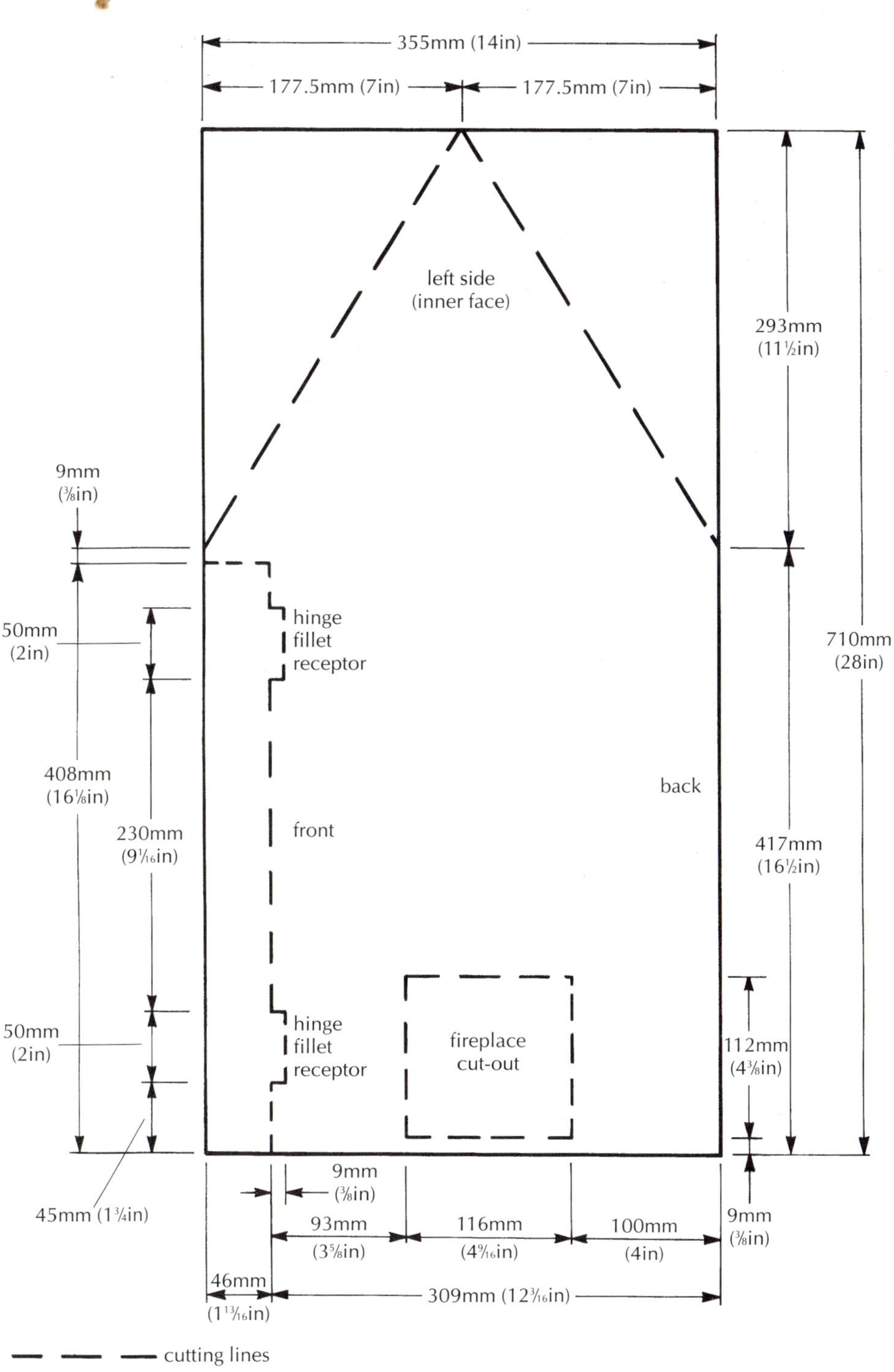

Side wall left – cutting lines.

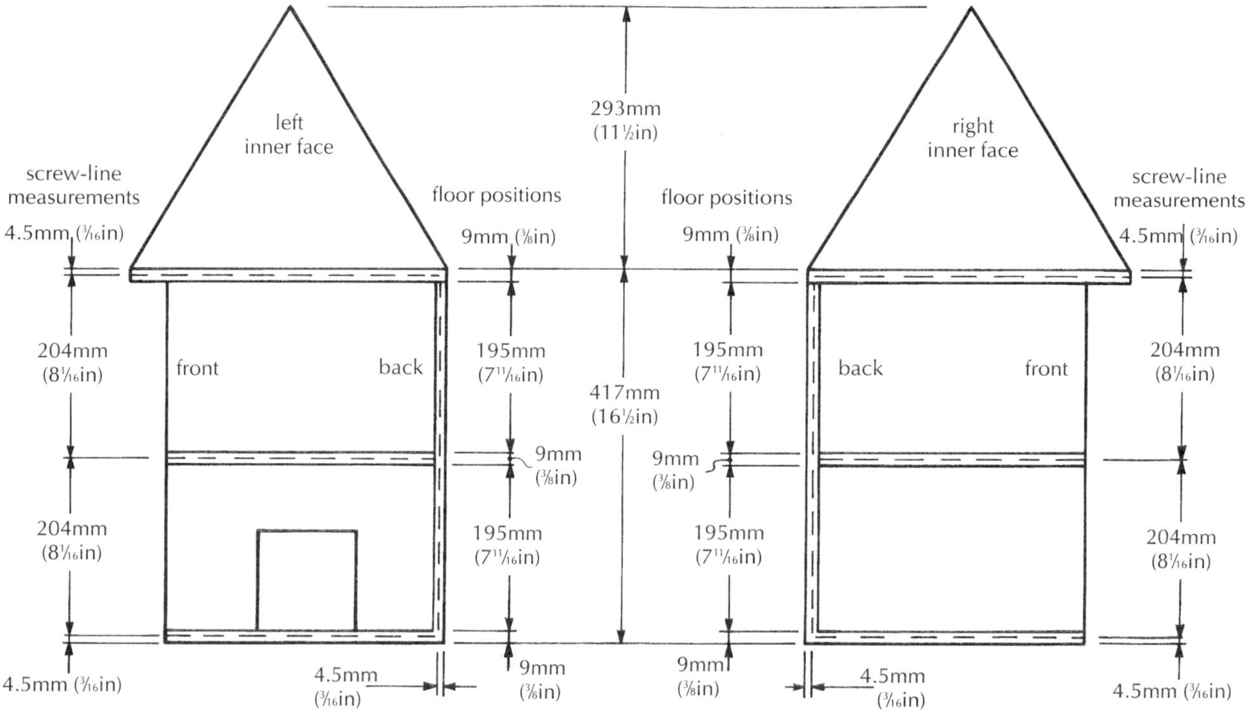

Screw lines for sides.

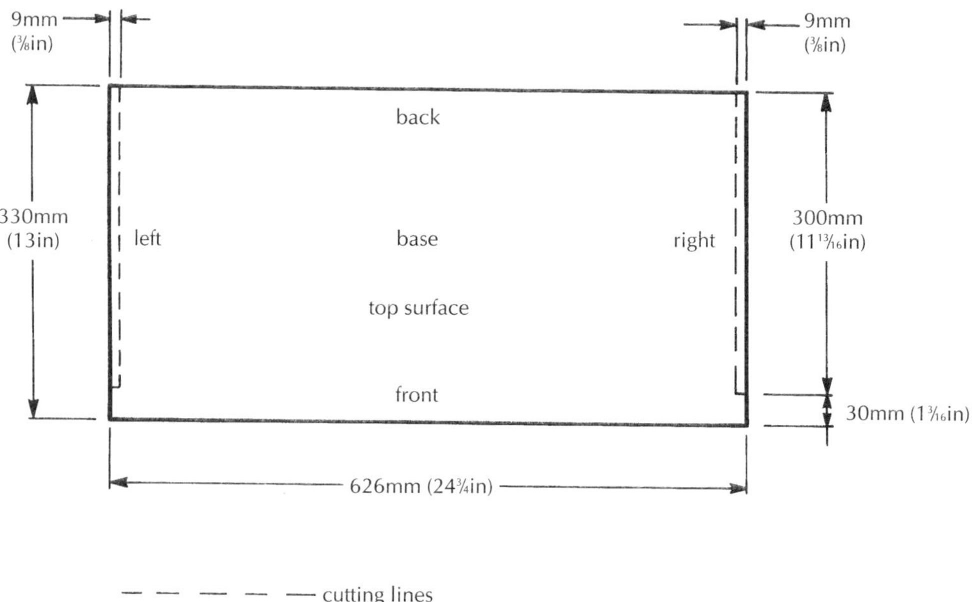

Base – cutting lines.

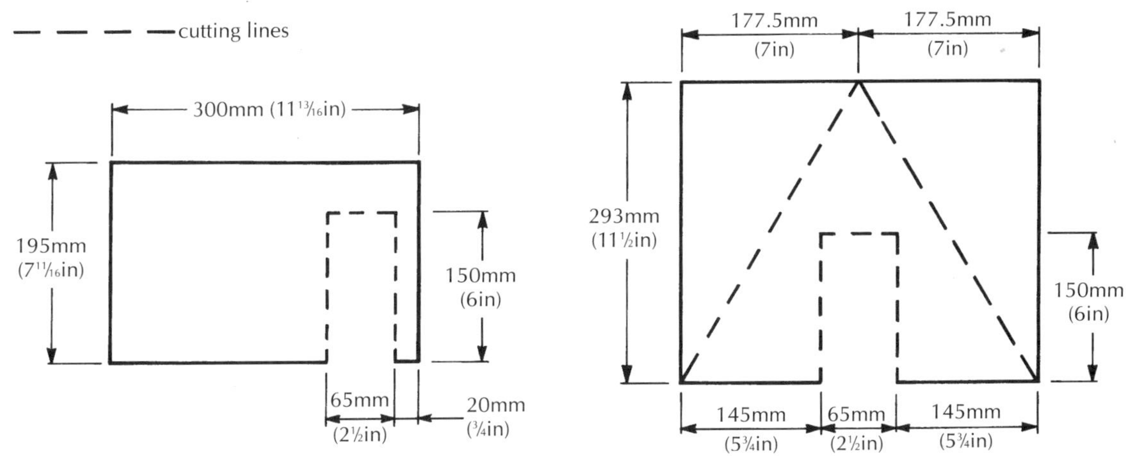

Main walls – cutting lines.

Triangular (top-floor) wall – cutting lines.

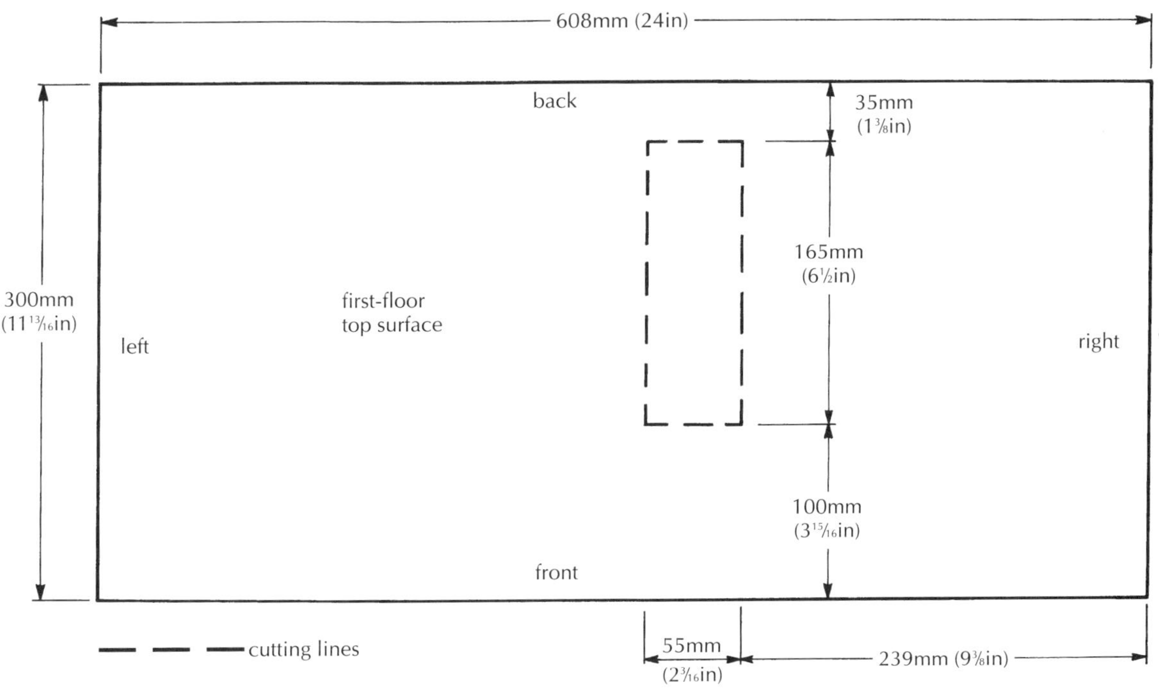

Cutting: first-floor top surface.

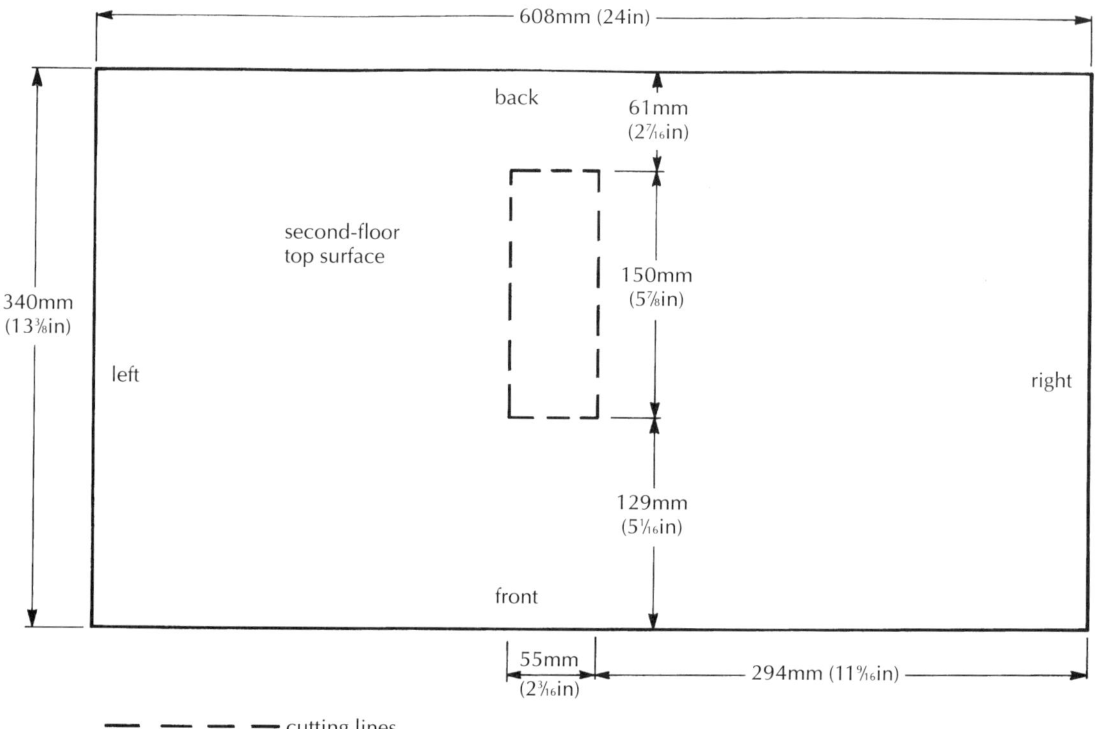

Cutting: second-floor top surface.

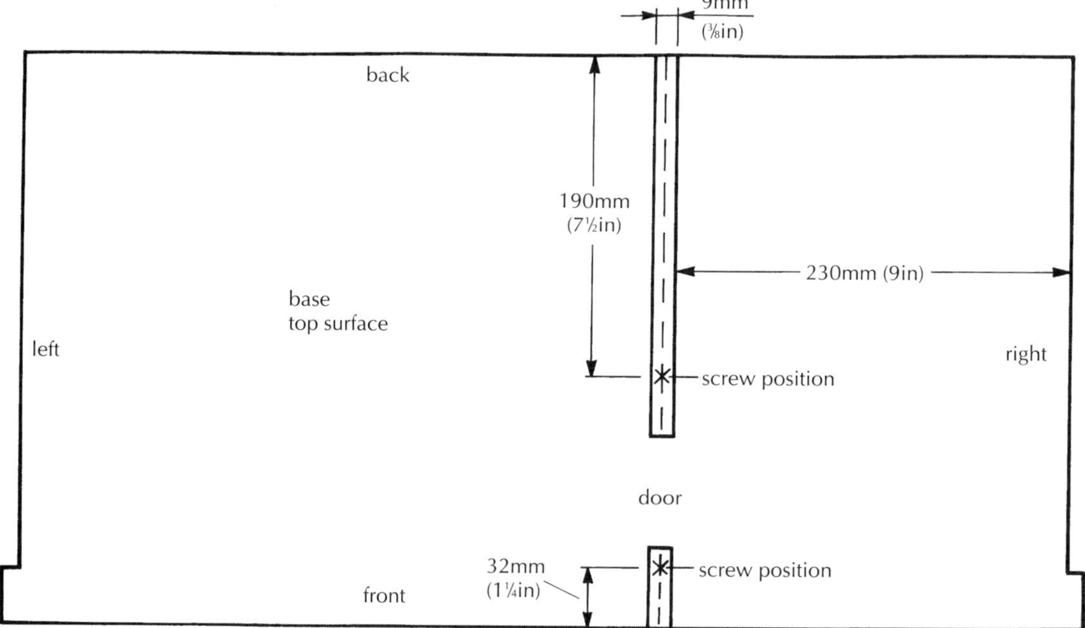

Screw lines for base – top surface.

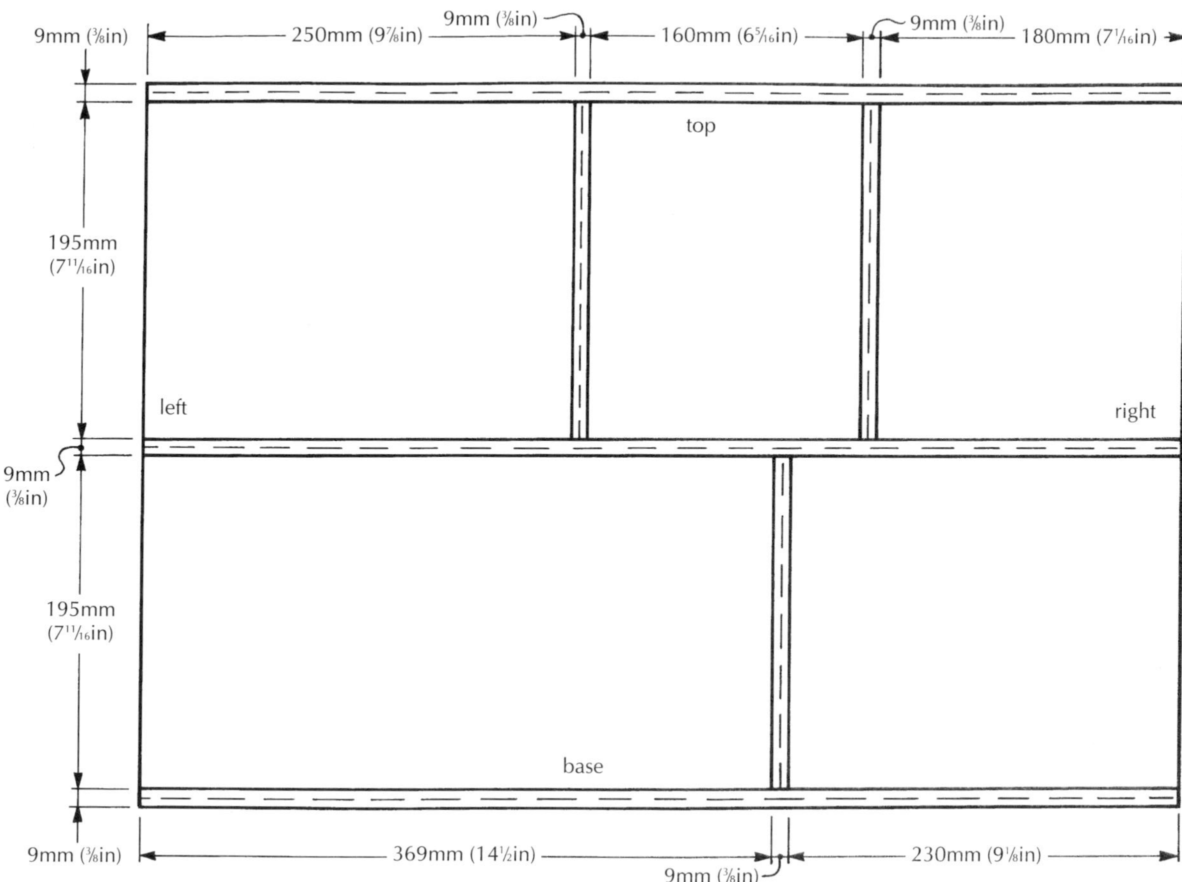

Screw lines: back.

surface to be uppermost, since this is to be carved, stained and sealed.

SCREW LINES FOR THE BASE AND BACK

Mark the position of the walls and floors as above, then mark the screw lines. Drill holes along the screw lines where shown, or at 100mm (4in) centres when not otherwise directed.

SCREW LINES FOR THE FIRST FLOOR

Top surface: Mark the wall positions as shown in the diagram, then mark the screw lines and drill holes where indicated. Where precise measurements are not shown for holes, anywhere along line is suitable.

Underside: Mark the position of the single wall against the ceiling, and then the screw line. Drill two holes only. These two screws are to be inserted from the top (floorboard) side, and will need to be countersunk and filled to match the dark wood stain. Bonding in a section of veneer to cover the screw heads is not necessary in this instance as dark-coloured timber can be filled with dark wood filler unobtrusively.

SCREW LINES FOR THE SECOND (TOP) FLOOR

Top surface: Mark the wall positions and screw lines, and drill holes where indicated.

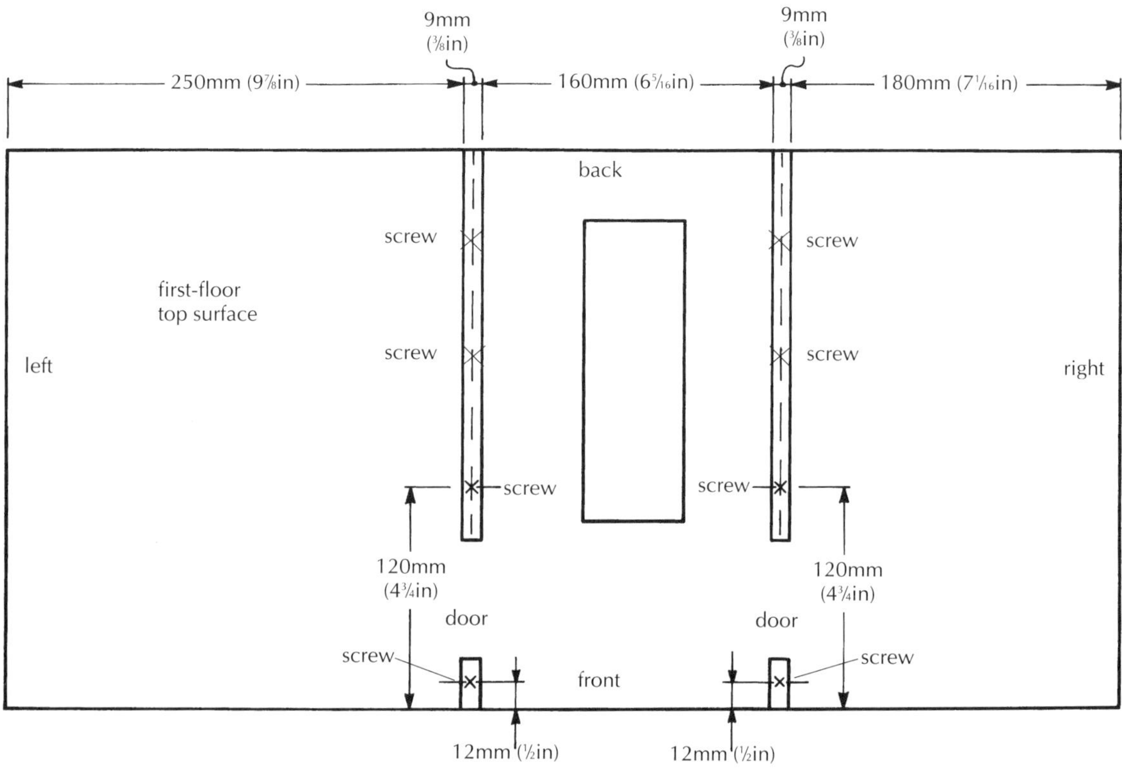

Screw lines for first floor – top surface.

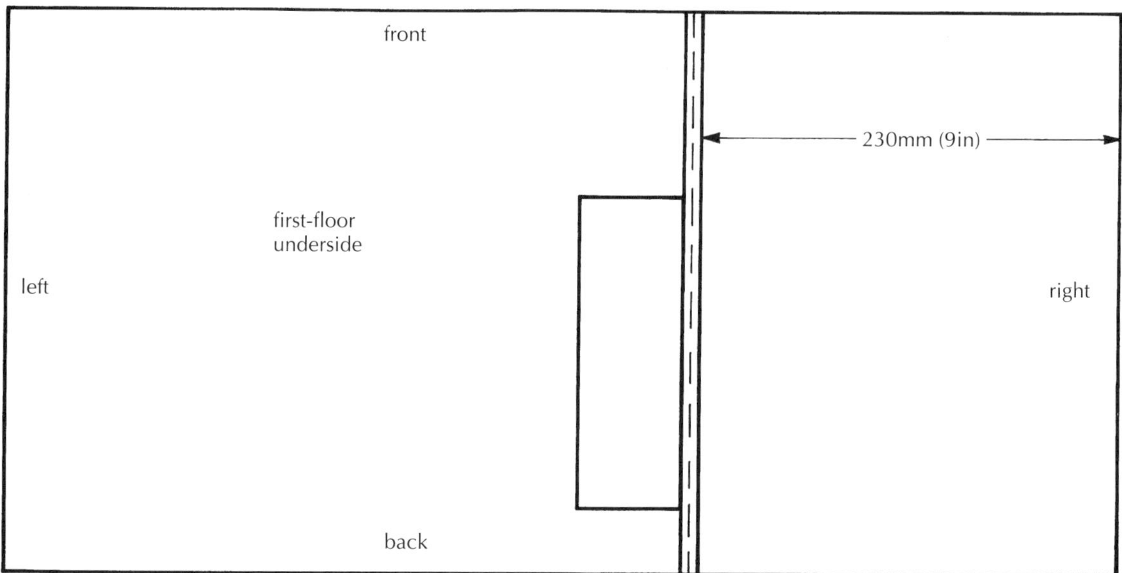

Screw lines for first floor – underside.

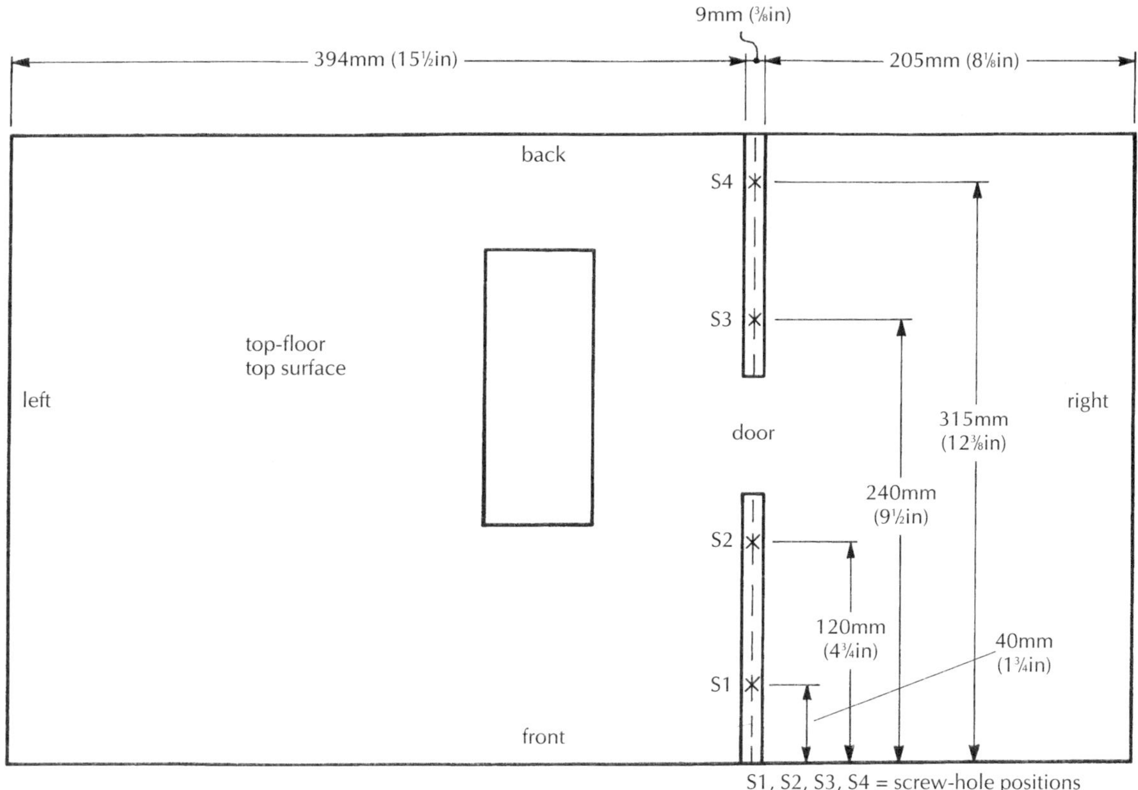

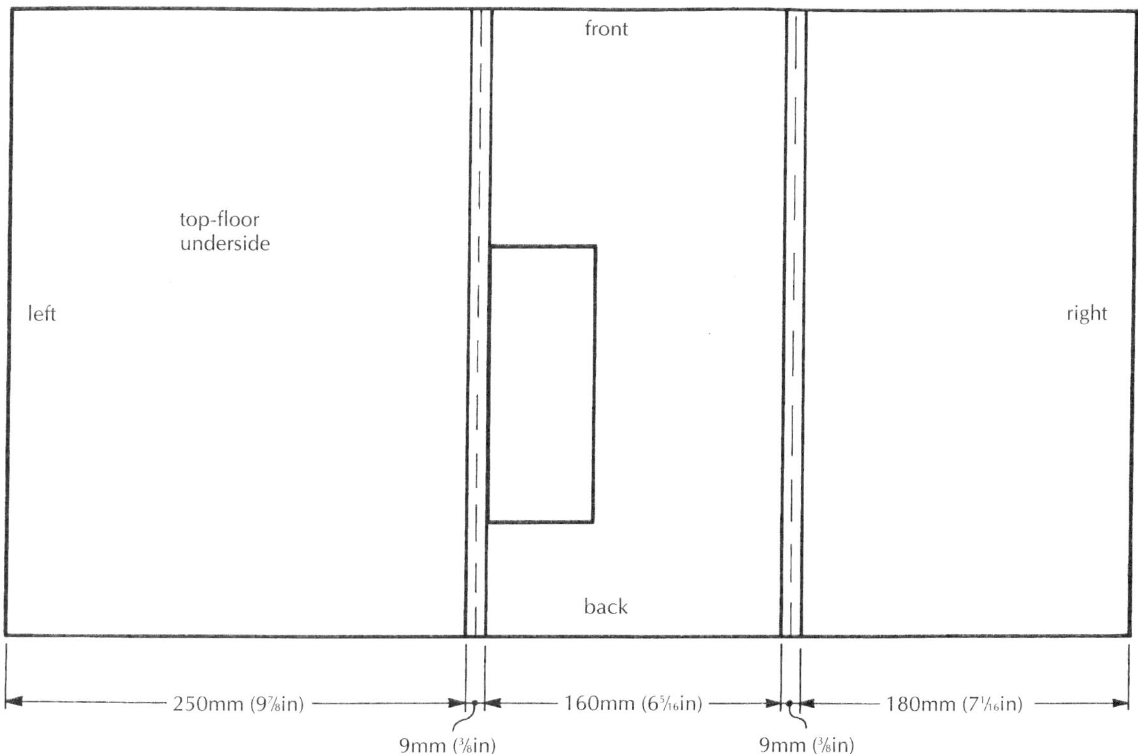

(Top) *Screw lines for top floor – top surface.* (Bottom) *Screw lines for top floor – underside.*

Underside: Proceed as above, using only two screws for each wall.

ASSEMBLING THE MAIN STRUCTURE: FIRST FIX

1. (C) With the base on a firm surface, fit the bottom edge of the back to the back of the base, then mark one screw destination hole in the edge of the base with a sharp-pointed bradawl. Pilot drill this hole, enlarge the host hole and screw the panels together.
2. Mark and drill all other screw holes similarly, and insert screws.
3. Fit the left side as shown and mark the screw destination holes; fix in the same way.
4. Screw the right side panel to the structure in the same manner.
5. Fit the ground-floor wall (W1) in place, screwing from the bottom of the base and the rear of the back, as shown in the diagram opposite.
6. Screw the two first-floor walls (W2 and W3) to the first floor as above, screwing from underneath (what will eventually be the ground-floor ceiling). This becomes the first-floor assembly (FFA).
7. Screw the FFA into the shell of the house. There are five lines of screws to be inserted:
   (i) From the right side into the right-hand edge of the floor.
   (ii) From the left side into the left-hand edge of the floor.
   (iii) From the back into the rear edge of the floor.
   (iv) From the back into the rear edges of the first-floor walls.
   (v) Two screws from the top of the first floor into the top of the ground-floor wall.

Construction of main structure.

   (vi) The heads of these screws are to be countersunk, and the floor depressions eventually filled to blend with the floorboard finish.
8. Fit the top floor in place, and insert the screws as shown; again, there will be five lines:
   (i) From the left side into the left-hand side edge of the floor.
   (ii) From the right side into the right-hand side edge of the floor.
   (iii) From the back panel into the rear edge of the floor.
   (iv) Two screws from the top surface of the floor into the top edge of the left wall.
   (v) Two screws from the top surface of the floor into the top edge of the right wall.
9. Trim off the front parts of the left- and right-hand sides where they project in front of the front edge of the floor, so that the front of the projecting part of the house forms a continuous line.
10. Fix the triangular wall (W4) within the marked lines on the floor, then, using

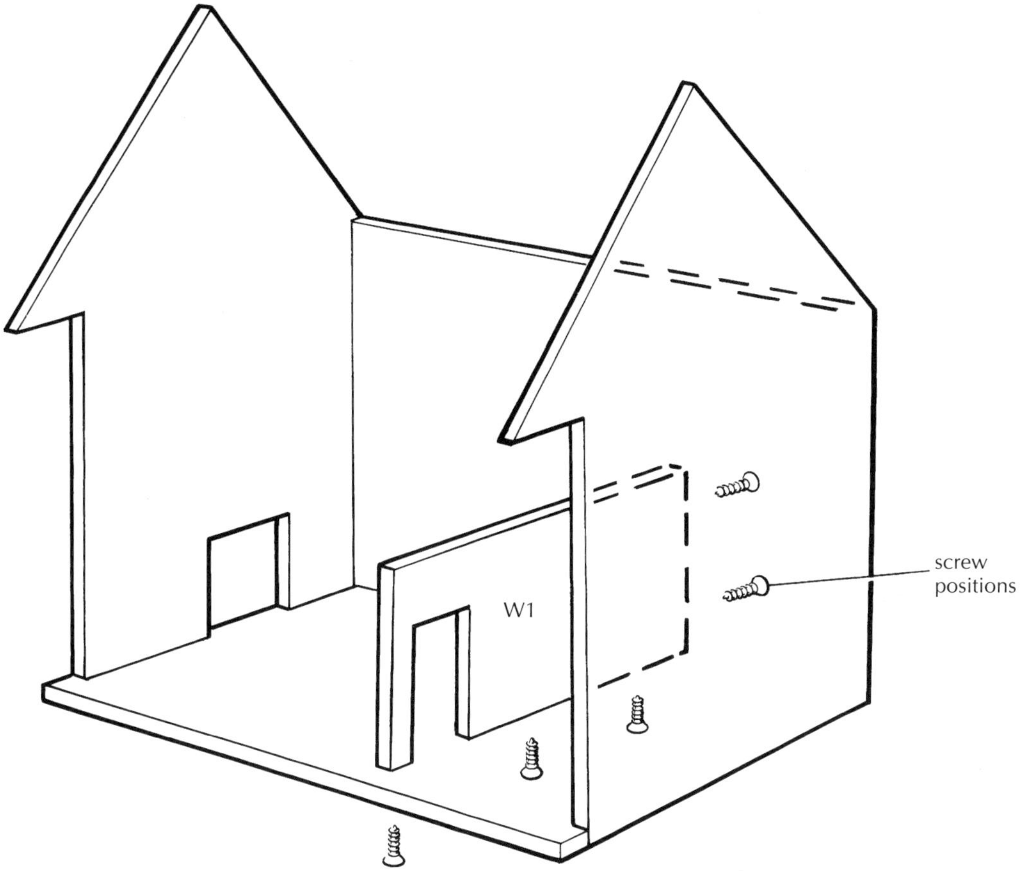

Assembling the main structure – adding W1.

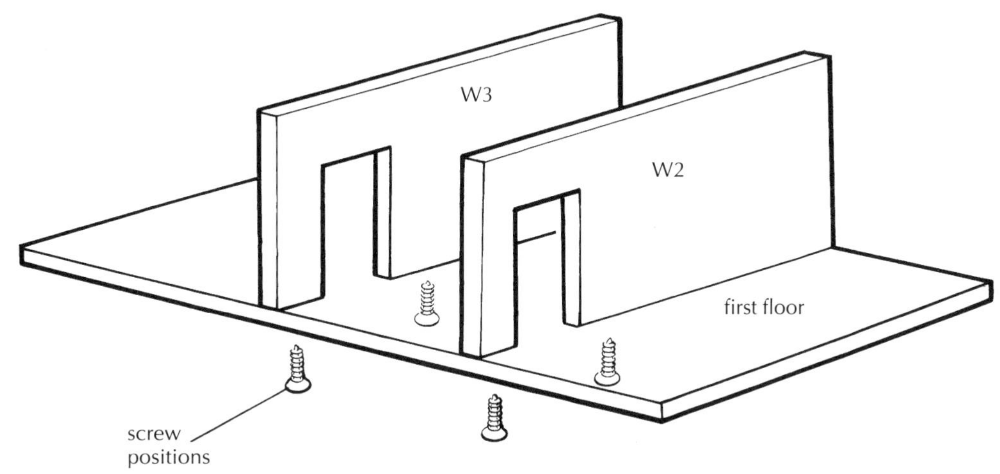

Assembling the first-floor assembly (FFA).

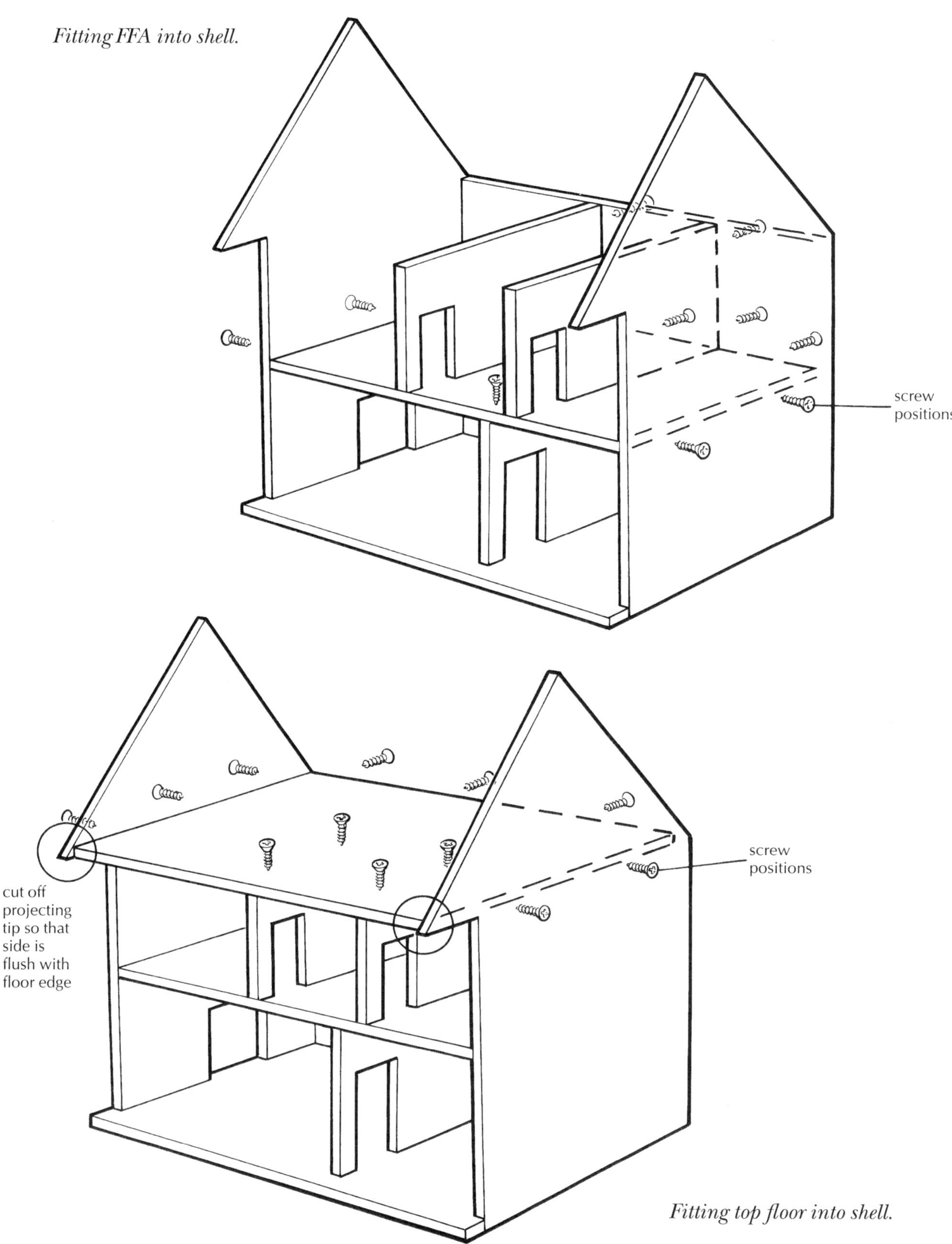

Fitting FFA into shell.

Fitting top floor into shell.

a straight-edge, check for continuity along the front and back sides, sliding the wall into position so that the face edges are in line with the side faces. When in the correct position, mark the screw destination holes and screw the wall into place.

11. If necessary, plane any of the edge faces that project above the other two, so that a continuous roof-line is presented at the front and back.

THE ROOF AND GABLES

Parts involved:
Main roof panel; back panel upper strip; rear roof panel; 4 gable panels; front gable panels; 9mm (⅜in) MDF or plywood roof bracing blocks; timber mouldings – 12mm (½in) dowel, 15 × 9mm (⅝ × ⅜in), 12 × 12mm (½ × ½in).

MAIN ROOF CONSTRUCTION

1. Set the bevel square to the same angle as that of the roof pitch: the angle formed at the apex of the left and right sides.
2. Mark and cut four pieces of 9mm (⅜in) ply or MDF as shown to the same angle, measuring down 75mm (3in) along the two lines and marking across. Cut along the lines, identifying the measured angles in some way. These are the roof bracing blocks.
3. Mark the screw lines as shown on the main (front) roof panel and the rear roof strip. Drill 2mm (5/64in) holes, as shown in the diagram overleaf.

Inside view of removable roof, to show roof bracing blocks.

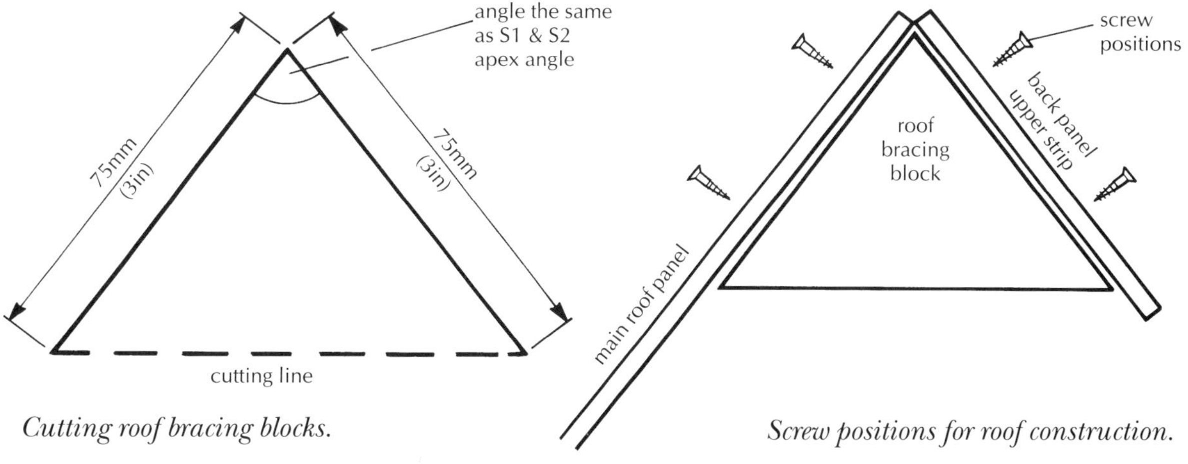

Cutting roof bracing blocks.

Screw positions for roof construction.

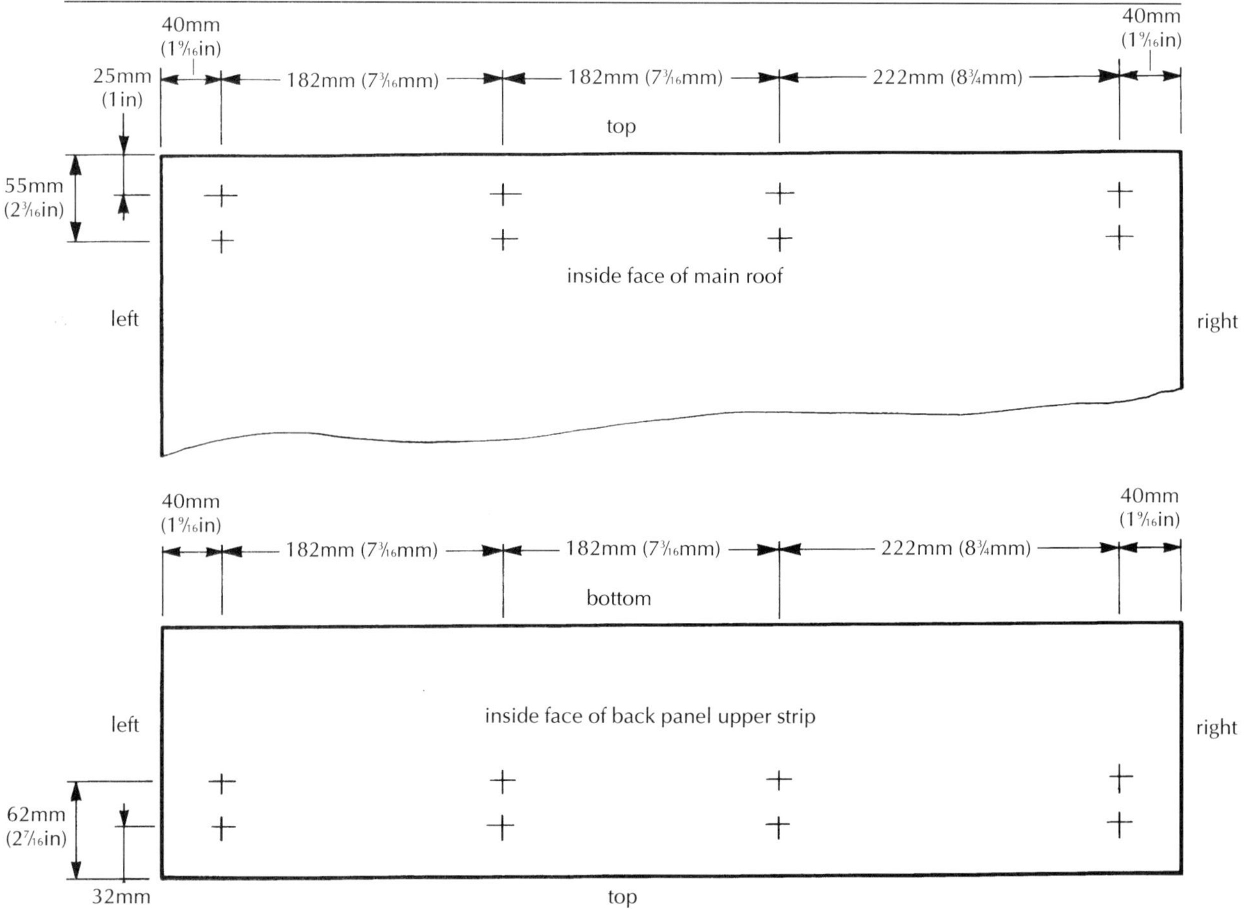

Screw-hole positions for the main roof panel and back panel upper strip.

4. Screw the fixing blocks to the roof panels as shown.
5. Place the roof in position, and check that it fits correctly. It should overlap the front edge of the top floor by approximately 12mm ($\frac{1}{2}$in).
6. Dismantle the unit, countersink all the host screw holes and reassemble, bonding the surfaces with PVA glue.
7. Place the roof in position again, ensuring that the overlap on each side is equal (20mm/$\frac{3}{4}$in), then position the rear roof panel as shown, its top edge against the bottom of the back panel upper strip and the sides in line.
8. Draw a line on the inside face of the roof on each side, to mark the position of the sides of the house.
9. Remove the rear roof, mark lines at 4.5mm ($\frac{3}{16}$in) inside these lines, and then drill screw holes at 100mm (4in) centres.
10. Replace the rear roof in its correct position and fix in place with screws.
11. With the roof removed, stick a 15 × 9mm ($\frac{5}{8}$ × $\frac{3}{8}$in) timber underneath the front edge of the top floor, so that it projects underneath the side panels to finish flush with the side of the house, thus allowing 9mm ($\frac{3}{8}$in) extra length at each end. Use PVA glue (no nails or screws) and clamp it with G-clamps until set. When the clamps are removed, replace the roof and check that the base of the batten is below the bottom edge of the roof.

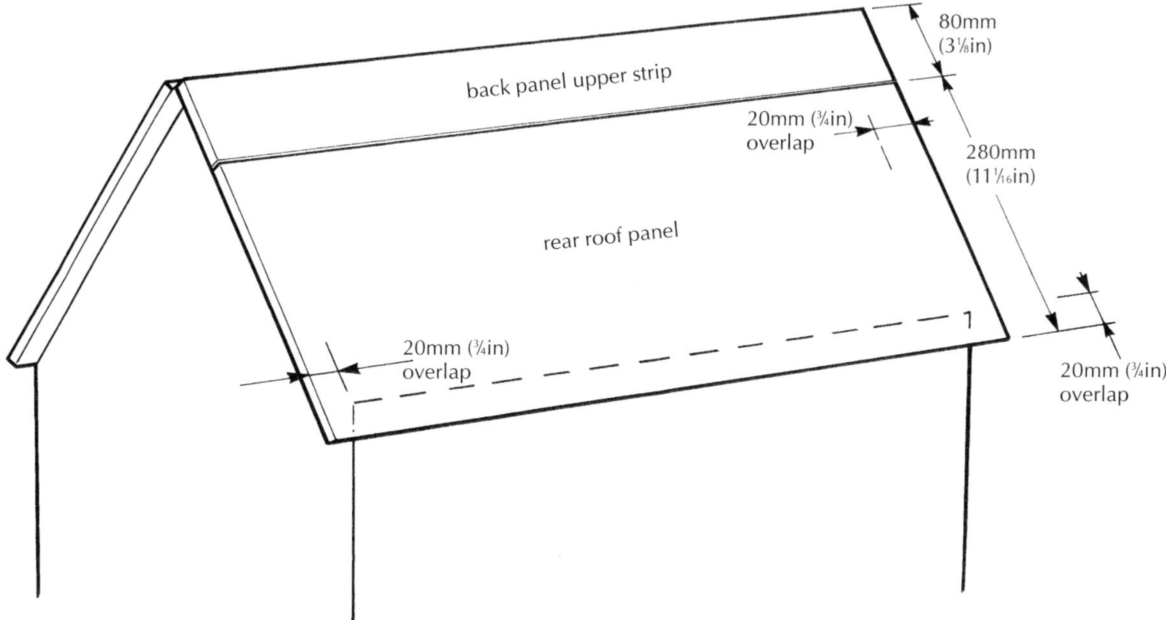

Positioning of rear roof panel.

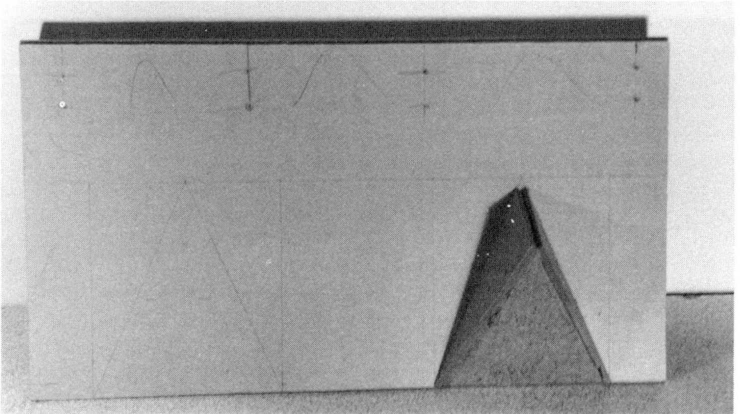

Gable, showing component parts.

12. Cut a suitable length of 12mm (½in) dowel to run along the complete length of the ridge. Using a junior hacksaw or tenon saw, cut shallow grooves around the circumference at 20mm (¾in) intervals, so as to indicate the edges of curved ridge tiles.
13. Stick this dowel in place in the valley formed at the juncture between the panels at the roof's ridge, using PVA adhesive. Clamp with several large G-clamps until the adhesive is set.

GABLE CONSTRUCTION

1. Mark the front of the main roof as in the diagram overleaf.

For each gable:

2. Using the measurements on diagram, mark and cut two pieces of 6mm (¼in) MDF, clearly identifying the ridge side and the side that meets the roof. These become the Gable Roof Panels (GRPs).
3. Place these panels as in the diagram, the outside edges of the panels meeting the marked lines on the roof. Mark

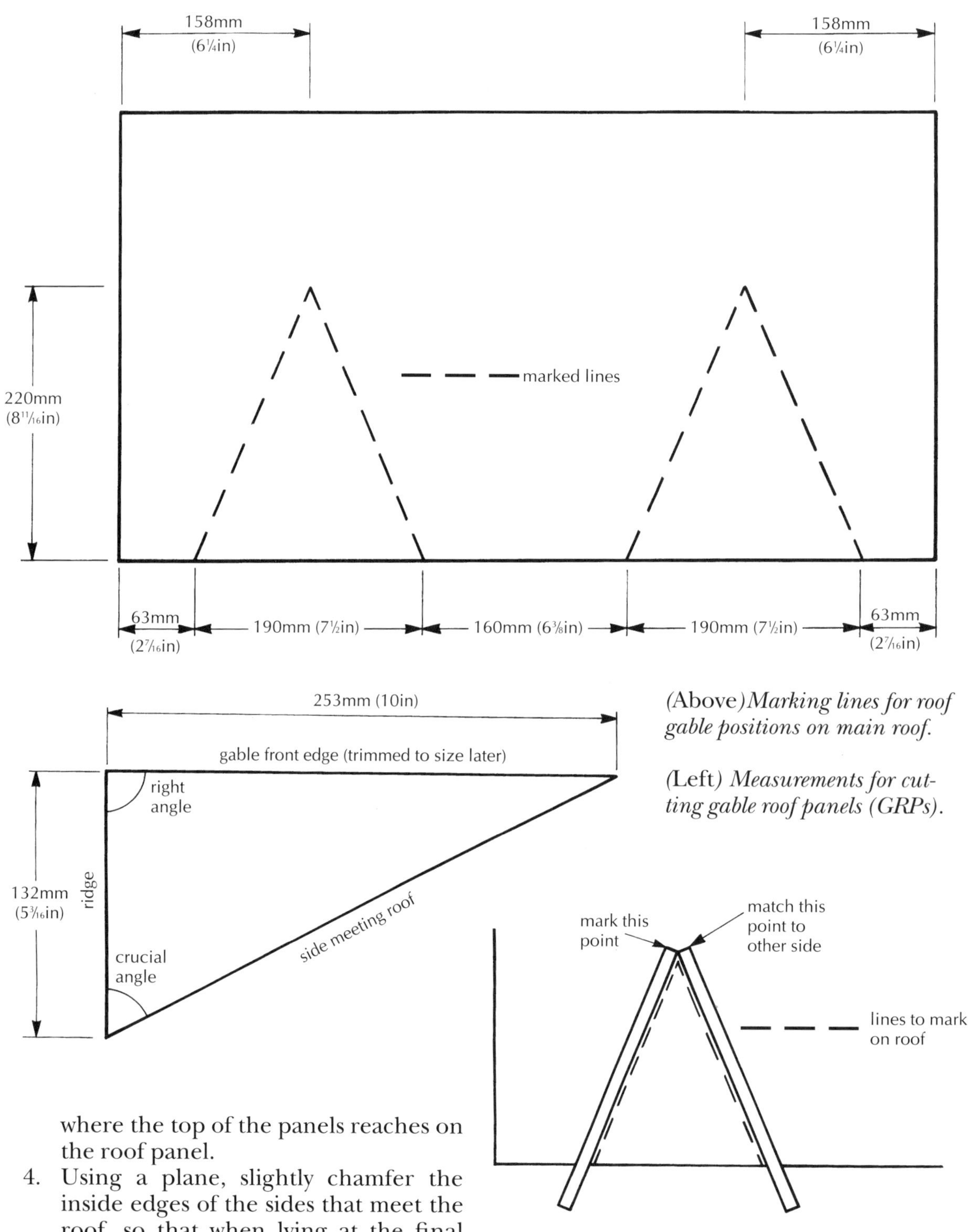

(Above) *Marking lines for roof gable positions on main roof.*

(Left) *Measurements for cutting gable roof panels (GRPs).*

Marking inside edges of GRPs on main roof.

where the top of the panels reaches on the roof panel.

4. Using a plane, slightly chamfer the inside edges of the sides that meet the roof, so that when lying at the final angle (the ridges of both meeting as in

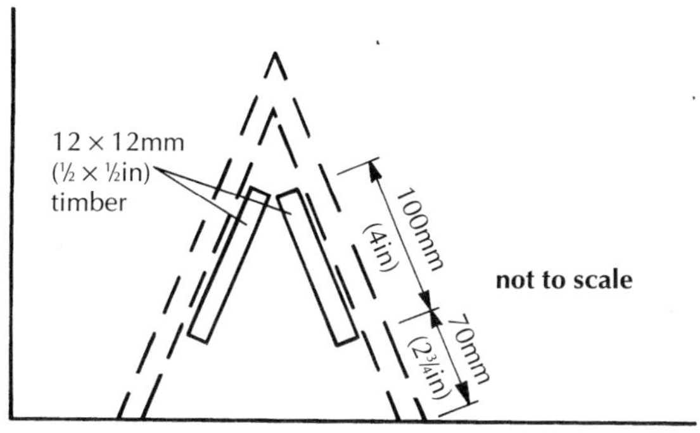

Position of timber GRP fixing blocks on main roof.

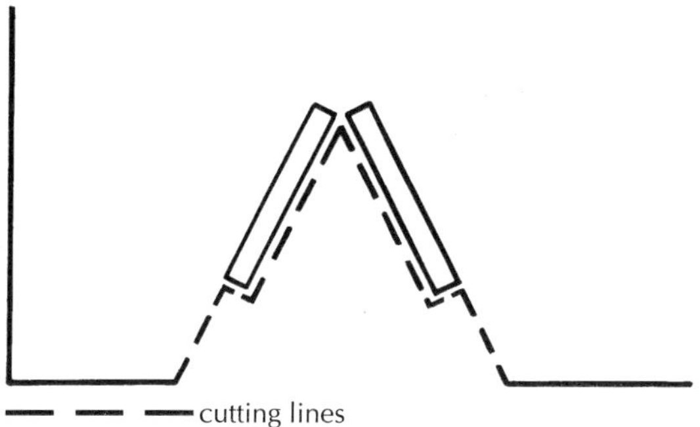

Cutting lines for main roof.

the diagram) there is no appreciable gap between the roof planes.

5. Place one of the GRPs in its final position and mark a line on the main roof that denotes the inside edge (i.e. fractionally more than 6mm/¼in away from the outer line).
6. Fix a 100mm (4in) length of 12 × 12mm (½ × ½in) batten along this line as in the diagram, using two screws inserted from the rear of the roof. Repeat for the other side.
7. Chisel these timber lengths until they slope to give correct support to the panels when they are in position.
8. Fix the panels to these battens, using two screws for each. The ridge of both should meet from front to back.
9. Mark a point along the ridge, 110mm (4⁵⁄₁₆in) from its juncture with the main roof. Place a ruler against this mark at one end and the bottom edge of the main roof at the other. Draw along this line, then cut along it to remove waste. Repeat for the other GRP.
10. If necessary, plane the panels at their front (freshly cut) edges, so that they meet neatly at the ridge.
11. Unscrew the GRPs, then cut away material from the main roof panel, as in the diagram. Refit the GRPs.

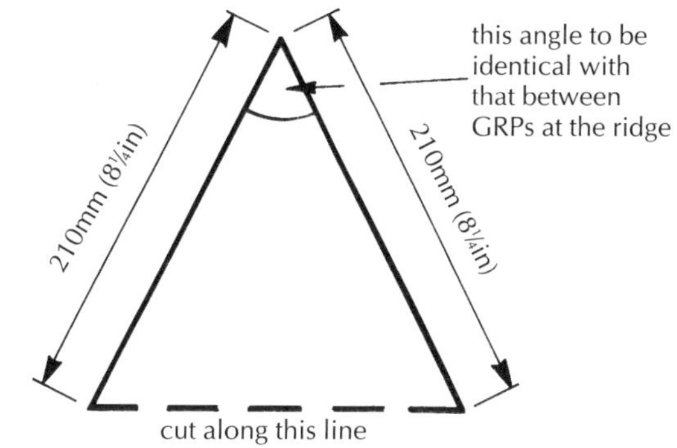

Marking and cutting the gable window fronts (GWFs).

Inside view of gable, showing section of roof to be removed.

12. Set the bevel square to the same angle as that between the gable roof panels, then mark this onto a piece of 6mm (¼in) MDF (the gable window front: GWF). Measure 210mm (8¼in) along the two lines so formed, draw a line to join these points and cut off the waste.
13. Using the marking gauge, scribe a line on the inside faces of the gable roof panels, 10mm (⅜in) from the front (open) edge.
14. Place the GWF in position, its front face against the scribed lines. Mark behind on the inside face of the GRPs to show the position of its rear face.
15. Fix 70mm-length (2¾in-length) 12 × 12mm (½ × ½in) battens against these lines so as to form fixing blocks for the GWF. Use two screws to fit the blocks as near to the top (ridge) as possible.
16. Screw the GWF in position, taking care to select screw sites in the batten that are not too close to the screws already in place.
17. Trim the GWF at its lower edge so that it is flush with the rest of the main roof, bearing in mind that it is still going to stick below this level because of its different angle of approach.
18. Rehang the roof on the house and plane the underside of the GWF until the angle is such that the GWF does not hold the roof away from the front of the house.
19. Dismantle the gable roof assembly, identifying all parts for reassembly.
20. Cut a window aperture in the GWF as in the diagram.
21. Countersink all host screw holes and reassemble the gable permanently, bonding the mating surfaces with PVA adhesive.
22. Cut a suitable length of 12mm (½in) dowel for the ridge, trimming the end that abuts the main roof to the correct angle, and using the bevel square to mark this. Cut ridges along the dowel as with the main roof ridge, then stick it in place with contact adhesive.

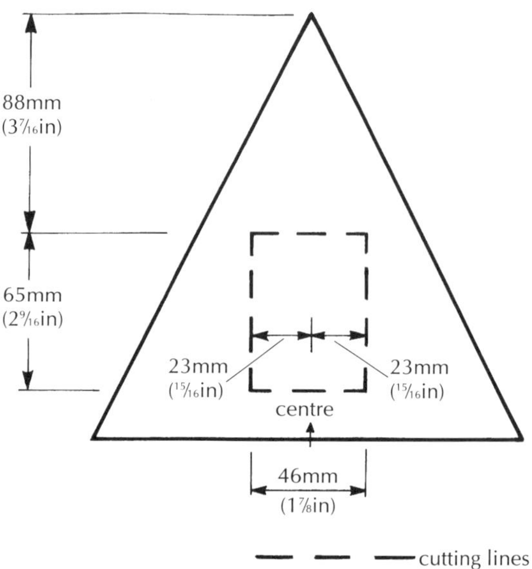

Cutting window aperture in GWF.

FRONT GABLE WINDOWS AND TIMBER BEAMS APPLICATION

Parts involved:
Metal mesh for windows; 0.8mm (1⁄32in) plywood; timber mouldings: 9 × 9mm (⅜ × ⅜in), 6 × 6mm (¼ × ¼in), 12 × 12mm (½ × ½in), 12 × 6mm (½ × ¼in).

GABLE WINDOWS

Fit the windows in the same way as for the cottage: rebate 6mm (¼in) around all four sides of the opening, to a depth of the thickness of the metal mesh. Then cut the mesh to the size of this larger hole, and glue in place using contact adhesive.

TIMBER BEAMS APPLICATION

To stick the timbers to the gable front, use PVA adhesive only. There is no need to clamp the joints as the materials should form an immediate suction bond. Apply the beams in the order given below, judging their length and the angles of each end by eye and cutting with a jigsaw.

1. 9 × 9mm (⅜ × ⅜in) **horizontal** along the base line of the panel.

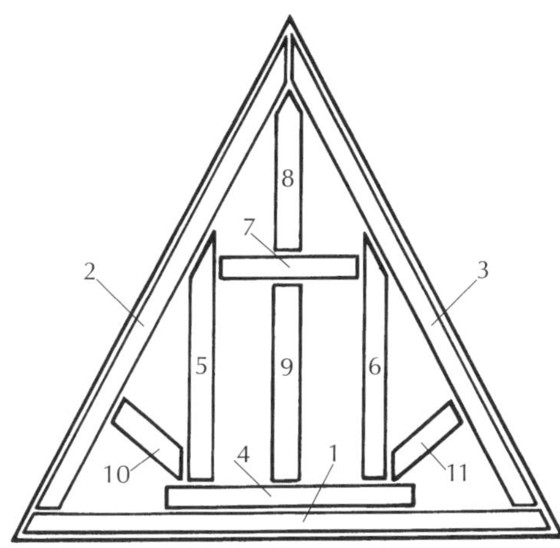

Timber beam application on GWF.

2. and 3. 6 × 6mm (¼ × ¼in) diagonals fitting under the eaves and angled to meet at the top and to join **1** at the base.
4. 12 × 12mm (½ × ½in) **horizontal** window-sill, 90mm (3½in) long, fitted centrally above **1**.
5 and 6. 12 × 6mm (½ × ¼in) **verticals** fitted to form the side window frames, aligned with the window aperture and angled at the top to meet **2** and **3**.
7. 12 × 6mm (½ × ¼in) **horizontal** between **5** and **6** to form the top of the window frame.
8. 6 × 6mm (¼ × ¼in) **vertical**, centralized along **7** and cut at the top to fit under the joint of **2** and **3**.
9. 6 × 6mm (¼ × ¼in) **vertical** window bar in line with **8** to fit between **7** and **4**.
10 and 11. 6 × 6mm (¼ × ¼in) **diagonals** angled at the ends to meet **2** and **5**, and **6** and **3** respectively, as in the diagram.

ROOF AND GABLE ROOF TILING

Parts needed:
0.8mm (1/32in) plywood.

Proceed as with the cottage roof, using the same measurements and method. Cut the tile strips with a junior hacksaw, as this is ideal for such fine material. Tile the main roof panels first, afterwards the gable roofs; this way, the cut ends of the rows of tiles as well as cavities on the main roof will be covered up. Afterwards fill any gaps where rows of tiles meet with filler and sand smooth.

When fitting tile strips on the main roof to either side of the gables, and to the gables themselves, it can be difficult to successfully judge the angle to cut the ends. The bevel square is useful for marking one constant angle. Where a different angle for each end is required (between the gables), one end must be judged by eye and cut oversize. Remove the excess, using a junior hacksaw, a small amount at a time. Judgement improves with practice.

FRONT SECTIONS

Parts involved:
Front section left (FSL); front section right (FSR); FSR and FSL top section panels; strips for making upper storeys; window cavity spacer pieces; metal mesh for windows.

The opening front sections operate on the same principle as that of the cottage: 9mm (⅜in) MDF panels that overlap, the left side (FSL) chamfered at 45° from the front at its right-hand edge, the right side (FSR) chamfered from behind at its left-hand edge.

1. Ensure that the distance between the base of the batten under the top floor and the surface of the ground floor is constant along the width of the house. It is difficult to measure this accurately as the top edge is set forward from the lower. Trim the underside of the top-floor batten if necessary to make the distance constant.

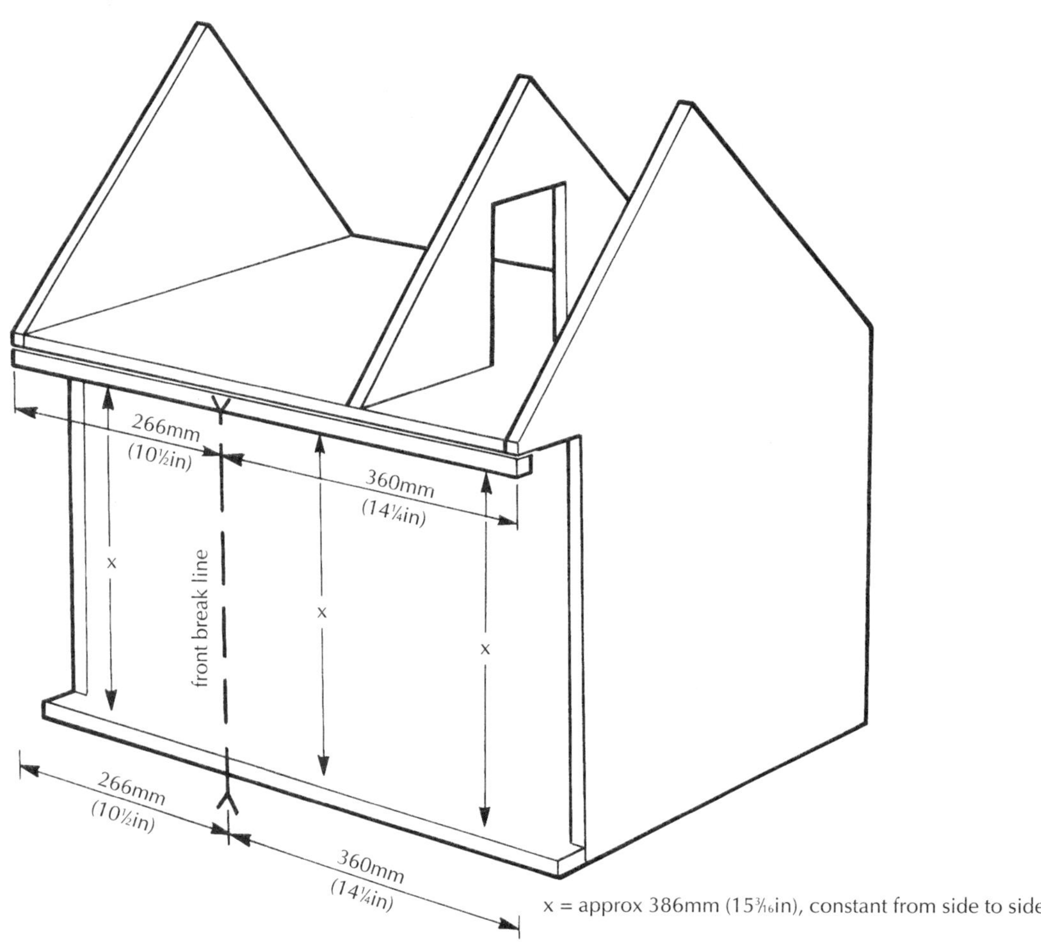

Establishing constant distance between the bottom of the top-floor batten and the base, and also the front break line.

(Above) *FS units attached and open.* (Above right) *FS units attached and closed.*

2. Establish the front break line (FBL) as diagram, marking the points above and below.
3. Trim and plane the FSL and FSR until they are the correct height for the opening.
4. Using the method described in Chapter 4, The Country Cottage, hang and trim the FSL and FSR to size so that the two sections overlap, their visible meeting line being the FBL.
5. Remove the front sections from the house.

For the FSL:

6. Working on the outside face of the FSL (as diagram right), mark a line 190mm (7½in) from the top edge, and parallel to

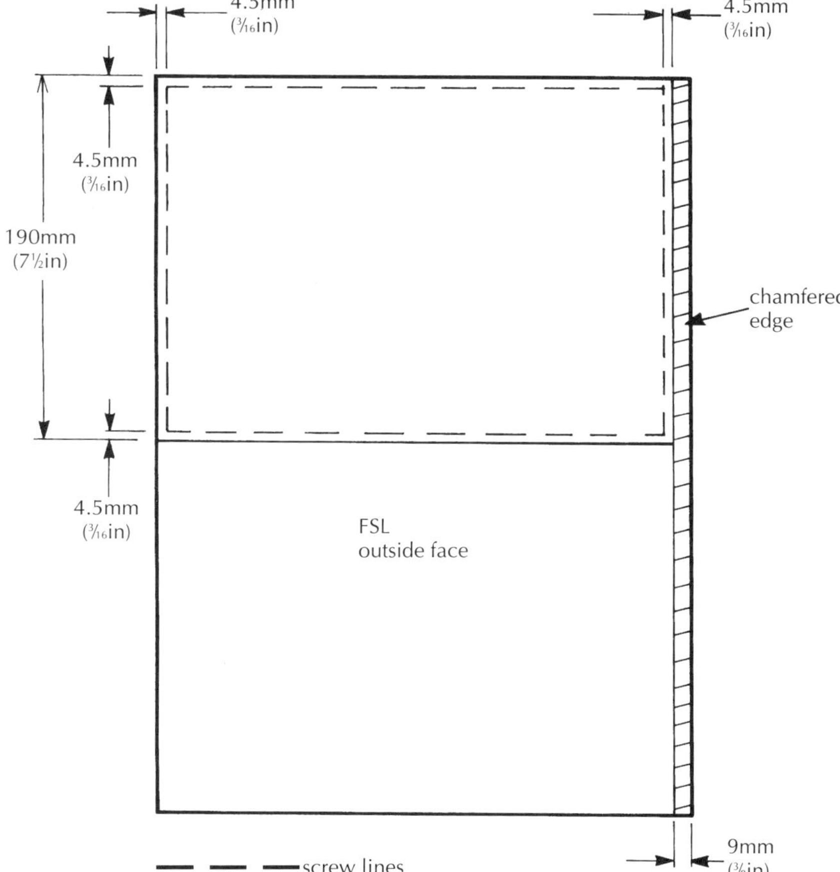

Marking base of jetty and screw lines on FSL.

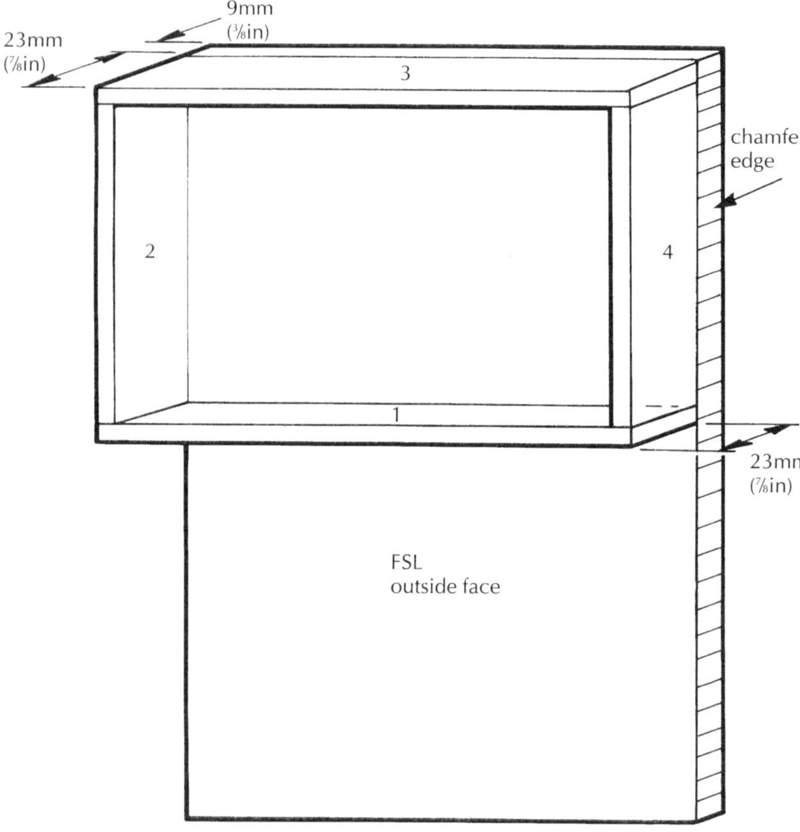

Fitting upper storey strips to FSL.

it. This coincides with the position of the underside of the first floor in the house.

7. Mark the screw lines as in the diagram on page 79 and drill 2mm (5/64in) holes along them, at 75mm (3in) centres, avoiding drilling within 25mm (1in) of the end of any line.
8. Permanently bond 23mm (⅞in) wide strips of 9mm (⅜in) MDF onto the front of the panel as shown in the diagram above, using PVA adhesive and countersinking all screws (inserted from behind).
9. If necessary, plane the edges of the strips so that they present a flat surface.
10. Place the 6mm (¼in) MDF upper-storey front panel onto the surface so formed, and mark and trim off any overlapping material.
11. Scribe a line with the marking gauge, 4.5mm (3/16in) in from the inside edge of the upper front panel on all four sides. Drill 2mm (5/64in) holes at 75mm (3in) intervals along these screw lines, avoiding the final 25mm (1in) of any line, as before.
12. Screw the panel in place without gluing.
13. Repeat steps 6–12 for the FSR.
14. Plane the sides and edges of the assemblies to remove unwanted projections.
15. Rehang the front sections and check that they close correctly.
16. Mark the window and door apertures as shown. Take measurements from the base of the top-floor batten, thus including any gap above the FS sections in the measurements.
17. Remove the FS sections, and cut the lower window and door apertures in the usual way. Unscrew the upper front panels and cut the window apertures in them.
18. Replace the upper front panels, then transfer the size of the window openings to the back (9mm/⅜in) panel by drilling small holes in the corners. Marking from the back side, draw lines to connect the four holes, then remove the front panel again and cut the apertures.

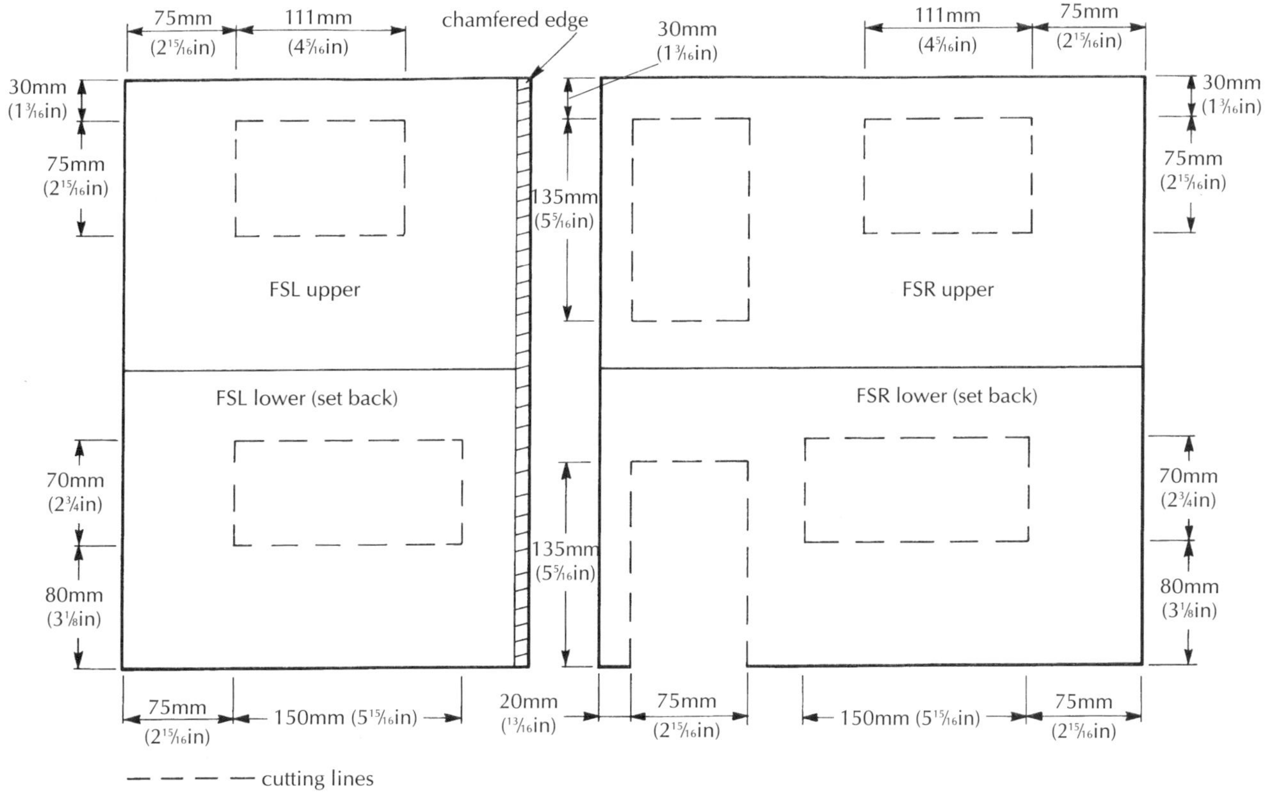

75mm (2 15/16in)
111mm (4 5/16in)
chamfered edge
30mm (1 3/16in)
111mm (4 5/16in)
75mm (2 15/16in)
30mm (1 3/16in)
75mm (2 15/16in)
135mm (5 5/16in)
30mm (1 3/16in)
75mm (2 15/16in)
FSL upper
FSR upper
FSL lower (set back)
FSR lower (set back)
70mm (2 3/4in)
135mm (5 5/16in)
70mm (2 3/4in)
80mm (3 1/8in)
80mm (3 1/8in)
75mm (2 15/16in)
150mm (5 15/16in)
20mm (13/16in)
75mm (2 15/16in)
150mm (5 15/16in)
75mm (2 15/16in)
– – – – cutting lines

Cutting window and door apertures of FSL and FSR.

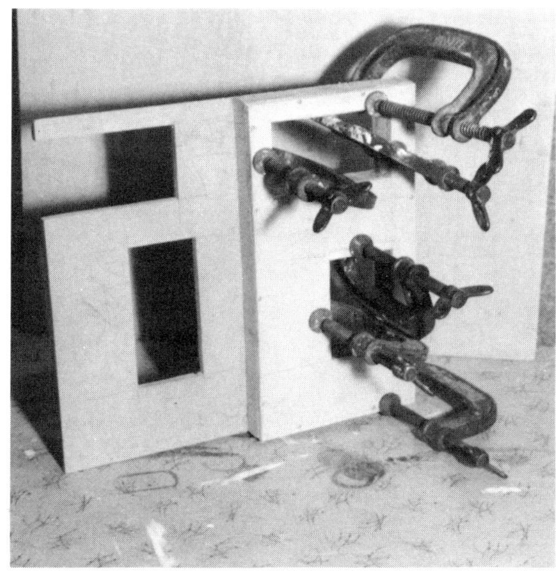

FSR with front jetty panel clamped in place.

For the FSL:

19. Use 23mm (7/8in) wide strips of 9mm (3/8in) plywood to frame the upper-storey window aperture. Cut the pieces so that the shorter pieces butt against the longer ones and pin and glue them in position, using 19mm (3/4in) panel pins and 2mm (5/64in) pilot holes.
20. Countersink all screw holes in the upper panel, and screw permanently in place, using PVA glue to bond all adjoining surfaces. Do not panel pin the front panel to the ply, as this is the area that is to be rebated for accepting the metal window mesh. Instead, clamp with G-clamps.
21. Repeat steps 19 and 20 for the FSR.

(Above) *FSL timber framing (detail).*

(Left) *Front view showing timber framing FS units.*

TIMBER FRAMING ON FRONT SECTIONS

Parts involved:
Timber mouldings – 34 × 6mm (1 5/16 × ¼in), 12 × 6mm (½ × ¼in), 6 × 6 (¼ × ¼in), 12 × 12mm (½ × ½in).

1. (C) Rebate a ledge around all the window apertures for receiving the window mesh. It should be 4mm (3/16in) wide and to a depth of the thickness of the metal mesh used.
2. Cut the metal mesh for each window to fit the larger (rebated) aperture, with the cells square- (not diagonal-) shaped. Stick the mesh in place, using clear contact adhesive.
3. Rehang FSR and FSL so that the timber framing can be done with the FS units *in situ*. This allows for the possibility of closing gaps at the top and where the units meet.

TIMBER FRAMING

Just as with the timber framing on the gable fronts, all the moulding pieces are stuck to the MDF panels using PVA glue alone, applying a layer to both surfaces. No pressure is required normally during the drying process in most cases, but occasionally some of the longer timbers need one or two screws (later removed) to keep them in place until the glue dries. Additional

> **Cutting Timbers**
>
> It is quickest to judge and mark the angle of cut by eye, using a jigsaw rather than a tenon for slicing. If the jigsaw can be slowed down, this can sometimes be helpful when intricate cutting is required.

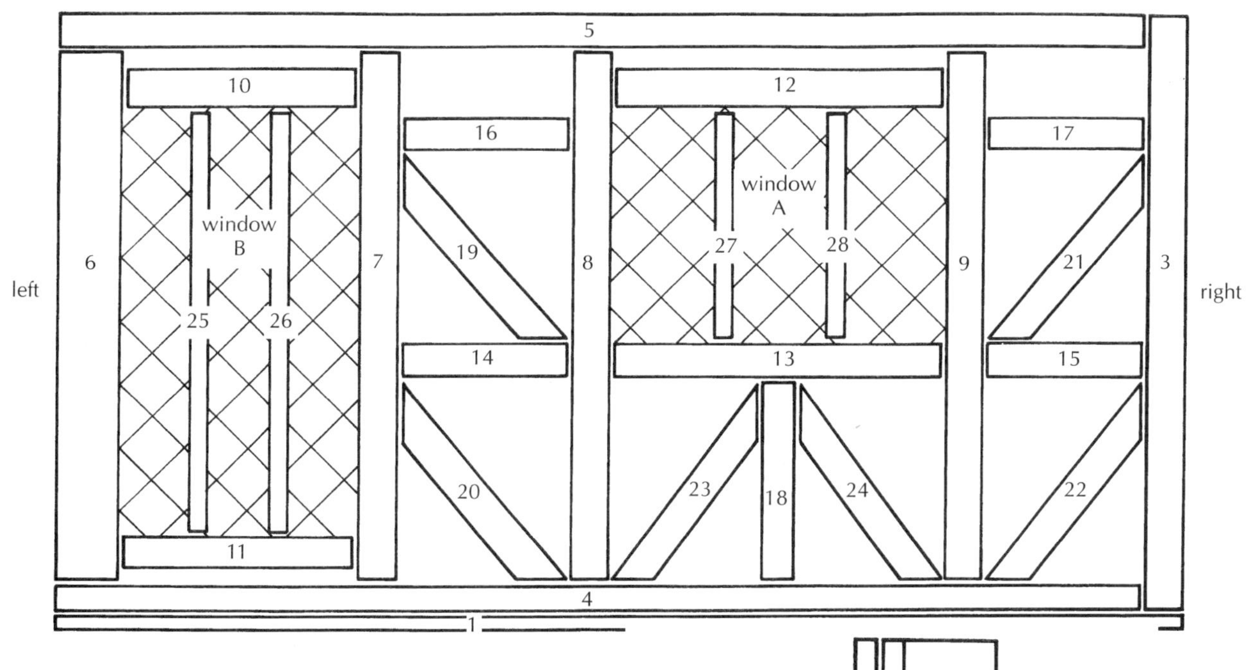

FSR. Timber framing of upper storey – front view. Order of fixing timbers.

pressure is only required when an initial suction bond is impossible: where heavy pieces are involved, or if warping pulls the surfaces apart. Below, where it says 'fix' an item, it means trim to the correct size, and stick.

FSR: ORDER OF FIXING TIMBERS

Refer to the diagram above for the numbered notes below; the numbers refer to the numbered timbers.

FSR upper storey:
Note that timbers are 12 × 6mm (½ × ¼in) unless stated otherwise, and that 34 × 6mm (1⁵⁄₁₆ × ¼in) timbers are referred to as LARGE timbers below, to avoid repetition.

1. LARGE timber **horizontal** flat underneath the jetty, the front edge forming a lip. The right-hand edge must project beyond the panel by 10mm (⅜in).

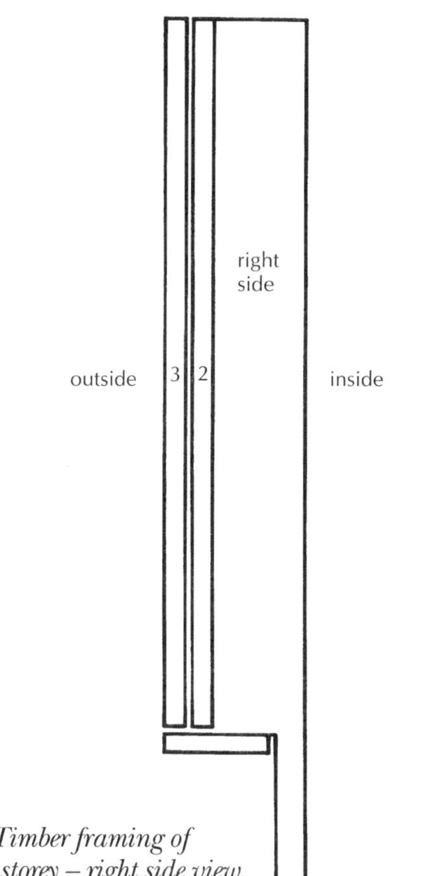

FSR. Timber framing of upper storey – right side view.

It will probably be necessary to fix this in place with two screws until the adhesive has set, to avoid the possibility of one end springing away.

2. 6 × 6mm (¼ × ¼in) **vertical** to the edge of the right side of the panel, its base resting on **1**, its front surface flush with the front.
3. **Vertical** on the front right hand of the upper panel, half-fixed to **2**, half to panel, its base resting on the projecting lip of **1**.
4. **Horizontal** flat along the base of the panel, its lower edge bonded to the projecting front lip of **1**.
5. Top **horizontal**. Right-hand end meeting **3**, left-hand end flush with the left side of the panel. This piece can be adjusted to fill any gap between the top of the opening front and the body of the house.
6. LARGE **vertical**, flat along left-hand side of window B, trimmed off at edge of panel, fixed between **4** and **5**.
7. **Vertical** along the right-hand side of window B, fixed between **4** and **5**.
8. **Vertical** along the left-hand side of window A, between **4** and **5**.
9. **Vertical** along the right-hand side of window A, between **4** and **5**.
10. **Horizontal** along the top of window B, between **6** and **7**.
11. 12 × 12mm (½ × ½in) **horizontal** window-sill along the base of window B, between **6** and **7**.
12. **Horizontal** along the top of window A, between **8** and **9**.
13. 12 × 12mm (½ × ½in) **horizontal** window-sill along the base of window A, between **8** and **9**.
14. **Horizontal**, in line with **13**, between **7** and **8**.
15. **Horizontal**, in line with **13** and **14**, between **9** and **3**.
16. **Horizontal**, between **7** and **8**, its top edge 25mm (1in) below the bottom edge of **5**.
17. **Horizontal**, in line with **16**, between **9** and **3**.
18. **Vertical**, centralized between **8** and **9**, and parallel to them. Fixed between **13** and **4**.
19. **Diagonal** within box formed by **16**, **8**, **14** and **7**.
20. **Diagonal** within box formed by **14**, **8**, **4** and **7**.
21. **Diagonal** within box formed by **17**, **3**, **15** and **9**.
22. **Diagonal** within box formed by **15**, **3**, **4** and **9**.
23. **Diagonal** within box formed by **8**, **13**, **18** and **4**.
24. **Diagonal** within box formed by **18**, **13**, **9** and **4**.

25 and 26. 6 × 6mm (¼ × ¼in) window bars, dividing window B widthways equally into three.

27 and 28. 6 × 6mm (¼ × ¼in) window bars, dividing window A widthways equally into three.

FSR lower storey:

Jetty support pieces (JSPs) are made from 34 × 6mm (1⁵⁄₁₆ × ¼in) softwood timber, marked to size as below and cut to shape with a jigsaw. Nineteen are required in all, eleven for FSR, and eight for FSL. Use a jigsaw set to a low speed if possible, and

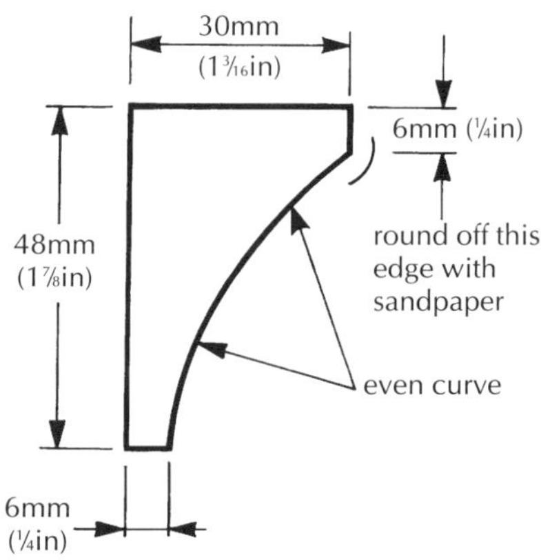

Cutting jetty support pieces NB: not actual size.

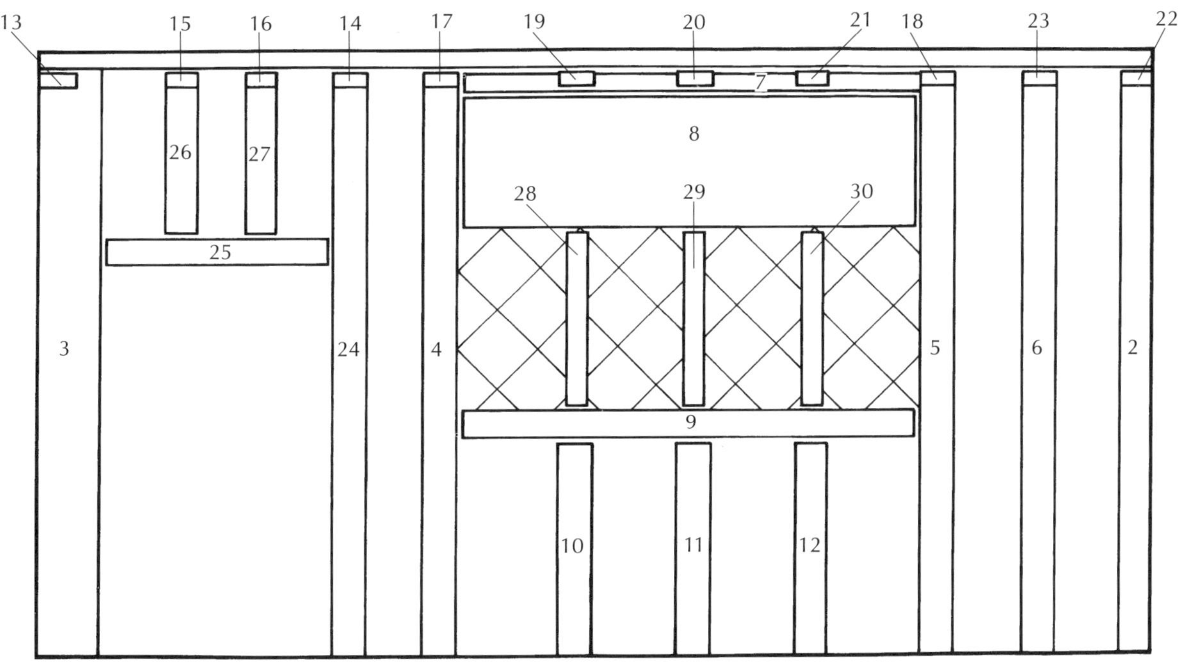

FSR. Timber framing of lower storey – front view. Order of fixing timbers (see also *next page*).

cut carefully as the soft timber splits across the grain very easily. Cut from the outer surface in, approaching the cut from two directions that meet in the middle, where the timber is strongest.

1. 6 × 6mm (¼ × ¼in) **vertical** fixed to the side edge of the panel, flush with the surface of the lower storey but continuing up along the side edge of the top storey; total length approximately 384mm (15¼in).
2. **Vertical** fixed to the front face of the panel at the right-hand side, half of its width covering **1** and bonded to it, the other half fixed to the panel. In line with the upper storey vertical, **3**.
3. 21 × 9mm (13/16 × ⅜in) **vertical** fixed to the left side of the door aperture, from the base of the panel to butt up to the LARGE panel fixed to the underside of the jetty overlap (upper-storey number **1**).
4. **Vertical** to the left of the window, butting to the underside of LARGE, upper-storey number **1**.
5. **Vertical** to the right of the window, fixed as **4**.
6. **Vertical**, positioned parallel to **2** and **5**, and bisecting the area between them.
7. 6 × 6mm (¼ × ¼in) **horizontal** fixed to the underside of the upper-storey number **1** and the FSR surface. Between **4** and **5**.
8. LARGE **horizontal** fixed underneath **7**, glued lengthways to this timber and the panel front. Positioned between **4** and **5**. This denotes the top of the window frame.
9. 12 × 12mm (½ × ½in) window-sill fixed **horizontally** at the base of the window, between **4** and **5**.

10, 11 and 12. All **verticals** fixed beneath the window-sill and positioned so as to divide the space between **4** and **5** equally into four.

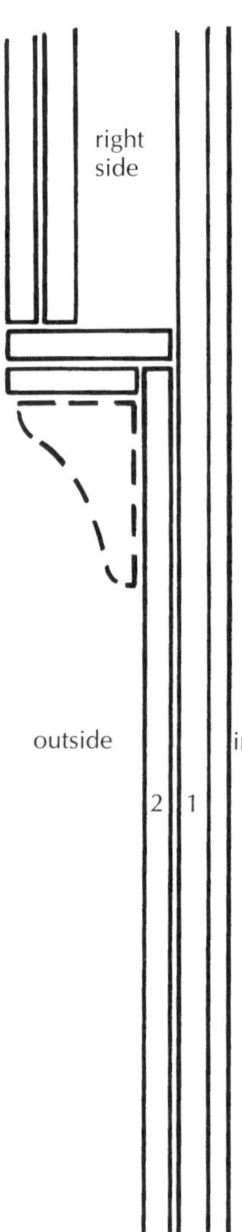

FSR. Timber framing of lower storey – right side view.

Note: 13–23 inclusive are short pieces of 12 × 6mm (½ × ¼in) fixed flat to the underside of the upper-storey number **1** timber. Some are longer (L), at 35mm (1⅜in), meaning they continue for the full width of the panel, but most are shorter (S), meaning that one end butts up against another (vertically placed) timber that is already in position.

Short pieces:

13. (S) At the far left side of the panel, its left-hand edge in line with the edge of **3**.
14. (L) To the right side of the door aperture, its left-hand edge lined up with the right side of the door aperture.

15 and 16. (Both L) Fixed parallel with **13** and **14**, so as to divide the space equally into three.

17. (S) One end to butt up against **4**.
18. (S) One end to butt up against **5**.

19, 20, 21. (All S) All to be fixed with one end butting up against the length of **7**, arranged so as to divide the length of **7** and **8** equally into four.

22. (S) One end to butt up against **2**.
23. (S) One end to butt up against **6**.

The remainder of the timbers:

24. 9 × 9mm (⅜ × ⅜in) **vertical** to the right-hand side of the door aperture, the top end butting up against **14**.
25. 9 × 9mm (⅜ × ⅜in) **horizontal** to go at the top of the door aperture, between **3** and **24**.

26 and 27. 9 × 9mm (⅜ × ⅜in) **verticals** fixed between **25** and **15** and **16**.

28, 29 and 30. 6 × 6mm (¼ × ¼in) **vertical** window bars fixed between **8** and **9**, and arranged so that they are in line with **10** and **19**, **11** and **20**, and **12** and **21** respectively.

FSR jetty support pieces (JSPs):

Finally, the jetty support pieces, described above, are fixed underneath the short pieces and against the vertical timbers, as in the photograph. Cut a piece of 6mm (¼in) MDF as in the top diagram opposite to form a curve that slopes equally on both sides. This forms an arch to place over the top part of the closed door. Fix this in place underneath **25** and between **3** and **24**, with its back face on the same plane as the surface of the main FSR panel.

Close-up of FSL to show jetty support pieces.

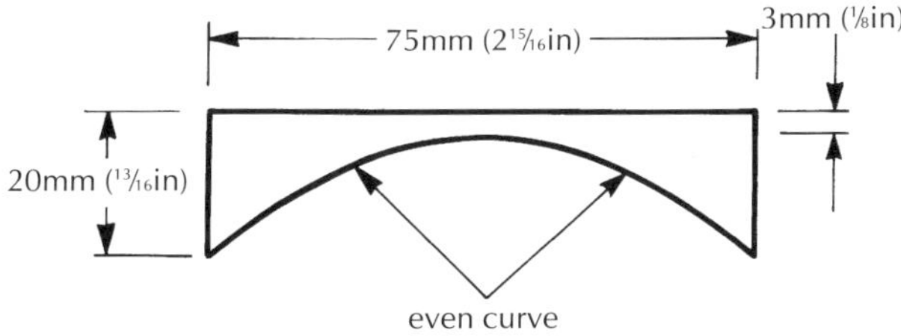

Arch over front door. Not actual size.

FSL: ORDER OF FIXING TIMBERS

FSL upper storey:

1. LARGE (34 × 6mm/1 5/16 × 1/4in) **horizontal** fixed flat underneath the jetty overhang, as in FSR, its front edge forming a lip and the left-hand edge projecting beyond the end of the house by 9mm (3/8in).
2. 6 × 6mm (1/4 × 1/4in) **vertical** fixed to the left-hand edge of the panel, its front face flush with the panel and the lower end resting on **1**.
3. **Vertical** along the left-hand side, the base resting on the projecting lip of **1**, half of its width fixed to **2**.
4. **Horizontal** along the base, bonded lengthways to the projecting lip of **1**. The right-hand end terminates at the front break line.

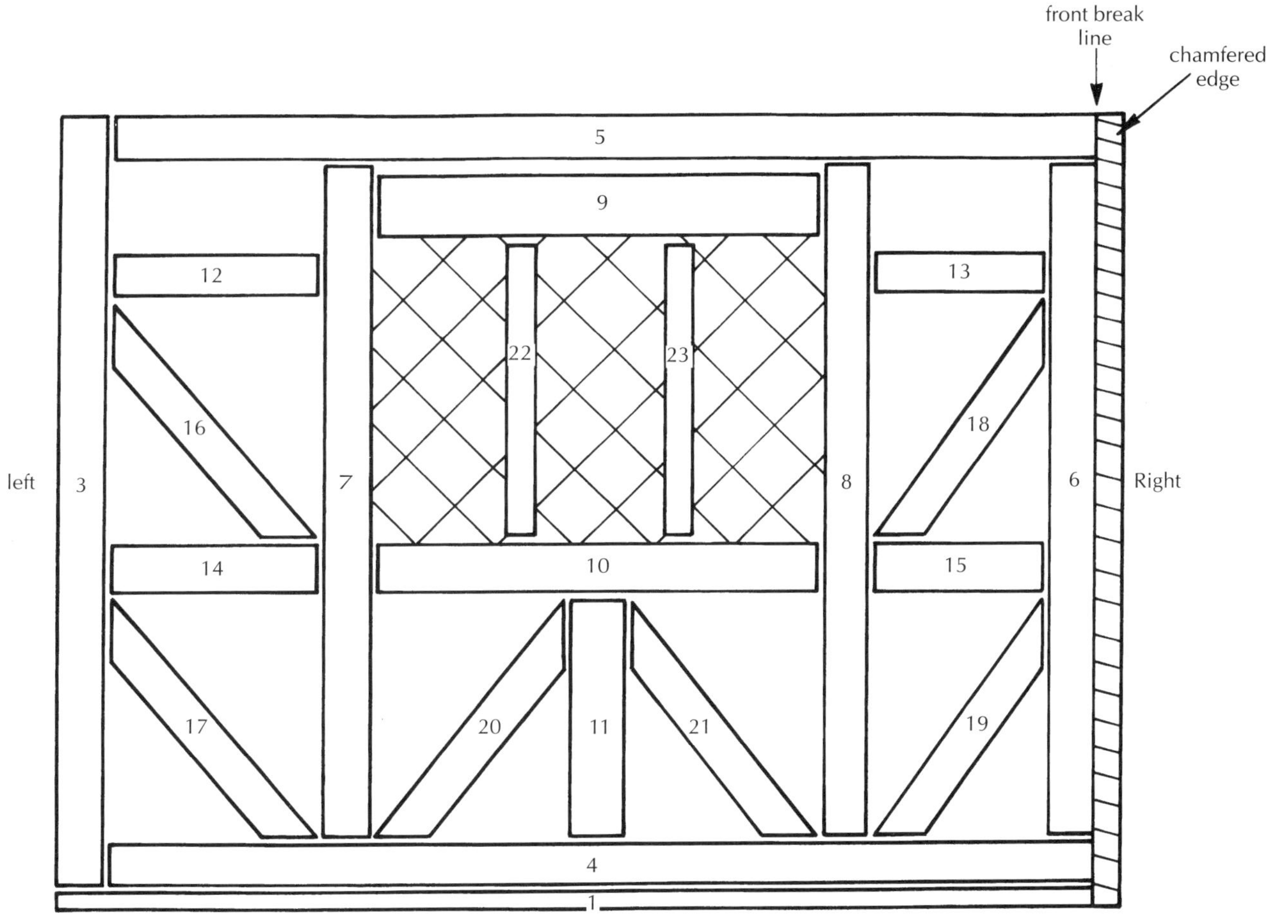

FSL. Timber framing of upper storey – front view. Order of fixing timbers (see also *next page*).

FSL. Timber framing of upper storey – left side view.

5. **Horizontal** along the top, the left-hand end butting up to **3**, the right-hand end terminating at the front break line FBL. This beam may be adjusted so as to fill any gap between the house and the FSL unit.
6. **Vertical** along the right-hand side, alongside the FBL, between **5** and **4**.
7. **Vertical** along the left side of the window, between **5** and **4**.
8. **Vertical** along the right side of the window, between **5** and **4**.
9. **Horizontal** along the top of the window, between **7** and **8**.
10. 12 × 12mm (½ × ½in) window-sill. Between **7** and **8**.
11. **Vertical** bisecting the length of the window-sill and running between **10** and **4**.
12. **Horizontal**, its top edge 25mm (1in) below the bottom edge of **5**, in line with corresponding beams on FSR. Between **3** and **7**.
13. **Horizontal**, its position in line with **12**. Between **8** and **6**.
14. **Horizontal**, in line with **10**, and between **3** and **7**.
15. **Horizontal**, in line with **10** and **14**, and between **8** and **6**.
16. **Diagonal** across box formed by **3**, **12**, **7** and **14**.
17. **Diagonal** across box formed by **14**, **7**, **4** and **3**.
18. **Diagonal** across box formed by **8**, **13**, **6** and **15**.
19. **Diagonal** across box formed by **15**, **6**, **4** and **8**.
20. **Diagonal** across box formed by **10**, **11**, **4** and **7**.
21. **Diagonal** across box formed by **10**, **8**, **4** and **11**.

22 and 23. 6 × 6mm (¼ × ¼in) **vertical** window bars fixed on mesh so as to divide the window into three equal areas. Between **9** and **10**.

FSL lower storey:

1. 6 × 6mm (¼ × ¼in) **vertical** fixed to the side edge of the panel, flush with the surface of the lower storey but continuing up along the side edge of the top storey; the total length is approximately 384mm (15¼in).
2. **Vertical** along the left side of the panel, half of its width to cover **1**, the other half fixed to the panel. Its top end butts up to the LARGE piece fixed beneath the jetty overhang.
3. **Vertical** along the right side of panel,

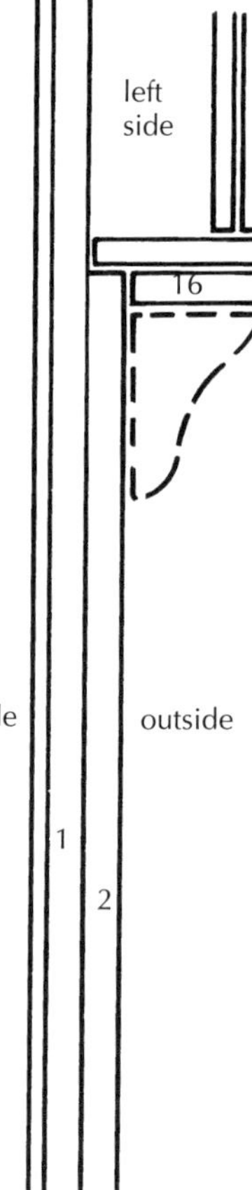

FSL. Timber framing of lower storey – left side view.

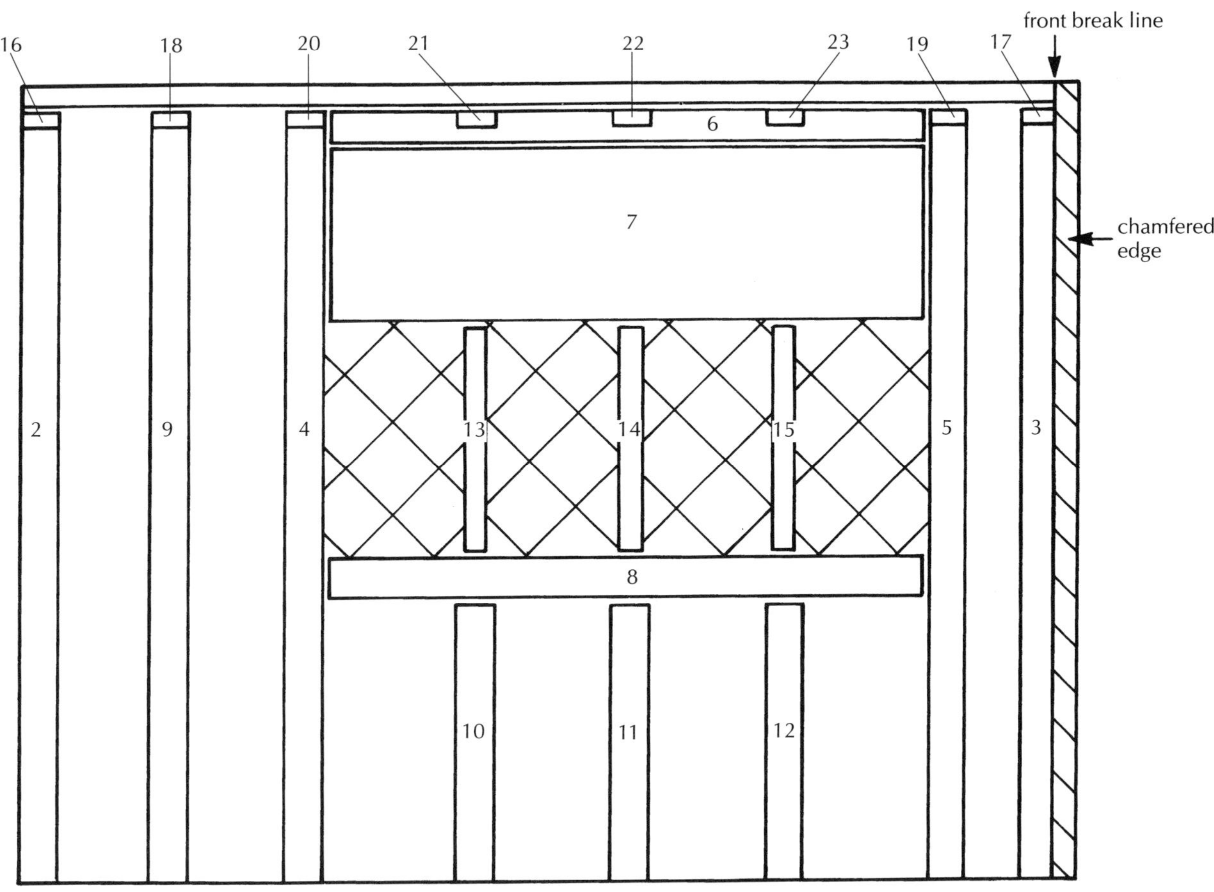

FSL. Timber framing of lower storey – front view. Order of fixing timbers.

its top end fixed as **2**, and its right-hand side against the front break line: away from the chamfered part.

4. **Vertical** on the left side of the window.
5. **Vertical** on the right side of the window.
6. 6 × 6mm (¼ × ¼in) **horizontal** fixed to the underside of the 34 × 6mm (1⁵⁄₁₆ × ¼in) panel and the FSR surface, and between **4** and **5**.
7. LARGE **horizontal**, its top long edge butting up to **6**, its lower long edge serving as the top of the window frame.
8. 12 × 12mm (½ × ½in) window-sill (**horizontal**), between **4** and **5**.
9. **Vertical**, parallel with **2** and **4**, bisecting the distance between them.

10, 11 and 12. **Verticals**, dividing the space between **4** and **5** equally into four sections. The top ends butt against **8**.

13, 14 and 15. 6 × 6mm (¼ × ¼in) window bars fixed to the mesh, in line with **10, 11** and **12** respectively.

Note: all the short pieces fixed to the underside of the 34 × 6mm ((1⁵⁄₁₆ × ¼in) panel are 6mm (¼in) shorter than the jetty overhang, and fit with one end butted against one of the beams already in place.

16–23 inclusive are short pieces, fitted as in the diagram above. The final stage in fitting the FSL timbers is to fit the jetty support pieces, as given in the instructions for the FSR on page 86.

TRIMMING

Once the timber-beam fitting is completed for both sections, trim away all the sharp right-angled edges with a sharp chisel, then sand them. This ensures that the beams look rounded and in keeping with the medieval style of construction, rather than purpose-built modern joinery. Similarly, round off the edges of the window-sills rather than leaving them square.

INTERNAL DOORS

Parts involved:
Four internal doors; 6 × 6mm (¼ × ¼in) balsa strips; 13 × 6mm (½ × ¼in) balsa strips; brass pins; 6mm (¼in) dowel; hinges.

1. Dismantle the complete structure.
2. Hang the doors as shown in Chapter 3, Techniques. Design their opening so as to open into a room and away from stairs wherever possible.
3. Remove the doors with hinges attached, numbering the underside of each door and its respective frame wall for refitting.

For each door:

1. Mark one side A and the other B, so that the A side faces the room when the door is closed, and the B side faces the stairwell, hall or stairs when closed.
2. Cut grooves widthways in side B, using the technique employed for carving floorboard grooves. Space the grooves at 15mm (⅝in) intervals.
3. **Side B:** cut and fit the 13 × 6mm (½ × ¼in) balsa strips as shown, two widthways, one diagonally, using decorative brass pins (with heads) of a suitable length. Fit a 20mm (¾in) length of 6mm (¼in) dowel to make a doorknob as shown, first drilling a 2mm (5/64in) hole as a pilot for the brass pin.
4. **Side A:** cut six 6 × 6mm (¼ × ¼in) pieces of balsa to the length of the door and fit them as shown, again using decorative brass pins of a suitable length. Fit the doorknob as above, this time using a longer pin so as to penetrate the balsa strip as well as the door itself.
5. Trim away all the rough edges of the balsa with a sharp chisel, then sand smooth.
6. Stain the complete assembly with dark-oak wood stain.

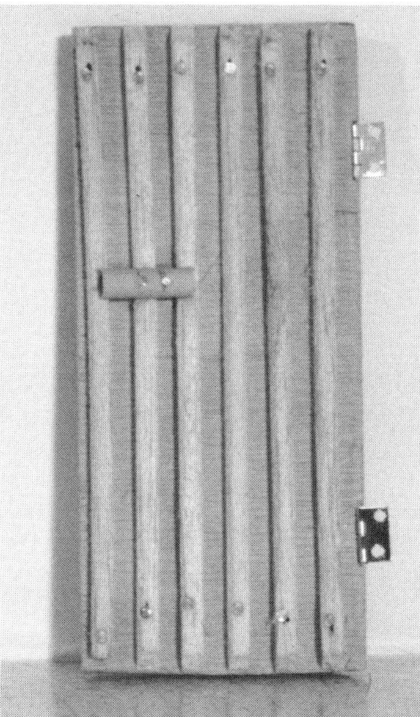

Internal door – view of both sides.

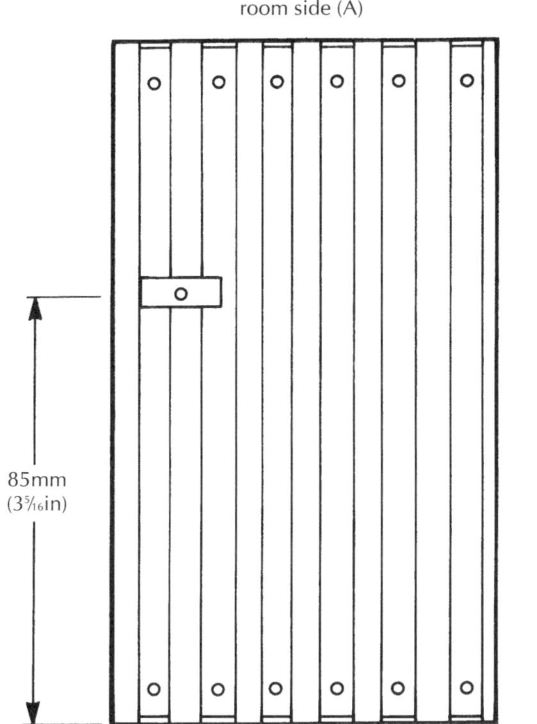

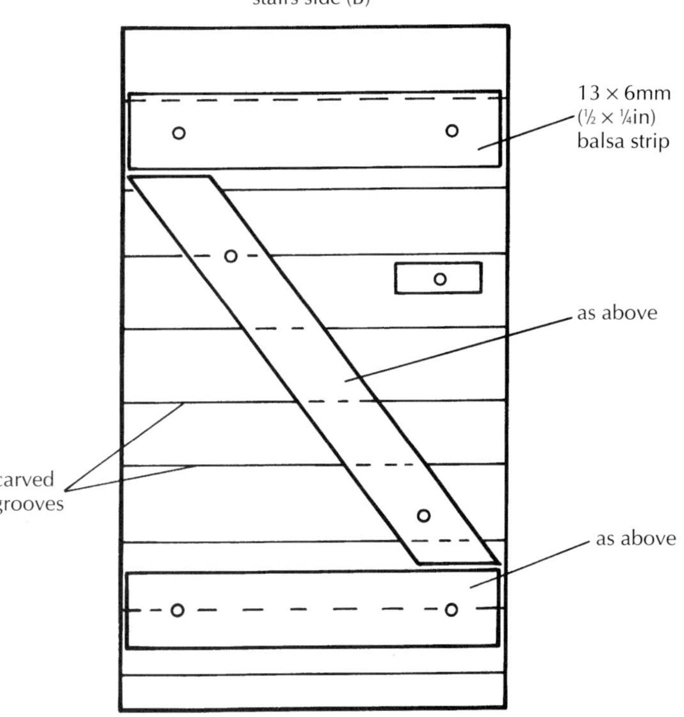

Internal door, view of both sides.

7. Seal the surface with polyurethane wood seal.

FLOORBOARDS

Carve the floorboards as described in Chapter 3, Techniques, then sand, stain with dark-oak wood stain and seal the surface. Make the boards 15mm (⅝in) wide, with the length 150mm (6in).

CHIMNEY STACK, BASIC STRUCTURE

Parts involved:
Eight strips of 9mm (⅜in) MDF; chimney top piece (9mm/⅜in MDF); 6mm (¼in) MDF stack side panel and top-piece lower tray; 12 × 12mm (½ × ½in) hardwood batten.

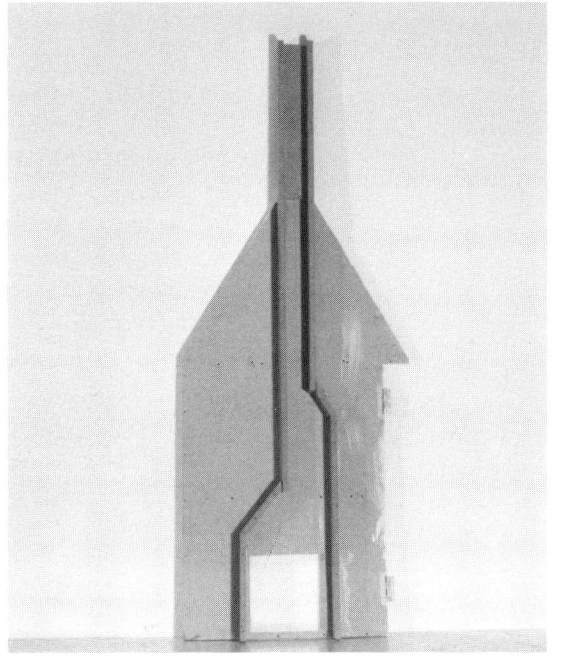

Chimney stack: side panels attached to side of house.

SCREW LINES

1. Mark the outside face of the left side panel as below. The lines denote the exterior shape of the chimney stack.

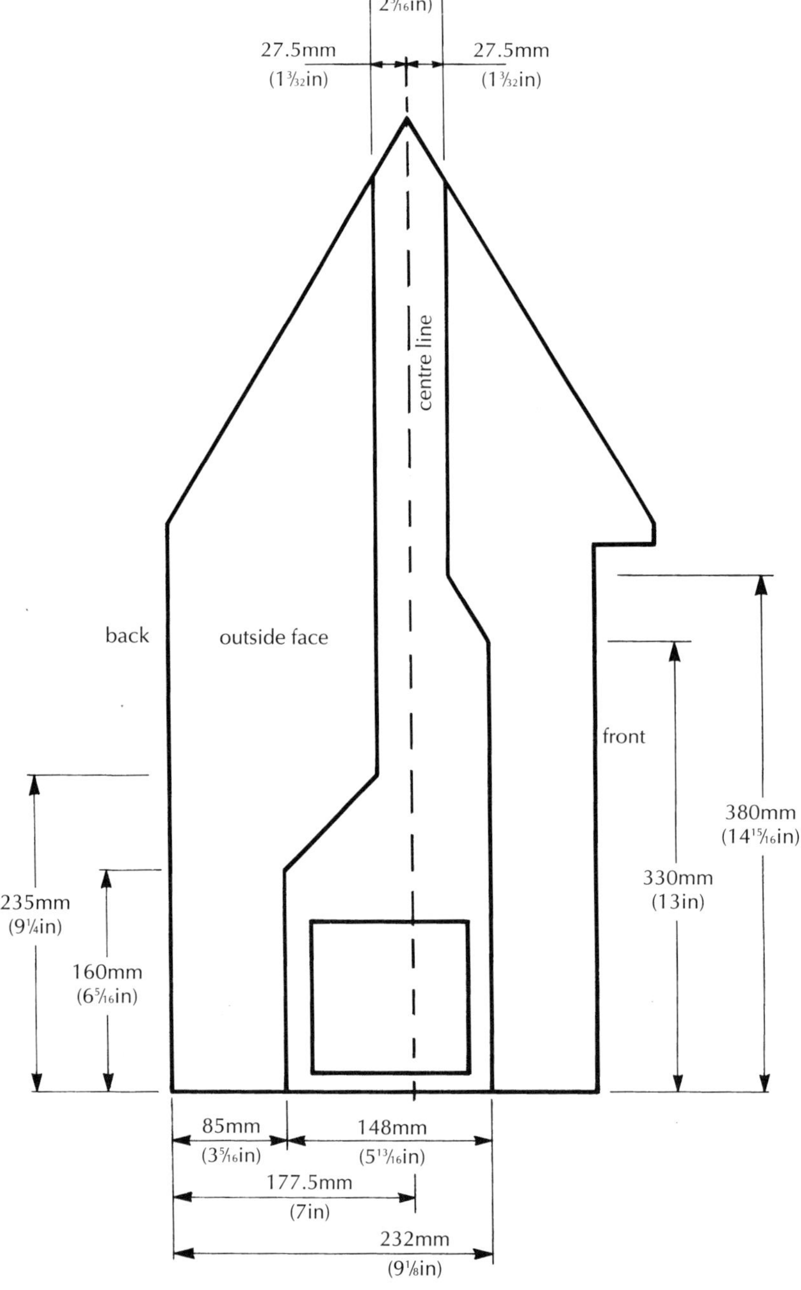

2. Mark lines 4.5mm (³⁄₁₆in) inside these exterior lines: these are screw lines.
3. Drill pilot holes along the screw lines at 100mm (4in) centres. For the shorter panels make sure there is provision for a screw at each end.

Note: all 9mm (⅜in) MDF strips used in making the chimney stack sections are 44mm (1¾in) wide unless otherwise stated.

SIDE PANELS OF STACK TO SIDE OF HOUSE: FIRST FIX (NO ADHESIVE)

1. **700mm (27⅝in)**. Mark a line 195mm (7¹¹⁄₁₆in) from the top. Position the strip in place, ensuring that this line is parallel with the *highest point* (triangle apex) of the side panel: the strip must project higher than the highest point of the house by 195mm (7¹¹⁄₁₆in). Fix the strip in place with screws in the usual way.
2. **560mm (22⅛in)**. Mark a line as with **1**, then fix as above.
3. **340mm (13⅜in)**. Fix in place, lining up the base with the base of the house.
4. **90mm (3⅝in)**. Cut the top and bottom edges to appropriate angles as in the diagram opposite, then fix in place between **2** and **3**. Small gaps do

Eventual position of chimney stack on left side panel.

not matter, as the structure is later to be covered with air-hardening clay.

5. **180mm (7⅛in)**. Fix in place, lining up the base with the base of the house.

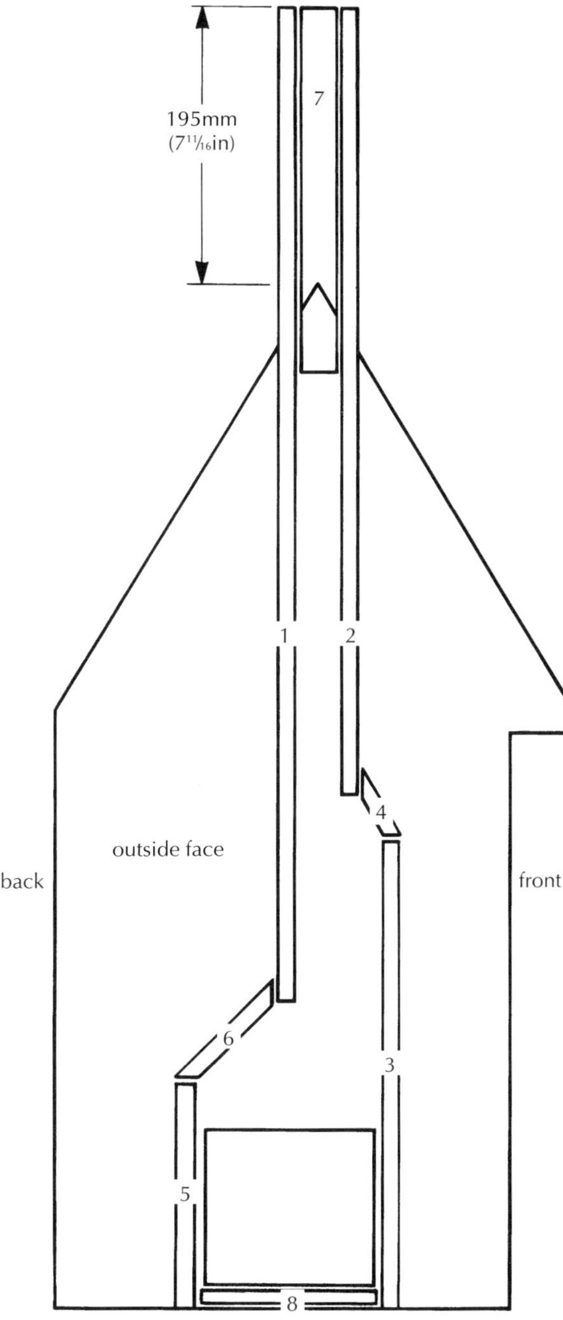

6. **130mm (5⅛in)**. As with **4**, trim the top and bottom edges to angles, then fix between **5** and **1**.
7. **270 × 37mm (10⅝ × 1½in)**. This is the closing piece that fits between **1** and **2**, lying flat against the side panel. Screw in position, first drilling pilot holes along the edges of **2** and **1**.
8. **134mm (5⅜in)**. The 'floor' of the chimney, screwed between **5** and **3**, and held by screws at each side.

COMPLETING THE CHIMNEY STACK

1. Dismantle the structure, countersink all clearance screw holes and then reassemble, bonding all mating surfaces with PVA adhesive.
2. Place the 6mm (¼in) MDF stack side panel (SSP) on top of the open side of the structure, then draw a line on it to denote the shape of the chimney stack.
3. Remove the SSP and trim away excess material, so that the panel is of the same dimensions as the stack.
4. Scribe a line 4.5mm (³⁄₁₆in) inside the outer edge of the SSP, and drill screw holes at 100mm (4in) intervals.
5. Screw and glue in position, having countersunk all clearance screw holes first.
6. Using a plane or chisel, trim off all excess material, so that corners and edges are flush with the main stack.
7. Measuring from the *highest point* of the house (the apex of the triangle on the house side), mark a line 190mm (7½in) above this on the stack, and continue this line around all four sides using a try-square. There should be approximately 5mm (³⁄₁₆in) of material above this line.
8. Using a cross-cut or tenon saw, cut along this line for all four sides, so that the top of the chimney stack is now perfectly square.

Fixing order for component parts of chimney stack.

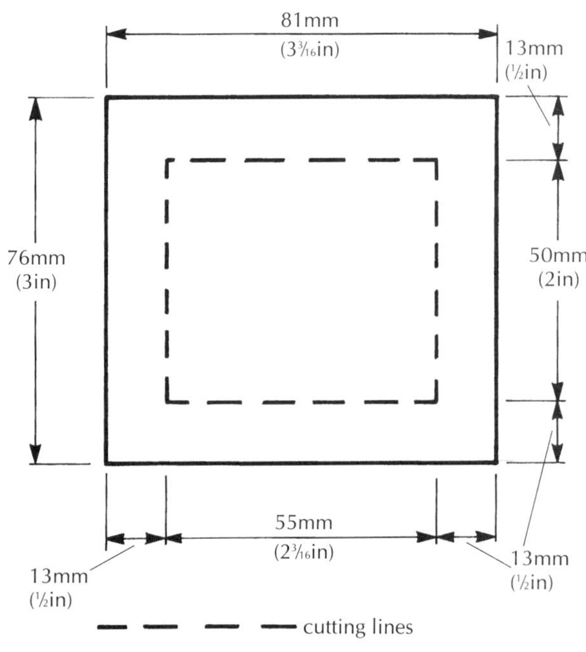

Cutting lines for chimney top piece lower tray.

CHIMNEY UPPER SECTION AND TOP

1. Cut the 6mm (1/4in) MDF top-piece lower tray, as shown in the diagram above. The hole should be of the same dimensions as the stack.
2. Slide the tray onto the stack.
3. Cut pieces of 13 × 13mm (1/2 × 1/2in) batten: in length, four @ 50mm (2in), and four @ 81mm (3 3/16in).
4. Lay two of the 50mm (2in) battens and two of the 81mm (3 3/16in) battens in place on the lower tray, as in the diagram above right. Then lay the remaining four battens above them in the same way, adjusting the height of the tray down the chimney as necessary, so that the battens are flush with the top.
5. When the tray is at the correct height, remove all the battens, cover the surfaces to be joined with PVA adhesive, and then reassemble the parts. If necessary, clamp

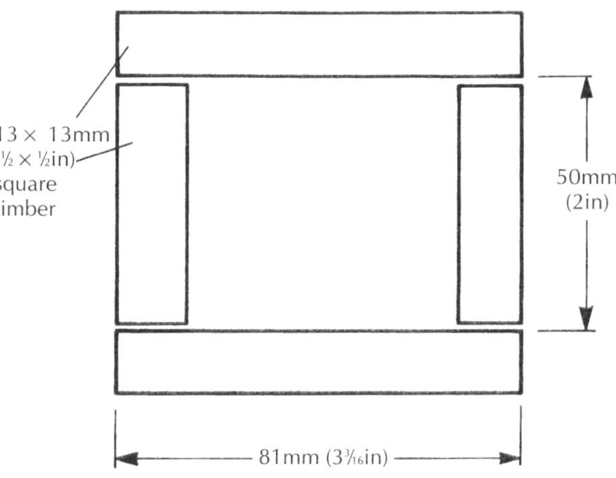

Formation of timbers on the lower tray to make chimney top.

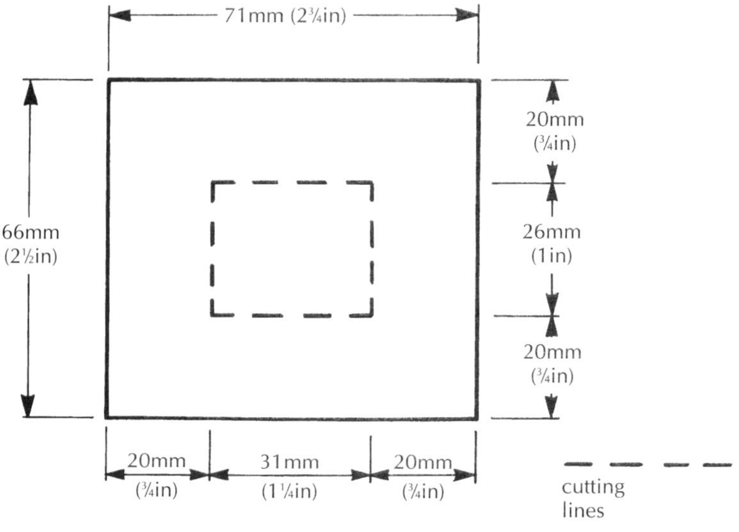

Cutting lines for chimney top.

all the pieces together until the glue is set. Fitting clamps onto the narrow outcrop may be tricky, but can be achieved with patience; in fact, clamping may not be necessary if the parts form a suction bond without drawing apart. Try to fix the battens both to the chimney side and to the tray, thus ensuring that the complete structure is bonded as a whole.

6. Plane the top and side surfaces of the chimney unit until they are reasonably flat. Extreme precision is unnecessary since the whole unit is to be covered with air-hardening clay.
7. Cut the chimney top (9mm/⅜in MDF) as in the diagram below opposite, then stick it on the top surface and clamp it in position. Ensure that it is reasonably well centralized within the larger area.
8. Use a marking gauge set at 8mm (5⁄16in) to scribe a line onto the top surface of the chimney top. Hold the gauge's block against the side of the chimney-top unit, thus marking this distance in from the widest part of the chimney stack and ensuring that the bonded area is absolutely central.
9. Cut along the four lines with a tenon or cross-cut saw to remove the unwanted pieces of chimney top; only cut to a depth of 9mm (⅜in).

DECORATING THE INTERNAL STRUCTURE

Parts involved:
Timber mouldings – 12 × 6mm (½ × ¼in) and 19 × 9mm (¾ × ⅜in).

PAINTING WALLS AND CEILINGS

Fill the countersunk screw holes in the left side panel, and then any other unwanted holes or blemishes on other panels (interior faces). Use fine surface filler to fill the grain of plywood ceilings. Sand surfaces afterwards, then apply primer and emulsion to all interior wall and ceiling surfaces. White is used on the prototype.

CEILING BEAMS

Either prime and paint the complete uncut lengths of timber with black emulsion, or stain them with dark-oak wood stain and wood seal, according to taste. Black emulsion is used for the prototype.

When fitting beams, always bear in mind the position of the walls, which should be clearly marked. Ensure that a beam does not encroach on the area designated for the top of a wall; also make sure that there are no large gaps between each side of the top of a wall and a beam.

Ceiling-beam arrangement for upper-storey rooms.

FIRST-FLOOR CEILING

All beams are cut to size using a jigsaw.

1–7 are smaller beams: 12× 6mm (½× ¼in)

1. Fix the first beam as in the diagram overleaf, using brass pins of a suitable length, the host holes drilled with a 2mm (5⁄64in) drill, so as to avoid splitting the timber. Use no adhesive.

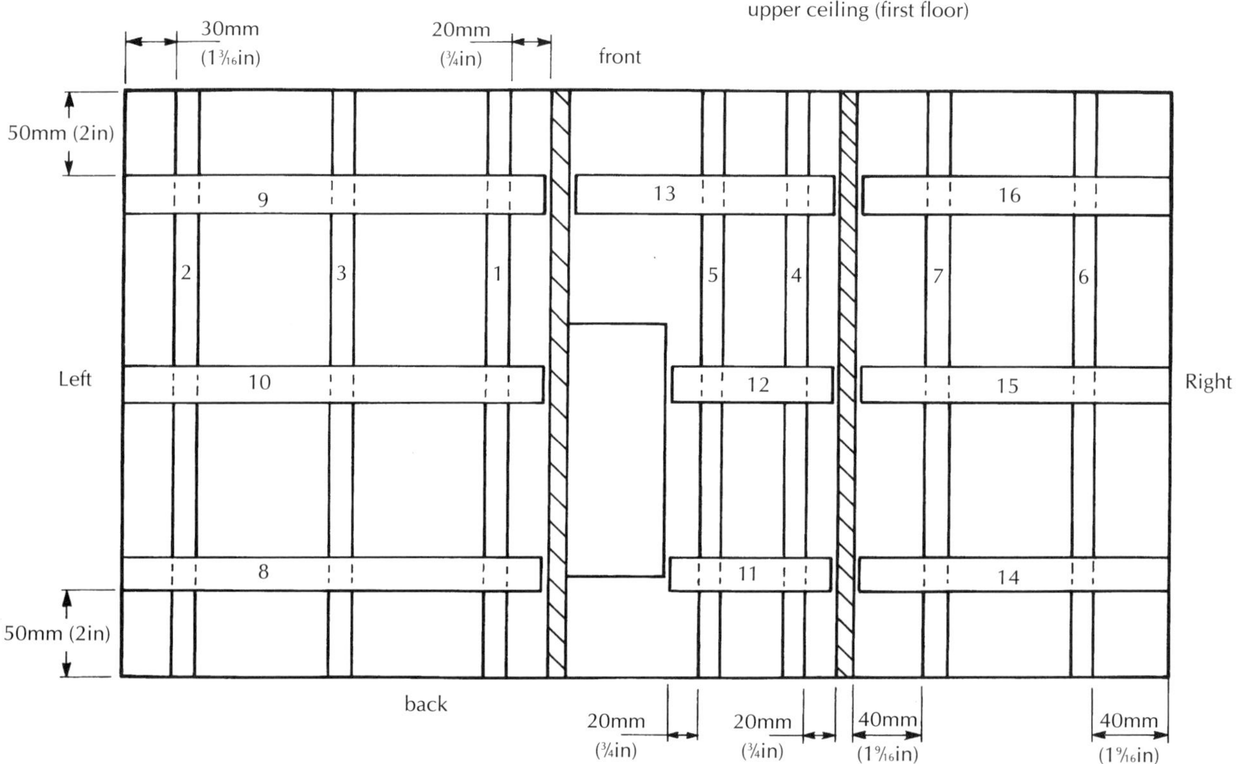

First-floor ceiling beams. Order of fixing.

2. Fix the second beam as in the diagram (left-hand side).
3. The third beam is positioned midway between **1** and **2**.

4 and 5. Positioned as in the diagram, beside the stairwell.

6 and 7. Positioned as in the diagram in the right-hand room.

8–16 are larger beams: 19× 9mm (¾× ⅜in)

Fit the larger beams over the top of the others. After cutting them to size, mark where the lower beams intersect, then cut away enough material from the large timbers for them to fit over the others. Make a saw-cut at each side of the area to be removed, then add several saw-cuts in between. Remove the resultant waste with a chisel, in the same manner as when rebating a hinge.

8. Fit this beam as in the diagram, ensuring it is parallel to the front and back of the house. Drill 2mm (5/64in) holes through both timbers in the centres of the areas of intersection, then nail with longer brass pins.
9. Fit as above in the same way as **8**.
10. Centralize this beam between **8** and **9**.

11, 12 and 13. Fit these parallel to **8**, **9** and **10**.

14, 15 and 16. As above, and parallel to **8**, **9** and **10**.

GROUND-FLOOR CEILING

1–8 are smaller beams: 12× 6mm (½× ¼in)

1 and 2. Positioned as opposite.

3. Centralized between **1** and **2**.
4. Centralized between **2** and **3**.
5. Centralized between **1** and **3**.

6 and 7. Fitted as diagram.
8. Centralized between **6** and **7**.

9–15 are larger beams: 19× 9mm (¾× ⅜in)
9 and 10. Fitted as in the diagram, with **11** centralized between them.
13, 14 and 15. Positioned so as to be in line with **10, 11** and **9** respectively.

Ceiling-beam arrangement for lower-storey rooms.

When all the beams are in position, touch up any visible cut ends or damaged areas with an appropriate finish.

FINAL ASSEMBLY OF HOUSE

1. Refit the doors to the walls, trimming 6mm (¼in) from the base of the ground-floor door to allow for the thickness of the air-hardening clay tiles.
2. Countersink all host screw holes.
3. Remove paint or wood seal from panels where floor and wall edges meet them, using a 6mm (¼in) chisel. The screw holes serve as a useful guide for this. Similarly, remove any surface finish from the wall and floor edges that are to be bonded, using sandpaper.
4. Apply PVA adhesive to the areas to be bonded, then, finally screw the structure together.

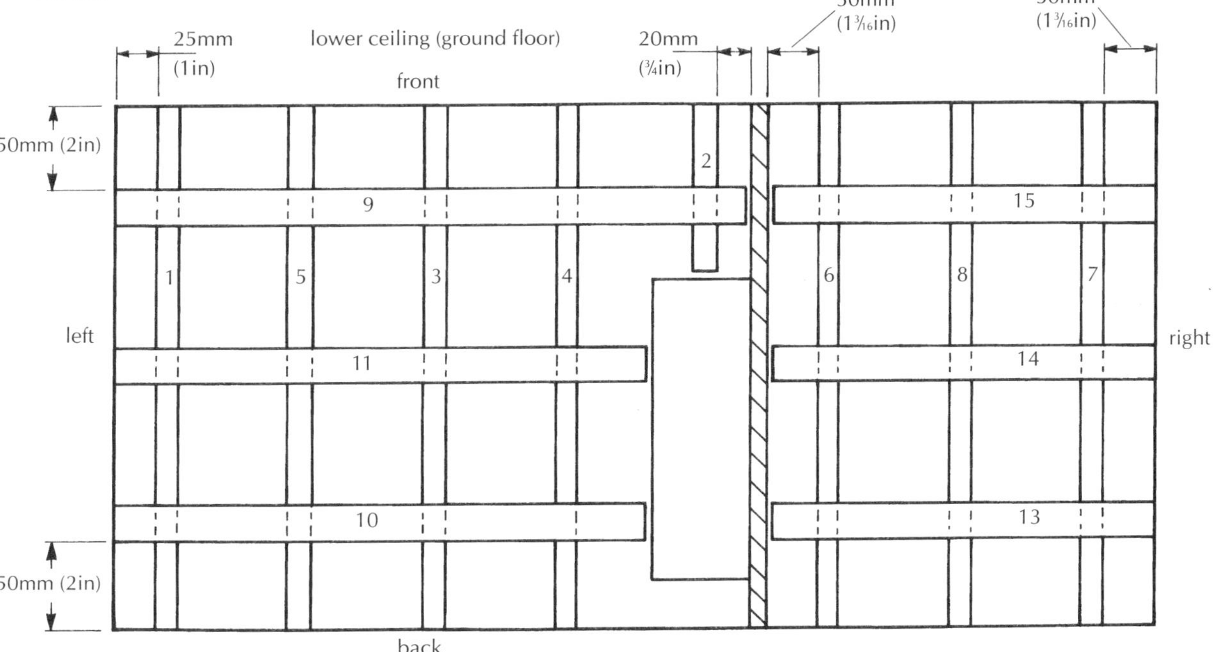

Ground-floor ceiling beams. Order of fixing.

CHIMNEY AND CHIMNEY-STACK BRICKWORK

Materials involved: Air-hardening clay; emulsion or acrylic paint; kitchen film (the type used for sealing food containers), enough to cover the entire surface of the chimney stack and chimney.

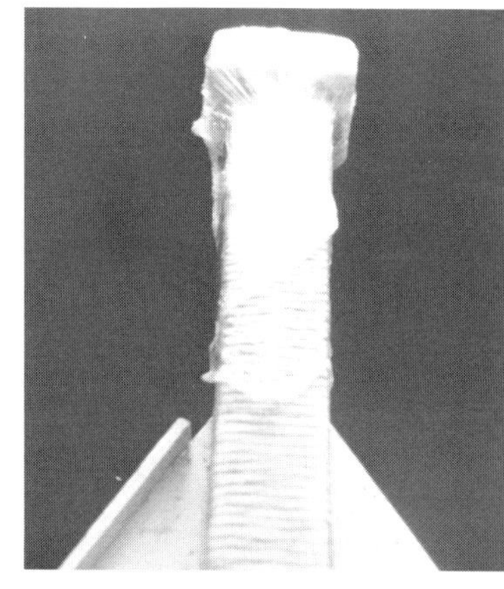

Clay-covered areas protected from drying too quickly by using kitchen film.

Completed chimney stack – upper section.

APPLYING CLAY TO MDF SURFACES

1. Using a rolling pin, milk bottle or similar, roll out some clay on a firm, flat surface to a uniform depth of approximately 3mm (⅛in).
2. Cut rectangular sections from this clay layer to the same width as the sides of the stack. Put these sections aside and cover them with kitchen film to prevent the onset of the drying process.
3. With the house lying on its back, apply a layer of PVA adhesive to the surfaces of the stack side that are uppermost.
4. Apply the sections of clay to these adhesive-covered surfaces and smooth over the joins. If the clay seems uneven at this stage, some small cylindrical container, such as a spice jar, can be used to level the clay by rolling it lightly along the surface.
5. Place the house on its front and repeat steps 3 and 4 for the other stack side.
6. Put the house on end so that the widest part of the stack is uppermost. Then roll out rectangular pieces of clay wide enough to cover this area plus the thickness of the clay affixed to the sides. As above, cover with acetate any pieces of rolled-out clay that are not to be used immediately.

Keeping Clay in a Workable Condition

Thin layers of air-hardening clay dry very quickly, especially in a warm atmosphere. To prevent this, for instance if the work has to be left for a while, wrap the clay-covered areas closely with kitchen film. When the material begins to dry while the clay is being marked to delineate lines of brickwork, spray the surface very lightly with water, using an atomizer.

7. Apply PVA adhesive to the stack surface and affix the clay sheets. Here, the rolling pin can be used (very lightly) to smooth out any unevenness, and the edges trimmed with a craft knife.
8. Wrap clay around the projecting bricks at the top of the stack, and cover the remaining inside face of the chimney which appears above roof level.

Close-up of brickwork.

MARKING BRICKS

1. Use a knitting needle or bodkin to mark parallel lines 6mm (¼in) apart horizontally, the full length of the stack. It is very hard to keep these lines parallel with the base. Measure and mark points at 25mm (1in) intervals on the house sides, and use these as a reference guide.
2. Mark vertical divisions for the individual bricks.

PAINTING

To achieve the appearance of mortar between the bricks, first paint the whole stack with a greyish or yellowish-white colour using emulsion or acrylic paint, mixing white with a little black or a little yellow ochre, and experimenting until a suitable shade is found. A reddish-brown colour would be suitable for the bricks, applied when the 'mortar' colour is dry. Once the whole stack is painted, a realistic appearance can be achieved by adding more red to the basic paint colour and painting two or three small groups of bricks in this shade, then adding more brown to the basic colour and picking out other small sections of bricks. A careful look at any brick wall will give a good idea of what shades to aim for when toning the bricks in this way.

> **Testing Paint Colours**
>
> For all air-hardening clay tasks it is useful to save a few leftover strips of rolled-out clay; leave them to dry and use them for testing paint colours.

FITTING TIMBER BEAMS TO THE SIDES AND BACK OF THE HOUSE

Parts involved:
Timber mouldings – 34 × 6mm (1⁵⁄₁₆ × ¼in), 12 × 6mm (½ × ¼in), L-shaped 34 × 34mm (1⁵⁄₁₆ × 1⁵⁄₁₆in) each side.

To avoid repetition, 34 × 6mm (1⁵⁄₁₆ × ¼in) moulding is referred to beneath as LARGE while 12 × 6mm (½ × ¼in) moulding is referred to as SMALL.

Although the timbers are stuck in position with PVA adhesive without clamping, in the same way as the beams are applied to the FS sections, some of the larger beams may require temporary screwing until the glue has set.

THE RIGHT-HAND SIDE

With the house standing on its chimney end:

1. LARGE **horizontal** to run along the base. Its right-hand (back) end

Timber-beam application for right side.

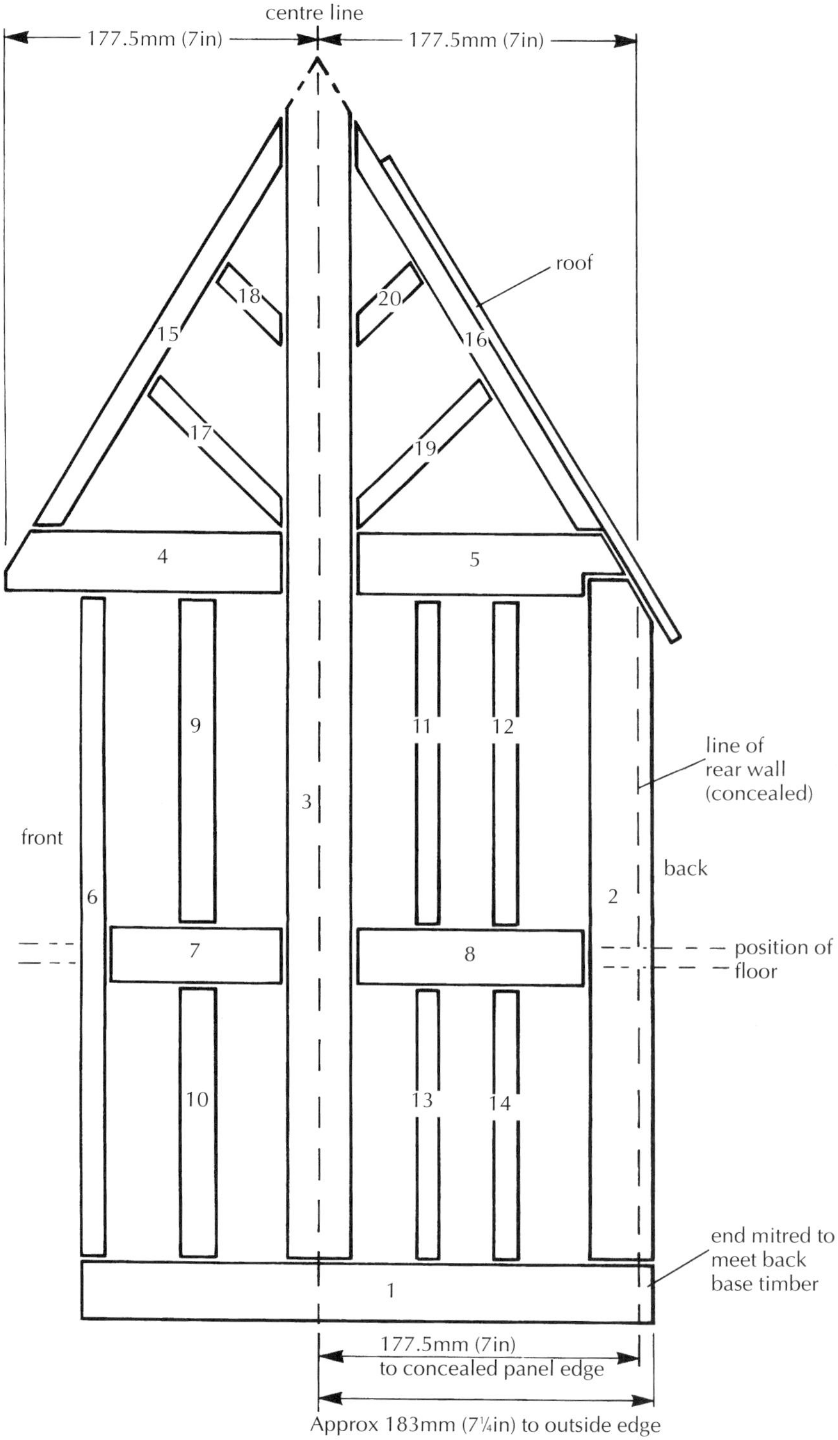

centre line
177.5mm (7in)
177.5mm (7in)
roof
15
16
17
18
19
20
4
5
9
11
12
3
front
6
7
8
2
back
line of rear wall (concealed)
position of floor
10
13
14
1
end mitred to meet back base timber
177.5mm (7in) to concealed panel edge
Approx 183mm (7¼in) to outside edge

Fitting timber beams to the right side of house exterior. Order of fixing.

should be mitred in order to join a similar beam that will run along the base of the back panel. For this reason it therefore needs to be proportionately longer than the panel.

2. 34 × 34mm (1⁵⁄₁₆ × 1⁵⁄₁₆in) L-shaped timber **vertical** from the top of **1** to fit underneath the eaves.
3. LARGE **vertical** along the centre of the side, from **1** to the apex of the triangle. The beam is in fact central to the upper, wider part of the panel, the centre of the base 183mm (7¼in) from the outermost point of **2** (at the back of house), and the centre of the top aligning with the apex of the triangle. Top overlaps are to be trimmed in line with the house side.
4. LARGE **horizontal**, its bottom edge parallel with the base and on a level with the top of FS units. It should be fitted so that it overlaps the sloping part, and the left-hand edge must be trimmed afterwards to the shape of the house side.
5. LARGE **horizontal** in line with **4**, its right-hand edge cut so as to fit over the top of **2** and under the roof overhang.
6. SMALL (12 × 6mm/½ × ¼in) **vertical** between **1** and **4**, its front edge aligned with the front of the house and cut to fit around the hinges.
7. LARGE **horizontal** between **6** and **3**. The height should be such that the centre of the beam corresponds with the centre of the middle floor.
8. LARGE **horizontal** in line with **7**, between **3** and **2**.
9. 20 × 6mm (¾ × ¼in) **vertical** between **7** and **4**. Positioned midway along **7**.
10. 20 × 6mm (¾ × ¼in) **vertical** between **7** and **1**, in line with **9**.

11 and 12. SMALL **verticals** between **5** and **8**, trisecting the length of **8**.

13 and 14. SMALL **verticals** between **8** and **1**, in line with **11** and **12** respectively.

15. SMALL fitted **diagonally** along the slope of the front roof line, the ends suitably angled to fit against **4** and **3**.
16. SMALL fitted **diagonally** along the slope of the rear roof line, the ends suitably angled to fit against **3** and **5**.
17. SMALL fitted as in the diagram opposite between **3** and **15**.
18. SMALL fitted as in the diagram opposite between **3** and **15**.

19 and 20. SMALLS fitted as **17** and **18** in the triangle formed by **3**, **5** and **16**.

THE BACK

1. LARGE **horizontal** along the base, mitred at both ends so as to fit against the mitred ends of the base beams on the sides.
2. 34 × 34mm (1⁵⁄₁₆ × 1⁵⁄₁₆in) L-shaped piece, fitted **vertically** on the right-hand side, in the same way as the one already in place on the left. The base fits against **1**, the top underneath the roof overhang.
3. LARGE **horizontal**, fitted as high as possible underneath the roof overhang, between **2** and the L-shaped beam on the left side.
4. LARGE **horizontal** between **2** and the left side beam, in line with beams, **7** and **8** on the right-hand side of house.
5. SMALL **vertical** between **4** and **3**, bisecting the length along **4**.

6, 7 and 8. SMALL **verticals** fitted between **4** and **3**, dividing the distance horizontally between the edge of **5** and the edge of the L-shaped beam equally into four.

9, 10 AND 11. SMALL **verticals** fitted between **4** and **3** in the same way as **6**, **7** and **8**, to divide the area to the right of **5** equally.

12–18 inclusive. SMALL **verticals** fitted between **4** and **1** and in line with the beams **5–11**.

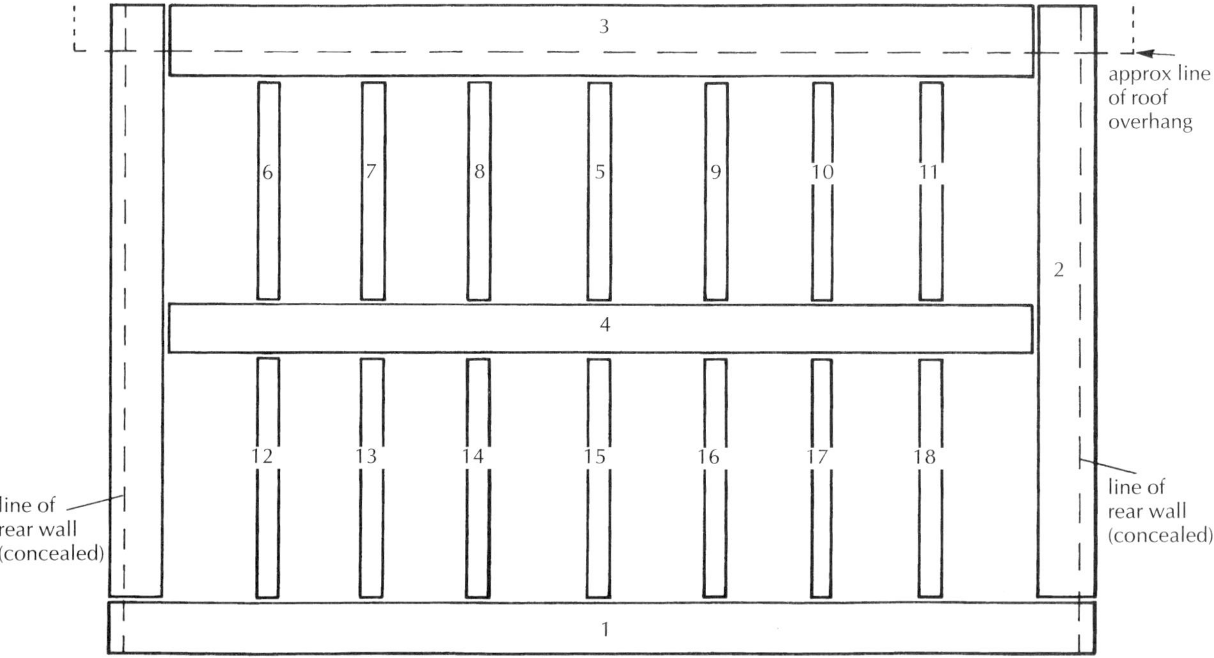

Fitting timber beams to the back of house. Order of fixing.

THE CHIMNEY SIDE

1. LARGE **horizontal** along the base, its left end mitred to fit the back horizontal base beam, and its right end butting against the chimney stack.
2. LARGE **horizontal** along the base, fitting between the chimney stack and the front edge of the house.
3. LARGE **horizontal** measured so as to be on the same level as the corresponding beam on the right-hand side. The front end to be trimmed afterwards to align with the roof slope, the back end meeting the chimney stack.
4. LARGE **horizontal** in line with **3**, one end meeting the chimney stack, the other cut to fit around the top of the L-shaped beam and underneath the roof overhang.
5. SMALL **vertical** between **3** and **2**, the front edge aligning with the front edge of the house, and cut to fit around the hinges.
6. LARGE **horizontal** between the L-shaped corner beam and the chimney stack. To be on a level with the back horizontal beam **4**.
7. LARGE **horizontal** in line with **6**, fitted between the chimney stack and **5**.
8. SMALL **diagonal** fitted along the roof slope underneath the roof eaves, the ends suitably angled to meet **4** and the chimney stack.
9. SMALL **diagonal** fitted along the roof slope at the front, the ends suitably angled to meet **3** and the chimney stack.

10 and 11. SMALLS fitted as in the diagram opposite between **8** and the stack.

12 and 13. SMALLS fitted as in the diagram opposite between **9** and the stack.

14. 20 × 6mm (¾ × ¼in) **vertical** between **4** and **6**, bisecting the distance along **4** between the stack and the edge of the L-shaped timber.

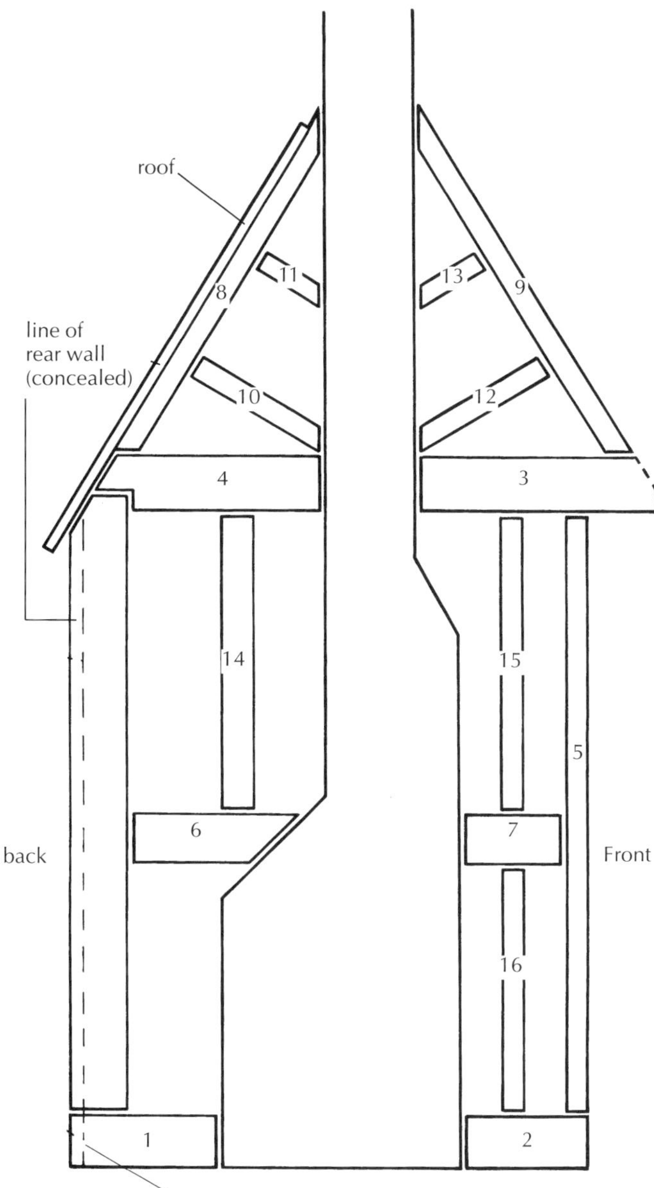

Timber-beam application for left (chimney) side.

(Left) *Fitting timber beams to the chimney side of house. Order of fixing.*

15. SMALL **vertical** between **3** and **7**, bisecting the distance along **7** between the stack and the edge of **5**.
16. SMALL vertical between **7** and **2**, and in line with **15**.

After completing the beam fitting, the sharp right-angled edges of the beams should be removed with a chisel, as with the FS units. Finally, sand the chiselled edges.

THE INTERIOR: FINAL TASKS

THE FIREPLACE

Parts involved:
6mm (¼in) plywood – two sides, back and base; 0.8mm (1/32in) plywood – two front flanges; air-hardening clay.

1. Bond the sides, back and base together as above, using PVA adhesive. Either clamp with G-clamps until the glue is set, or hold with pins, pre-drilling the host holes to avoid splitting the timber.
2. Glue the front flanges as above, clamping until set.
3. Check that the unit fits inside the hole in the house wall. If not, trim as necessary.

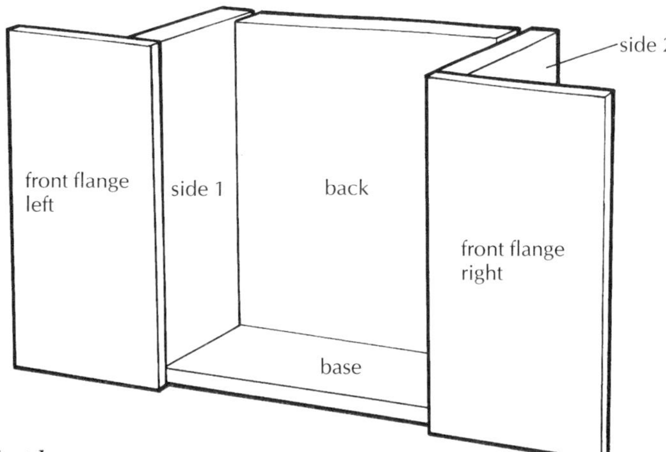

(Above) *Fireplace.* (Right) *Construction of fireplace.*

4. Roll out a thin layer of air-hardening clay approximately 5mm (3/16in) thick. Paint the inside faces and front of the flanges with PVA adhesive, and apply the clay to the surfaces, smoothing as flat as possible. Also cover the base and front of the base with clay in the same way.
5. Using a knitting needle or bodkin, mark out the horizontal and vertical lines to denote brickwork, following the procedure described for brick-marking on the chimney stack (*see* page 99).
6. Paint according to taste (as the chimney-stack brickwork was painted).
7. Glue the unit into place inside the house, using contact adhesive on the reverse of the front flanges and on the area of wall where they meet. It may be necessary to trim away excess clay in order for the fireplace to sit correctly on the floor, and for the flanges to meet the wall evenly.
8. Cut a 190mm (7½in) length of 34 × 6mm (1 5/16 × ¼in) timber for the mantelpiece. Either stain it with dark-oak stain and seal, or prime and paint with matt black (emulsion). Centralize it above the fireplace, bonding it into position with contact adhesive or countersunk screws, the holes for which must afterwards be filled and the resultant surfaces finished to match the rest.

REPRODUCTION STONE FLOOR TILES FOR THE GROUND FLOOR

Materials involved: air-hardening clay.

1. Measure the two ground-floor room floors accurately.
2. Use a large, flat surface such as a tray or a flat piece of MDF or plywood to roll out sections of clay that are slightly larger than the floor areas, to a depth of approximately 4mm (3/16in).
3. Trim round the edges of these areas to produce the exact dimensions of the floors, using a try-square to ensure right-angled corners.
4. Using a knitting needle or bodkin, mark out the tiles in random shapes, starting from one edge and always checking every corner with the try-square.
5. At this stage the tiles can be 'aged' by dabbing one or two with a dry sponge, make a slight depression in some with the fingers, or rub a wet forefinger over part of a tile to give it a slight sheen.
6. Put aside these panels and allow to dry out completely.
7. Paint with either emulsion or acrylic paint. The colour used for the prototype is light grey emulsion: black and

white mixed together with the addition of a very small amount of blue.

8. Check that the panels fit the rooms, trimming around the edges if necessary.
9. Paint the MDF floors and the underside of the clay panels with PVA adhesive, and stick the panels in position, if necessary weighing the corners with heavy objects until the glue has set properly.
10. Fill the cavity underneath the door aperture with clay, marking for a tile edge where appropriate. When dry, paint to match the rest.

The Finished Appearance of Air-Hardening Clay

Air-hardening clay is sold in terracotta or white. If terracotta has been used, it can be left in that colour if preferred, in which case a light varnish, sold by model shops for use with the clay, can be applied; this gives a slightly shiny finish to the surface.

STAIRCASES AND BANISTERS

Parts involved:
Timber mouldings – 21 × 21mm (13/16 × 13/16in), 4 × 4mm (3/16 × 3/16in), 12 × 12mm (1/2 × 1/2in); 6mm (1/4in) plywood panels.

STAIRCASES

Make the staircase tread and string assemblies as described in Chapter 3, Techniques, using the following dimensions:

1. Ground floor to first floor: height 192mm (7 9/16in), length at base 178mm (7in).
2. First floor to second floor: height 195mm (7 11/16in), length at base 150mm (5 15/16in).
3. The length of the treads to be cut from 21 × 21mm (13/16 × 13/16in) timber is 48mm (1 15/16in).

The above measurements allow 3mm (1/8in) for the thickness of the floor tiles, and ensure that the surface of the top step fit under the upper floor to be reached. The design uses only one side panel (the banister rail side) and no underneath panel.

BANISTERS

For each:

1. On the string side of the tread and string assembly, mark on the top surface 12mm (1/2in) from the front and

Staircase and banisters.

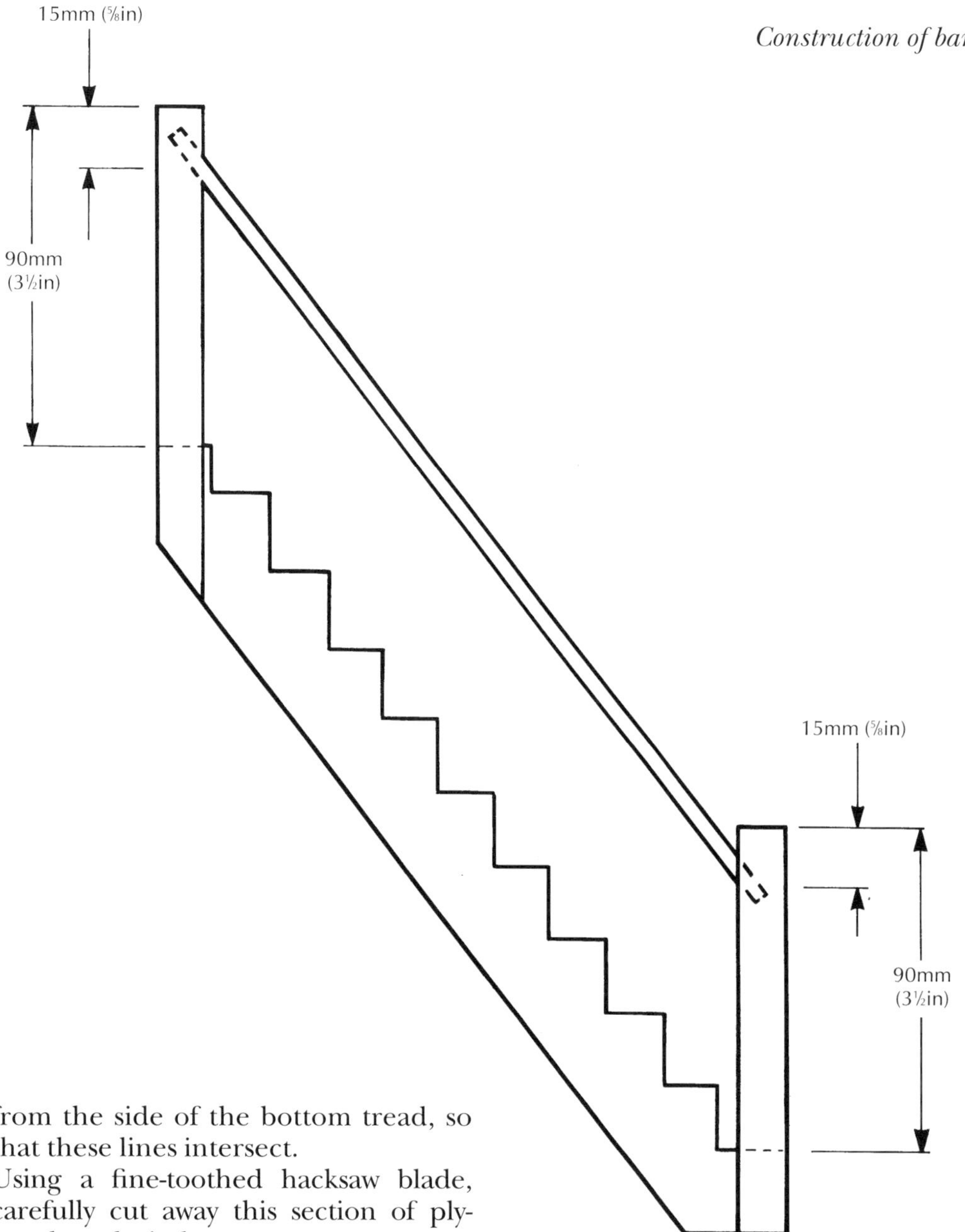

Construction of banisters.

from the side of the bottom tread, so that these lines intersect.

2. Using a fine-toothed hacksaw blade, carefully cut away this section of plywood and timber so as to create a square-shaped cut-out at the corner, size 12 × 12mm (½ × ½in). Repeat stages 1 and 2 for a square-shaped cut-out in the top tread, in the same relative position.
3. Cut a 111mm (4⅜in) length of 12 × 12mm (½ × ½in) timber, then mark a line 21mm (13/16in) from one end. This end will be the lower newel-post base.
4. Cut a 135mm (5 5/16in) length of 12 × 12mm (½ × ½in) timber, then mark a line 90mm (3½in) from one end: the top of the upper newel post.
5. Mark a line 15mm (⅝in) down from the top end of both newel posts on one of the surfaces: the banister rail face.

6. Set the bevel square to the angle of the slope of the stairs. Transfer this angle to the side of the newel posts and mark it, as in the diagram opposite.
7. Drill a 2mm (5⁄64in) hole on the banister rail faces of the newel posts, angling the drill to follow the same line as the marked slope.
8. Enlarge these angles holes to 6mm (¼in).
9. Cut a 270mm (10⅝in) length of 4 × 4mm (3⁄16 × 3⁄16in) timber (this is oversize) for making the banister rail.
10. Line up the marks on the upper and lower newel posts, and then place the posts into position in their cut-outs on the stairs.
11. Trim the banister rail so that it projects approximately 6mm (¼in) into the holes in the newel posts.
12. Fit the banister rail into the holes in the newel posts, then place the newel posts in position once more to check that everything lines up.
13. Bond everything in place using PVA adhesive. It will probably be necessary to clamp the pieces together until the glue has set.
14. Using a sharp chisel, remove all the sharp right-angled edges from the stairs, banister rails and newel posts to give them a rounded look, then sand these cut edges smooth.
15. Either stain with dark-oak stain, and seal, or prime and paint the assembly matt black (emulsion).
16. Fix the staircase and banister assembly in position using either screws or contact adhesive.

EXTERIOR PAINTING

Fill all the gaps in the beams with filler, then sand smooth. Prime all surfaces. First paint the main exterior panels, then finally the beams and window frames. The prototype was painted white for the panels and black for the beams. A particular shade of yellow can be used to very good effect, and an alternative to black could be dark brown. Study postcards and pictures of genuine Tudor houses for ideas. The prototype's roof tiles were painted dark red.

FINISHING OFF

The front door should be made from 9mm (⅜in) plywood, and beamed in the same way as the interior doors, with 6 × 6mm (¼ × ¼in) uprights fitted vertically and stuck in place rather than pinned, after the door has been hung. Place the door in position, then mark the curve of the upper door arch on the door beams and cut these unwanted beam pieces away. Finally, prime and paint the door to match the exterior beams. Fix a hook and eye to fasten the FSR to the first-floor ceiling, so that it is accessible from the open front door. Fit it in the same way as for the country cottage.

CHAPTER 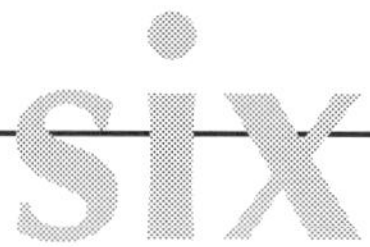

The Georgian House

This is a large house, and the discipline of the style of architecture means that it is necessary to aim for a high level of accuracy in order to maintain authenticity. Slight inaccuracies can be in keeping with country-cottage style dolls' houses, and with Tudor ones, as the originals were often less than meticulously planned and constructed. However, concomitant with Georgian values and styles are precision and accuracy, and therefore sharp, clean edges are important: different colours of paintwork should abut with a clean edge, and all surfaces need to appear sanded and perfectly smooth.

As long as the constructor uses care and patience, there is no reason why an excellent professional finish should not be achieved, as good or even better than the incredibly expensive examples that are found in exclusive dolls'-house shops. These houses are necessarily expensive, as will be realized when the length of time for construction is taken into account. The following design is loosely based on a dolls' house made for Mary Foster of Liverpool in the last century. There are many differences, of course. The Mary Foster design was purely a basis, chosen principally because it typifies the archetypal style of Georgian house that has always and always will be popular: large, with pleasing proportions and an air of clean-cut opulence.

DESCRIPTION AND DIMENSIONS

Shape: Rectangular, with a shallow plain roof that includes a central triangular-fronted gable section as a feature.

Size: Width 920mm (36¼in); depth 315mm (12⅜in); height 870mm (34¼in).

Rooms: Eight in all, plus one hall and two landing/stairs areas. The room dimensions are given below.

Ground floor

Room 1:	Width	170mm (6 11/16in)
	Height	230mm (9in)
	Depth	265mm (10 7/16in)
Room 2:	Width	170mm (6 11/16in)
	Height	230mm (9in)
	Depth	290mm (11 3/8in)
Hall with stairs:	Width	170mm (6 11/16in)
	Height	230mm (9in)
	Depth	290mm (11 3/8in)
Room 3:	Width	355mm (14in)
	Height	230mm (9in)
	Depth	265mm (10 7/16in)

First floor

Room 4:	Width	355mm (14in)
	Height	225mm (8 7/8in)
	Depth	265mm (10 7/16in)
Landing with stairs:	Width	170mm (6 11/16in)
	Height	225mm (8 7/8in)
	Depth	290mm (11 3/8in)
Room 5:	Width	355mm (14in)
	Height	225mm (8 7/8in)
	Depth	265mm (10 7/16in)

Second floor

Room 6:	Width	355mm (14in)
	Height	228mm (9in)
	Depth	265mm (10 7/16in)
Landing with stairs:	Width	170mm (6 11/16in)
	Height	228mm (9in)
	Depth	290mm (11 3/8in)
Room 7:	Width	170mm (6 11/16in)
	Height	228mm (9in)
	Depth	290mm (11 3/8in)
Room 8:	Width	170mm (6 11/16in)
	Height	228mm (9in)
	Depth	265mm (10 7/16in)

TOOLS

The same tools are used as those required for the country cottage, plus:

Extra chisels: 38mm (1½in), 19mm (¾in)

Bevel square

Six large G-clamps, 150mm (6in) or larger

Three approximately 1m (39½in) lengths of 50mm (2in) batten for clamping purposes

Large (builders') spirit level, or smaller would do

Grinding disc (metal cutting) for use with electric drill, or angle grinder, or pliers incorporating wire-cutting facility

Compasses for drawing semicircle (geometry-set type)

Large handsaw

Lathe (small lathe to be powered by electric drill is ideal) for turning finials. See relevant section if this tool is unavailable

Desirable but not vital:

Two large sash clamps (minimum jaw capacity 1m/39½in)

Model-makers' tweezers

Electric orbital sander

Splitting one of the large rooms into two on the ground and second floors will make provision for a kitchen and bathroom. If either of these is not required, the design should be adapted accordingly.

Floors: Carved to represent floorboards.

Walls: Plain painted with skirting boards.

Roof: Shallow pitch, four-sided, enclosed at its base. Triangular-faced pediment section at front. Five Grecian urn-type finials. Square chimney tops at each side.

Access to interior: Opening front, split to left of centre. The front assemblies to include the quoin (corner-stone) sections, so that the units are hinged 25mm (1in) further back, making a more stable structure and minimizing the obtrusiveness of the hinges.

Windows: Made from mitred, glass-bead moulding at the top and sides, abutting a straight-cut picture-frame moulding at the base to form a sill. One of the larger windows has a framed triangular section above, reflecting the roof pediment.

Front elevation: Fourteen windows, porticoed front entrance with semicircular fanlight. Palladian-style triangular section above the front door reflects the front part of the roof gable and one of the upper central windows. The exterior finish of the house is plain (no stipplecast).

MATERIALS

SHEET MATERIALS

9mm (3/8in) MDF

Sides 1 and 2	2 @ 792 × 305mm	31¼ × 12in
Back	902 × 792mm	35½ × 31¼in
Top	902 × 296mm	35½ × 11⅝in
Top front strip	920 × 83mm	36¼ × 3¼in
Party walls 1 and 2	2 @ 702 × 296mm	27⅝ × 11⅝in
Large front section (FSR)	702 × 699mm	27⅝ × 27½in
Small front section (FSL)	702 × 221mm	27⅝ × 8 11/16in
Single door wall (lower)	296 × 230mm	11⅝ × 9in
Single door wall (upper)	296 × 228mm	11⅝ × 9in
Interior doors	8 @ 165 × 65mm	6½ × 2½in
Chimneys: fronts	2 @ 320 × 50mm	12⅝ × 2in
Chimneys: sides	2 @ 320 × 32mm	12⅝ × 1¼in
Front door (oversize)	180 × 95mm	7⅛ × 3¾in
Chimney-breast sides	8 @ 235 × 30mm	9¼ × 1¼in
Portico top panel	146 × 60mm	5¾ × 2 5/16in

6mm (¼in) MDF

Front section overlap panel	710 × 488mm	28 × 19¼in
Chimney-breast fronts	4 @ 230 × 130mm	9⅛ × 5⅛in
Fireplace panels	4 @ 115 × 90mm	4½ × 3½in
Long roof panels	2 @ 902 × 212mm	35½ × 8 5/16in
End roof panels	2 @ 296 × 270mm	11⅝ × 10⅝in
Subsidiary roof panels	2 @ 270 × 170mm	10⅝ × 6¾in
Triangular pediment front	488 × 135mm	19¼ × 5 5/16in
Triangular pediment backing	488 × 83mm	19¼ × 3¼in
Portico back panel	283 × 146mm	11⅛ × 5¾in
Stair sides and backs	2 @ 320 × 100mm	12⅝ × 4in

9mm (3/8in) plywood. Grain to run lengthways

Base	920 × 320mm	36¼ × 12⅝in
Floors 1 and 2	2 @ 902 × 296mm	35½ × 11⅝in

TIMBER MOULDINGS

Finished sizes; the quantities are rounded up to the nearest half-metre or foot

12 × 12mm (½ × ½in) picture-frame moulding	5m (17ft)
12 × 9mm (½ × ⅜in) glass-bead moulding	13m (43ft)
32 × 9mm (1¼ × ⅜in) hardwood batten	1.5m (5ft)
12mm (½in) diameter dowel	0.5m (2ft)
12 × 12mm (½ × ½in) hardwood batten	2m (7ft)
34 × 34mm (1 5/16 × 1 5/16in) L-shaped moulding	2m (7ft)
12 × 12 × 12mm (½ × ½ × ½in) triangular moulding	1m (4ft)
6 × 6mm (¼ × ¼in) decorative moulding	2m (7ft)
12 × 6mm (½ × ¼in) plain moulding	1m (4ft)
65 × 65mm (2½ × 2½in) softwood batten for turning	1.5m (5ft)
or 55mm (2 3/16in) diameter dowel as above (expensive alternative)	
55 × 55mm (2 3/16 × 2 3/16in) batten	0.5m (2ft)
6mm (¼in) diameter dowel	2m (7ft)
3 × 3mm (⅛ × ⅛in) balsawood strips	5.5m (19ft)
19 × 19mm (¾ × ¾in) batten: soft- or hardwood	1.5m (5ft)
9mm (⅜in) diameter dowel	1.5m (5ft)
13 × 1mm (½ × 3/64in) strips of timber (*not* balsa) or equivalent ready-made skirting-board strips	11m (37ft)

METAL PARTS

- 18 13mm (½in) brass hinges
- Miniature screws for above
- 4 50mm (2in) brass hinges
- 12mm (½in) length suitable screws for above
- 200 25mm (1in) No 4 chipboard-thread, countersunk galvanized steel screws, with Pozidriv/Phillips heads
- 4m (14ft) 2mm (3/32in) diameter piano wire
- Small hook and eye fastening, *or* large magnetic catch
- 50mm (2in) piece of bendable steel or copper wire

ADHESIVES

- PVA
- Cyanoacrylate
- Nitrile (clear contact)
- Epoxy resin

PAINTS AND FINISHES

The colours used for the prototype are given in brackets; these are intended for general guidance only.

- Wood primer
- Metal primer
- Emulsion for window units/portico/exterior mouldings (white)
- Emulsion(s) for interior finish (white) overall or individual colours per room
- Emulsion for exterior house finish (sand)
- Gloss for metal banister rails (black)
- Gloss for interior doors (grey)
- Gloss for front door (red)
- Gloss for stairs (white)
- All relevant undercoats for the above gloss finishes
- Wood stain (if required) for floorboards and banister/guard bars (mahogany)
- Polyurethane wood-seal/varnish-type finish

SUNDRIES

- Clear acetate to cover nine areas of 160 × 90mm (6⅜ × 3½in) for large windows; five areas of 100 × 90mm (4 × 3½in) for small windows; and an area of 110 × 70mm (4⅜ × 2¾in) for fanlight
- Filler (ready-mixed)
- Fine surface filler (ready-mixed)
- Air-hardening clay
- Sandpaper: coarse, medium, fine and very fine
- Masking tape

THE MAIN STAGES IN CONSTRUCTION

1. Cutting the component parts from sheet materials.
2. Making the shell.
3. Party walls and floors assembly construction (W/F assembly).
4. Making and hanging the internal doors.
5. Decorating the major components, and final fit of the W/F assembly into the shell.
6. Construction and hanging of the opening front sections – the larger front section right (FSR), and smaller front section left (FSL).
7. Manufacturing and decorating the window units (WUs) and front-entrance portico.
8. Completing the front sections.
9. Constructing the main roof, the subsidiary roof and the pediment. Fitting the moulding to the exterior front and sides of the house.
10. Making and fitting the finials and the chimneys.
11. Interior fittings: stairs, fireplaces and skirting-boards; the manufacture and fitting of these.
12. Finishing off.

CONSTRUCTION

As with the other projects, the house is screwed and glued for the main part. Where clamping is an option, some parts are bonded with PVA adhesive alone, while for fitting mouldings and painted window and door frame assemblies, nitrile (clear contact) glue is the best choice.

Constructed shell.

CUTTING THE COMPONENT PARTS FROM SHEET MATERIALS: THE SHELL

Cut parts in the usual way, marking each with its final measurement for future reference.

Parts involved:
Base; back; two side walls; top.

Cut the base as in the diagram opposite along the dotted lines. Ensure that the best timber surface will be uppermost when the structure is assembled later.

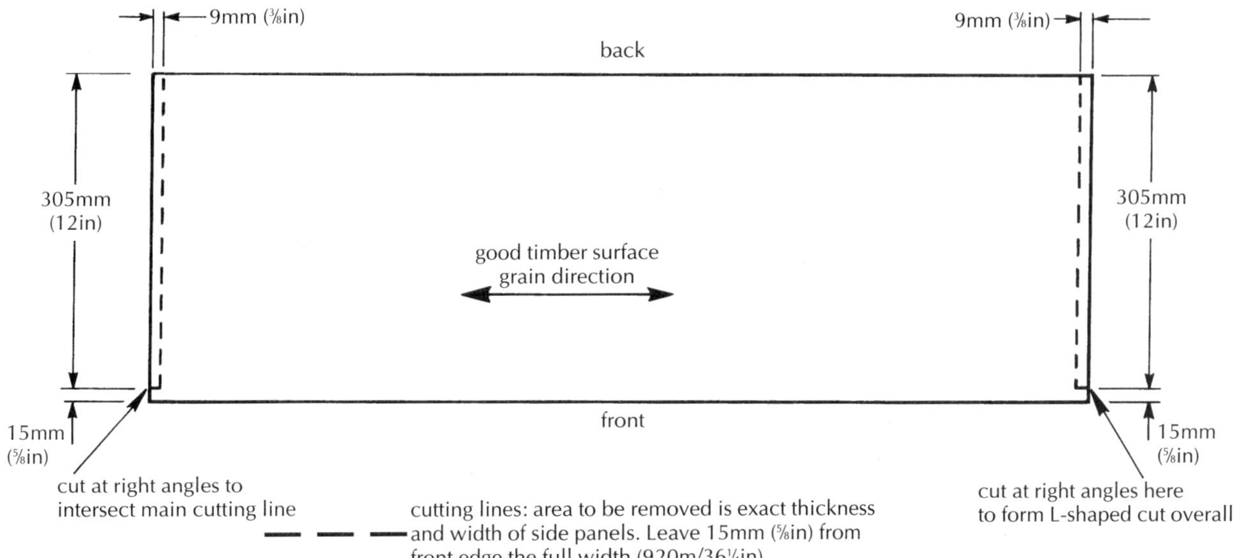

(Above) *Cutting lines for the base.*

(Below) *Screw lines and floor positions for the side panels.*

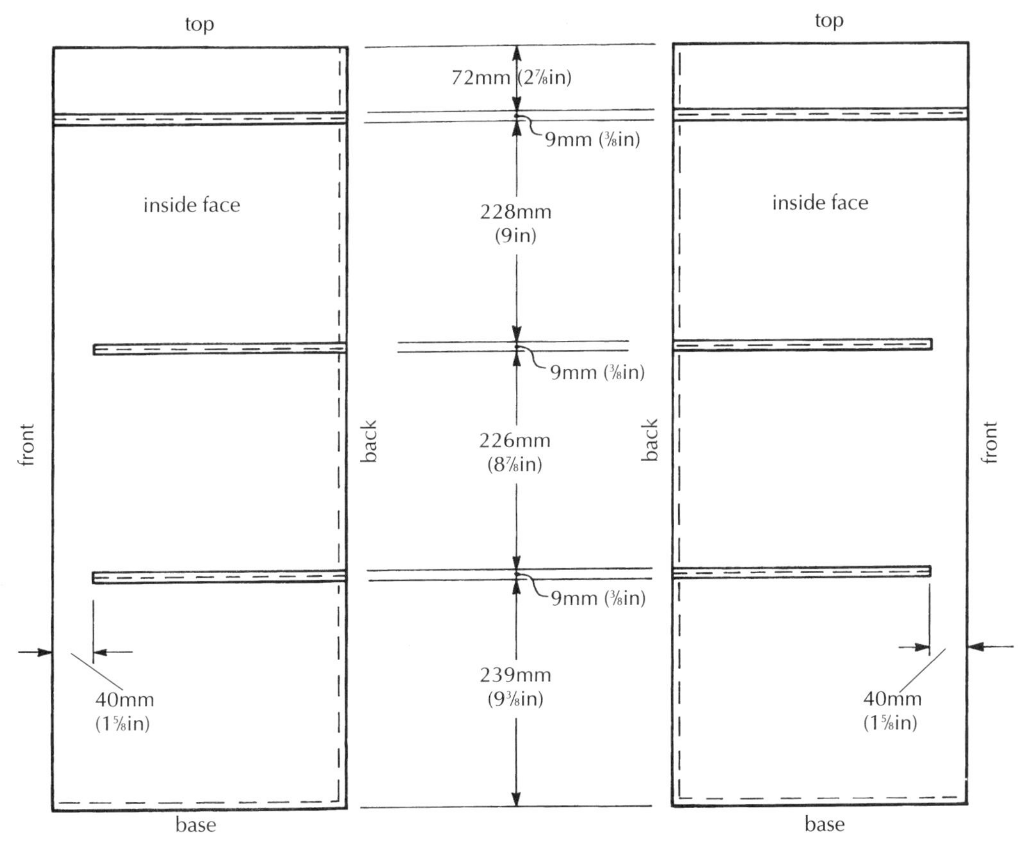

SCREW LINES

Side panels:

1. With the marking gauge set at precisely half the thickness of the panel (4.5mm/3/16in), scribe screw lines along the interior face of the long back edges and the short base edges, as shown.
2. Mark the other lines, as in the diagram on page 113: these lines denote the position of the widthways edges of the two floors, and also those of the top panel.
3. Mark lines midway between these lines: these are the screw lines.
4. Drill 2mm (5/64in) holes along the screw lines at 100mm (4in) centres. Do not drill holes closer than 50mm (2in) from the front edges for first and second floors.

Back panel:

1. Mark lines as in the diagram below on the inside of the back panel, using an HB pencil; these lines denote the position of the lengthways edges of the

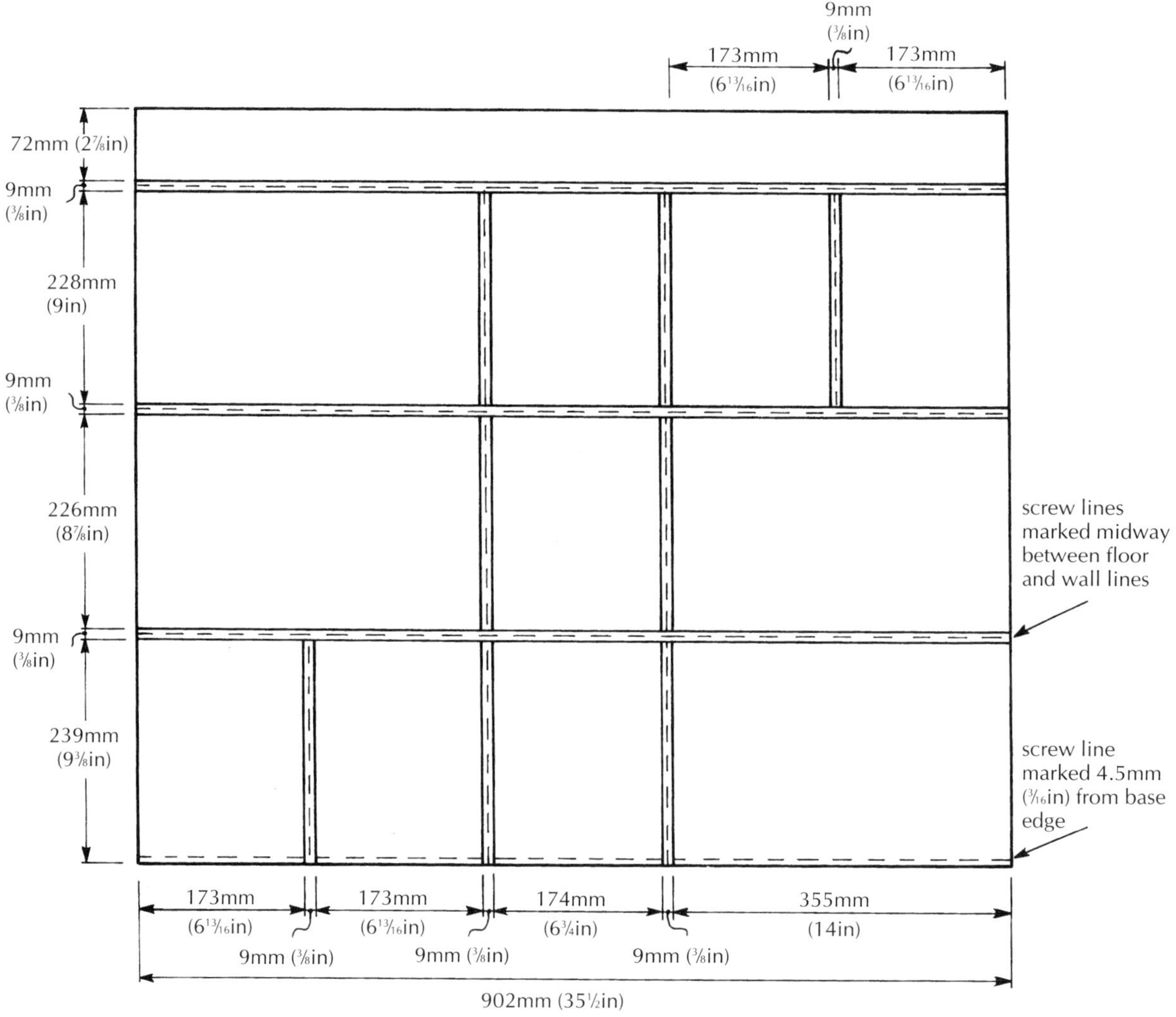

Screw lines and wall and floor positions for the back panel. Inside face shown.

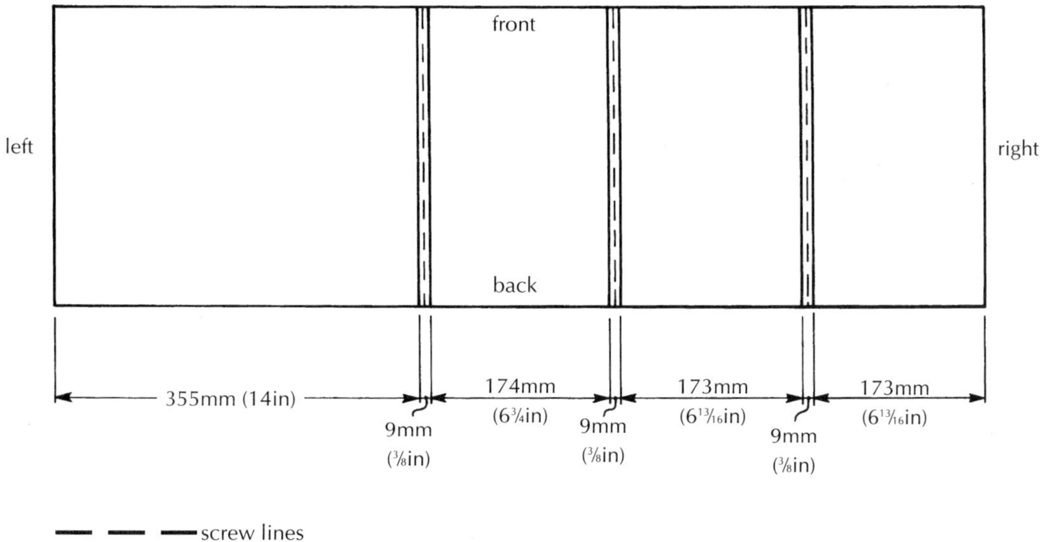

Screw lines and wall positions for the top panel. Inside surface (ceiling side) shown.

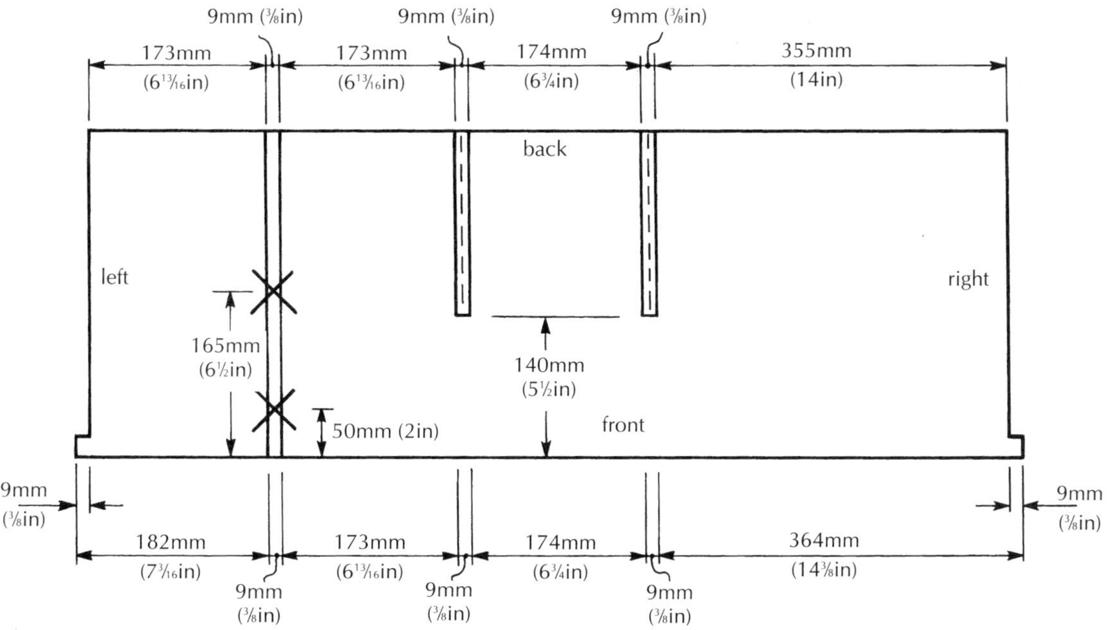

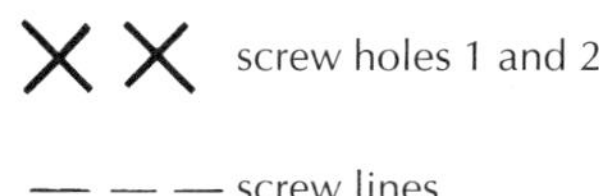

Screw lines and wall positions for the base. Top surface (floor side) shown.

floors and top panel, as well as the back edges of the walls.
2. Mark the screw lines midway between these lines, as shown in the diagram on page 114.
3. Scribe a screw line 4.5mm (3/16in) from the bottom edge, as shown.
4. Drill holes along the screw lines at 100mm (4in) centres.

Top and base:
1. Mark the position of the walls on the inside surface of the top and upper surface of the base as shown in the diagram (on page 115). Mark the screw lines midway between these lines.
2. Drill 2mm (5/64in) holes at 100mm (4in) centres along the screw lines of the top panel. For the base screw lines:
   (i) left hand: only two holes, in the positions shown.
   (ii) middle and right: no holes within 140mm (5½in) of the front edge.

SIDE PANELS TO BACK, TOP AND BASE: FIRST FIX

1. Lay the back panel flat on the working surface and position the right-hand side panel as below. Mark through two screw holes into the edge of the back panel, using a sharp bradawl in the usual way.
2. Remove the side panel and drill 2mm (5/64in) pilot holes at the marked sites to a depth of 15mm (5/8in). Enlarge the corresponding holes on the side panels to 3mm (1/8in).
3. Screw the panels together.
4. Repeat this procedure for joining the top panel to the side panel and to the back, using only a couple of screws for each panel joint.

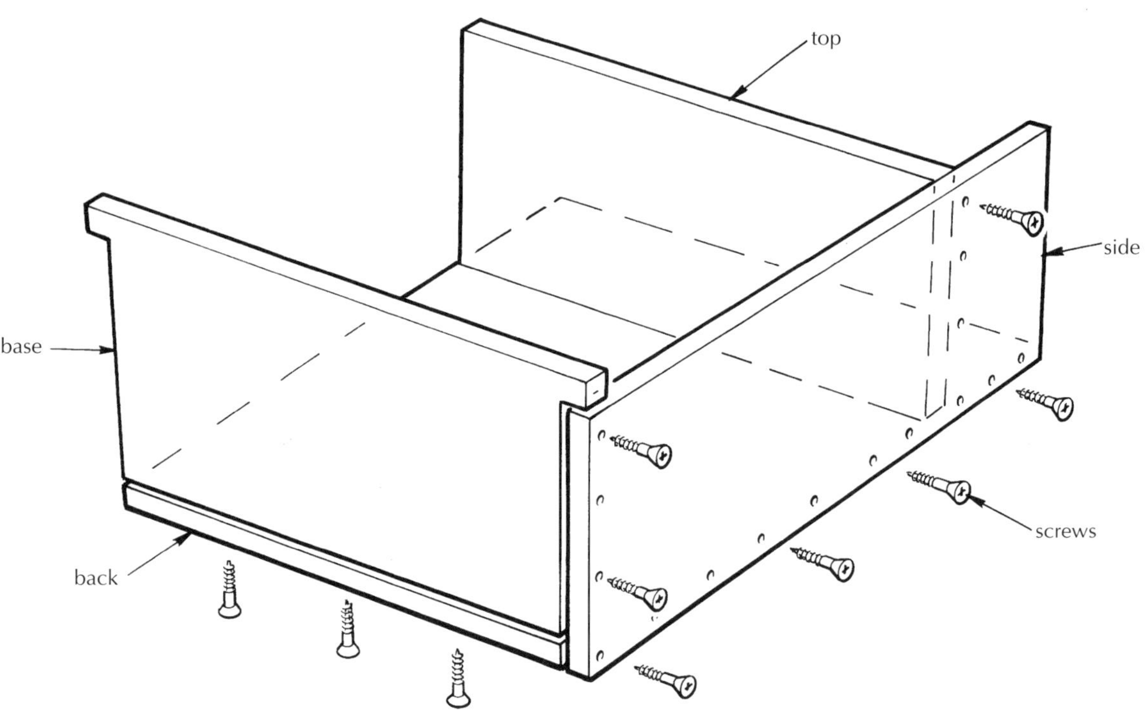

Fixing the side panels to the back, top and base, showing the screw entry points.

5. Fix the base in position in the same manner.
6. Fix the left-hand side panel to the structure by repeating steps 1 to 5.
7. Mark all the other screw-hole destination positions, then dismantle the structure and drill all the requisite holes. Reassemble, positioning and tightening all the screws.

Note: Do *not* fix permanently with adhesive at this stage.

FINAL ASSEMBLY

1. The base should project 9mm (3/8in) from the rest of structure, so as to fill the gap beneath the opening front sections. Measure and mark a line accordingly along the front of the base.
2. Take the structure apart, cut off the excess timber from the front of the base and then carve floorboard grooves into the top surface of the base floor panel (the process is shown in Chapter 3, Techniques), measuring from the front edge. The width of the floorboards should be 15mm (5/8in), and the length 203mm (8in). Sand and stain the surface according to taste, and then seal. The prototype was stained a mahogany shade, but natural wood or another shade may be preferred. Experiment with different shades of woodstain on offcuts, bearing in mind that the same finish should be applied to all the floorboards in the house.
3. Countersink all screw holes, then reassemble the complete shell permanently, using PVA adhesive.

Wall and floor assembly.

PARTY WALLS AND FLOORS (W/F) ASSEMBLY

Parts involved:
Floors 1 and 2, two party walls and two single-door walls.

CUTTING

1. Cut the two floor panels as indicated in the diagram overleaf, ensuring that the best timber surface is the top surface. The central part between the two slots is the landing/stair area, and the stairwell holes are to the right for the first floor (denoting that the stairs will be on the right side of the ground-floor hall). The stairwell hole is to the left on the second floor, indicating that the stair position is to the left of the floor below (the first floor).
2. Mark the first and second floors as in the diagram on page 118, and drill two 2mm (5/64in) holes only in each screw line, in the positions shown.
3. Cut the two wall panels (*see* diagram on page 119). Unlike the floors, the finished panels should be identical.
4. Slot the four pieces together in the final position. The fit should require gentle

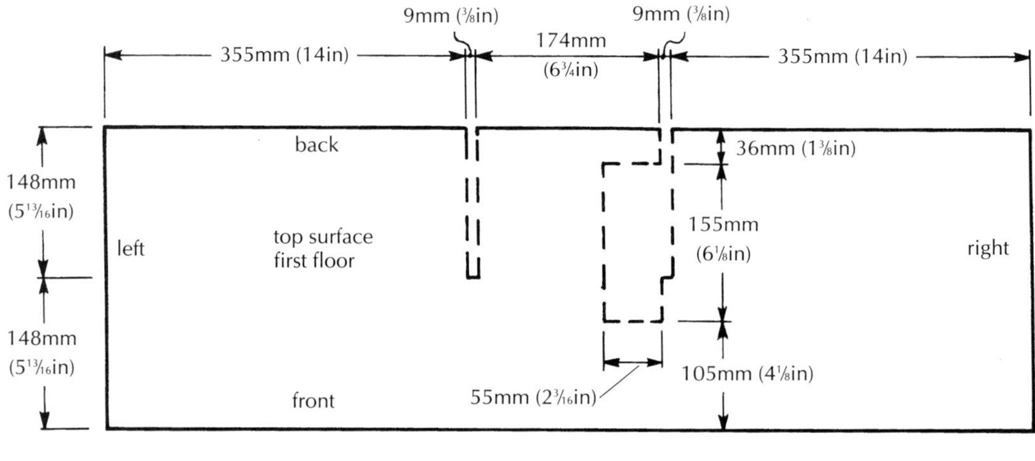

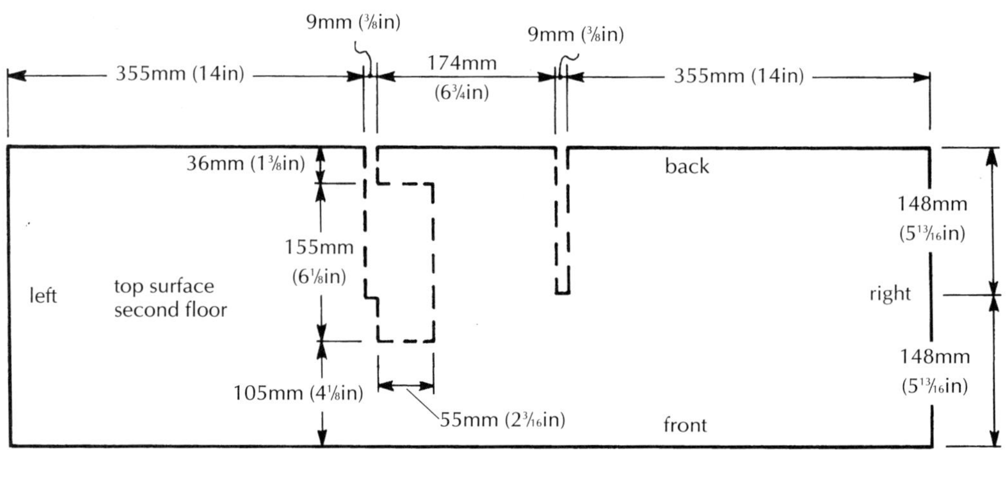

First- and second-floor cutting lines.

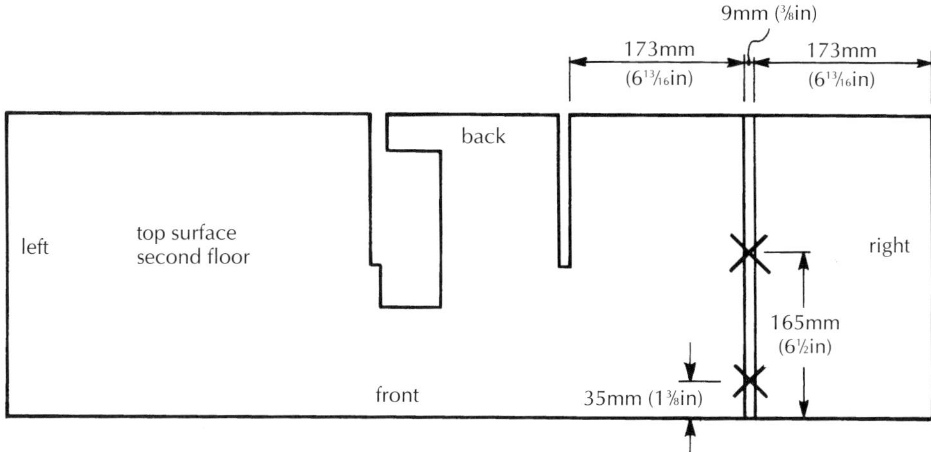

screwholes 1 and 2

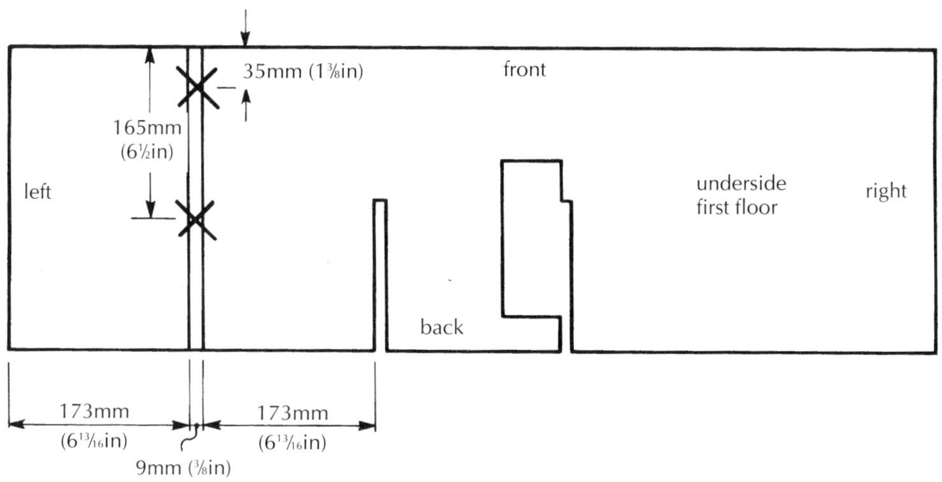

screwholes 1 and 2

First- and second-floor single door wall positions and screw holes.

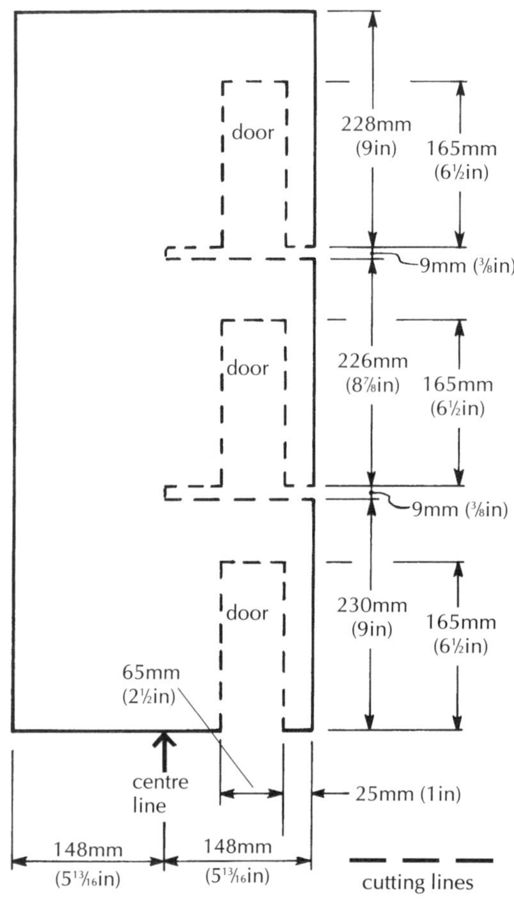

Wall 1 and wall 2 cutting lines.

pushing to slide all the way, but if the panel fit is too tight for easy assembly, dismantle and carefully enlarge the relevant slot(s) accordingly.

FITTING W/F ASSEMBLY INTO SHELL: FIRST FIT

1. Position this assembly inside the carcase, and mark some of the screw destination points from the back.
2. Remove the W/F assembly and drill pilot holes at these screw destination marks. Enlarge the corresponding holes in the back. Reposition the W/F assembly into the shell and screw tightly in place.
3. Mark the destination points for all the screw holes in the sides, top and bottom. Remove the W/F assembly, drill all the requisite holes for assembly, and then fix in place. Tighten all screws.
4. Check that the floors and walls meet the shell without gaps, especially at the back where it may be hard to see. If there are small gaps that cannot be eradicated, remember that certain discrepancies like this will be concealed by skirting-boards. Using a try-square, check that angles between walls and floors are reasonably close to 90°. Small variations are acceptable, and are possibly hard to avoid.

W/F assembly fixed inside the shell. First fit.

FITTING SINGLE-DOOR WALLS INTO THE SHELL

1. Cut door holes in the two single wall panels as shown in the diagram opposite. If

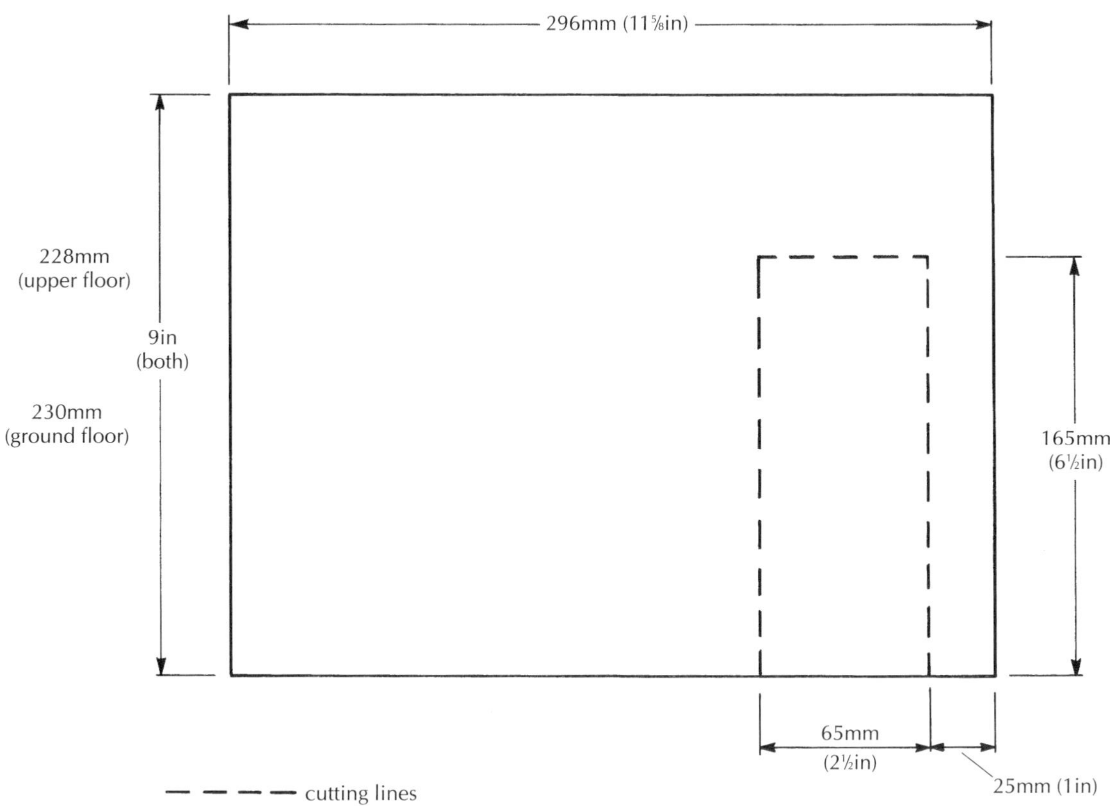

Single-door wall cutting lines.

using metric measurements, mark the panel 296 × 228mm as upper, and the one 296 × 230mm as lower. Using imperial measurements, both panels are identical: 11⅝ × 9in. This is because the fractional difference between 9mm and ⅜in adds up to a tiny discrepancy overall when several thicknesses of panel are taken into consideration.

For each panel:

2. Fit the wall in position, between the marked lines on the ceiling, back wall and floor. Using a bradawl, mark through two of the screw holes in the back panel; remove the wall, and drill destination and clearance holes. Replace the wall and screw it in position.
3. Repeat the procedure for all the other screw holes, and complete the drilling and screwing procedure for all holes.

SQUARING OFF AND DISMANTLING

1. Use a straight-edge to ensure that the front edges of the sides, floors, walls and top all finish in line with each other. Remove any projecting parts with a plane.

Note: The base is *intended* to project further than the rest in order to fill the space beneath the opening front sections.

2. Identify all six component panels by marking them with a pencil, taking care to keep any marking of the upper surfaces of the floors to a minimum, as the grain will later be stained and sealed (all the marks will have to be removed at that stage).
3. Remove all the screws, and then remove the W/F assembly and dismantle it.

INTERIOR DOORS

Parts involved: 9mm (⅜in) MDF interior doors; 6mm (¼in) dowel.

MAKING AND HANGING

1. Using a plane, trim each door in turn so that it fits a corresponding door-frame in the walls. Make the fit reasonably close, but not tight.
2. Number each door and its corresponding door-frame. Write the numbers on the thickness of the door's underside bottom edge; this is the only part that will not be painted. Similarly, write on the underside of the relevant wall section, inside the slots or on the panel base (for single-door walls).
3. Decide and mark the direction of opening on each door (always into a room, not into a landing or a hall), and also the hinge side. Fix doors leading off a hall or landing to the major section of the wall, never to the thinner strip section.
4. Hang doors, using 13mm (½in) hinges (the method is shown in Chapter 3, Techniques). Mount hinges 20mm (¾in) from the top and bottom.

Finished door, showing the carved panels.

PANELLING

For each door:
1. Remove the hinges.
2. Holding the door in a vice, mark surface as shown, using a 2H pencil. Measure from each edge and top: these are the crucial measurements; the central section and bottom part may vary slightly from door to door.

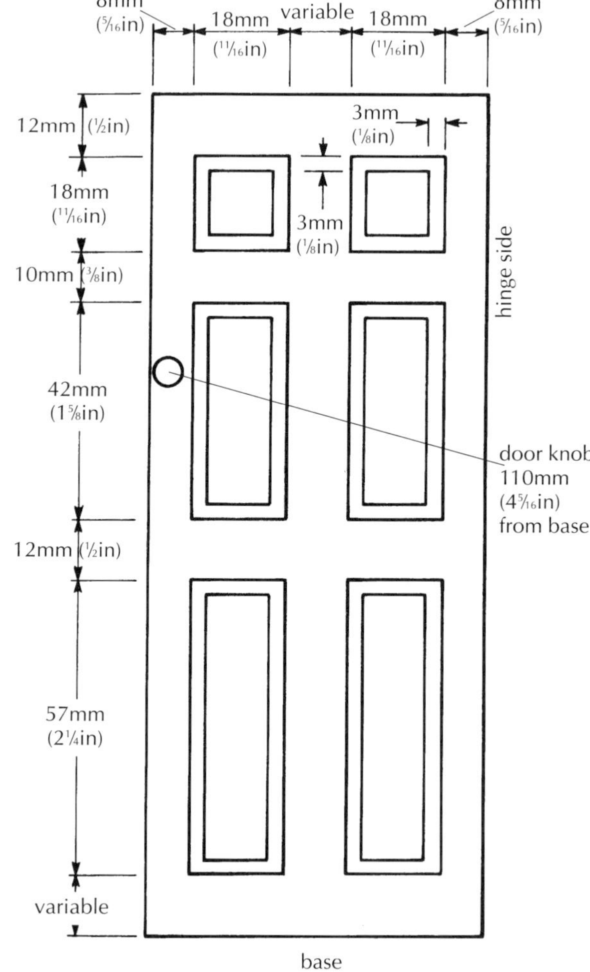

Interior-door panelling marking lines.

3. Using a sharp bradawl, mark the outermost corner of each square or rectangular shape; this serves to indicate the beginning and end of each cut.
4. Using a sharp craft knife and steel rule, cut along the outer lines.
5. With suitably sized, sharp chisels (38mm/1½in for the larger cuts, 13mm/½in for the smaller), slice fractionally to the inside of the initial groove in order to widen the groove widthways.
6. Cut with the knife again along the same outer lines, making a much deeper cut than was previously possible.
7. For each bevel cut, position the chisel exactly on the inner line at an angle of approximately 45°. Push hard to slice through material, aiming to produce a single cut that forms a neat bevel. This may require some practice initially on a scrap piece, but, if the chisel is sharp, MDF is ideally suited to carving in this way. Aim to produce a neat line at the corners, where cuts converge.
8. Slice along the outer line once more in order to remove any waste.
9. Clean all carved areas with sandpaper so that there is no rough or fibrous residue, especially in the corners (a pointed instrument such as a sharp bradawl is useful here).

MAKING HANDLES

1. Round off the top edge of a short length of 6mm-diameter (¼in-diameter) dowel with sandpaper.
2. Cut a 5mm (¼in) piece from this length, ensuring a 90° angle by using a mitre block or precision mitre saw.
3. Glue the handle 110mm (4⁵⁄₁₆in) from the base of the door as shown in the diagram, using cyanoacrylate adhesive. Hold the handle in position for a few seconds until the adhesive bonds.
4. When the glue is dry, carefully trim the handle so that it tapers inwards where it is joined to the door, so as to form an authentic handle with an outer knob and tapered shaft. Use a small chisel for this and afterwards sand off any sharp edges.
5. Prime, then sand with fine paper and apply undercoat and gloss coat according to taste. A light grey colour was used for the prototype.

DECORATING MAJOR COMPONENTS

Part involved:
12 × 9mm (½ × ⅜in) glass-bead moulding for architraving.

1. Mask the varnished surface of the plywood base with newspaper, its edges stuck in place with masking tape.
2. Prime all the interior MDF surfaces of the shell.
3. Fill the grain of the underside of floors 1 and 2, using a 'fine surface' type filler designed for filling wood grain

Decorated W/F assembly, fitted to the shell. Final fit.

and surface blemishes. Sand and prime these surfaces. An orbital sander is useful for this, but not vital.

4. Prime all the surfaces and exposed edges of the two, six-door walls. Do not paint the inside of the slots. Similarly, prime the two, single-door walls.
5. Sand all the flat areas and edges of the above, then apply emulsion paint according to taste. White and light colours tend to make rooms look bigger, and darker colours do the reverse. White was used throughout the interior of the prototype.
6. Sand the interior of the shell smooth and prime and emulsion paint it; if different rooms are to be different colours, the rows of screw holes serve to mark the room divisions.
7. Prime, sand and gloss paint approximately 8m (27ft) of 12 × 9mm (½ × ⅜in) glass-bead moulding that is to be used for door architraving.
8. Fit hinges to the painted doors and hang them in their correct apertures (matching pre-marked numbers).
9. Cut the moulding into mitred pieces to frame the door apertures (see Chapter 3, Techniques, for making mitres) with two side bars and a top. Stick this architraving in position using nitrile (clear) contact adhesive.
10. Carve the floorboard grooves into the top surface of the first and second floors, repeating the measurements and the methods used for the base. Do not stain or seal at this stage.
11. Using the method described in Chapter 4, The Country Cottage ('Using infill plywood veneer pieces to disguise screw heads in floorboards'), screw the lower single wall to the underside of the first floor, concealing the screw heads with plywood veneer.
12. Seal, or stain and seal the first and second-floor floorboard top surfaces to match that of the base.

FINAL ASSEMBLY OF W/F INTO SHELL

Part involved:
Top front strip.

1. Countersink all remaining host screw holes in the shell.
2. Slide the wall and floors together, making sure that all doors open correctly.
3. With a 6mm (¼in) sharp chisel, carefully remove paint from inside the shell where

TRIMMING SLOTS

It may be necessary to trim around the slots, as the thickness of the coats of paint on the panels could make assembly difficult. Use a craft knife for this.

W/F assembly glued to the shell and held with sash clamps.

CLAMPING WITH SASH CLAMPS

If large sash clamps are available, it is worthwhile clamping across the front of the house (widthways) to ensure that the front edges of the side panels are held in close contact with the floors until the adhesive sets. This is not crucial but it can be helpful, as the structure is large and heavy, and a good bond at the front edges is important. If such tools are not available and the joins at the front are not tight-fitting, fit extra (temporary) screws as necessary.

the walls and floors will join it (follow the lines of the screw holes). Dragging the blade along the line will normally successfully remove all paint back to the bare material; surfaces can be touched up later if too much paint is removed. PVA adhesive will not bond successfully over paint: it must penetrate the top surface of the timber. Similarly, use sandpaper to remove paint from all the panel edges that are to be bonded.

4. Apply PVA adhesive to all edges and surfaces to be joined, and slide the W/F assembly into its final position within the shell.
5. Insert all screws and tighten firmly.

FIXING THE TOP STRIP TO THE STRUCTURE

1. Scribe screw lines as shown in the diagram overleaf on the inside face of the top front strip, then drill 2mm (5/64in)

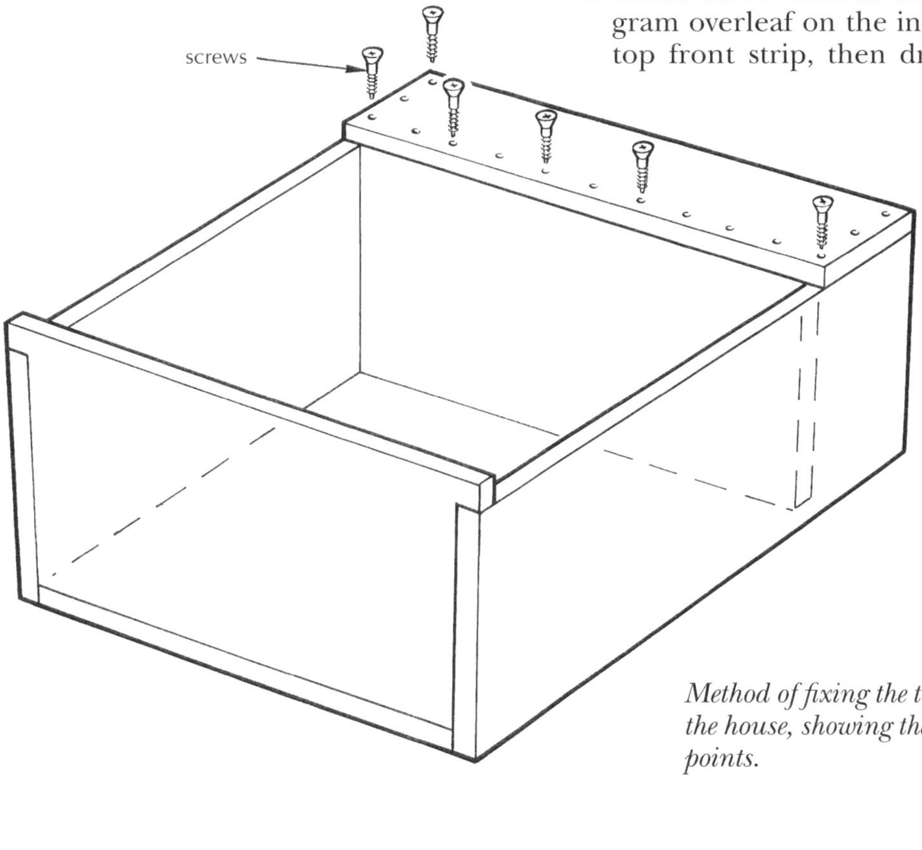

Method of fixing the top front strip to the house, showing the screw entry points.

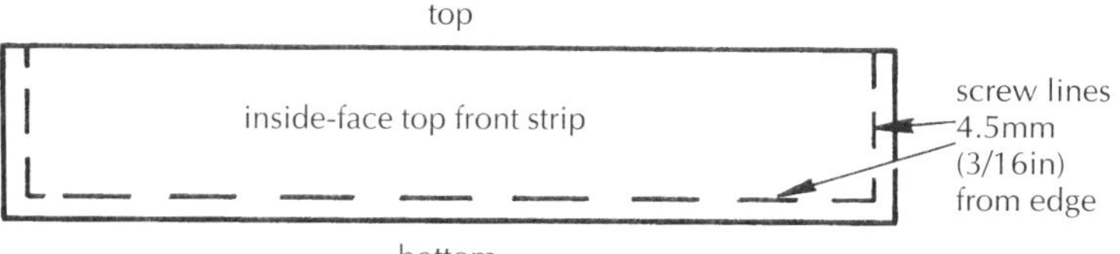

Screw lines for the top front strip.

holes, two at each side and at 100mm (4in) intervals along the bottom edge.
2. Fix the top front strip in position in the usual way.

CONSTRUCTING AND HANGING LEFT AND RIGHT FRONT SECTIONS

Parts involved:
Large front section (FSR); small front section (FSL); front-section overlap panel; 32 × 9mm (1¼ × ⅜in) hardwood batten; 12mm (½in) hardwood batten for hinge fillets.

ESTABLISHING THE FRONT BREAK LINE

Cutting panels to exact size:

1. Mark the top and bottom of the front break line on the house, as diagram. This is the line where the two front sections meet, and the marks should be on the front of the top section and the front of the base.
2. Fit the FSL (smaller) panel against the front of the house, between the bottom of the top section and the projecting lip of the base. If the panel is a tight fit, trim it at the top with a plane. Line up the right-hand edge of panel with the front break line marks, top and bottom, so that the left-hand edge overlaps the house.
3. Draw a line along the panel to correspond with the left-side external edge of the house: this denotes the final edge of the panel.

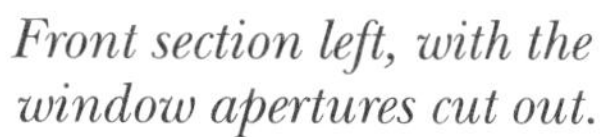

Front section left, with the window apertures cut out.

Front section right, with both the window and door apertures cut out.

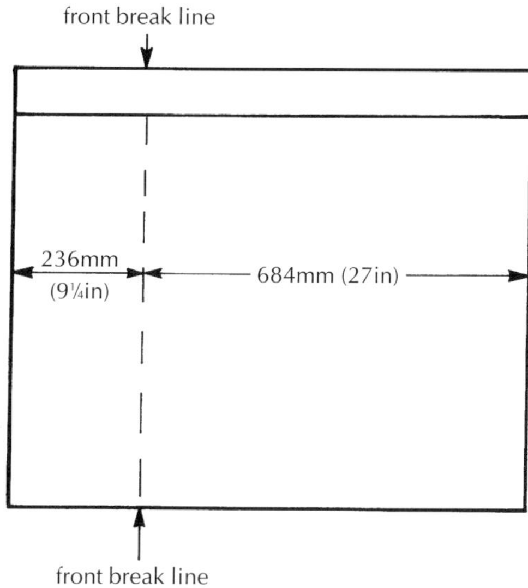

Establishing the front break line.

panel. The panels must be clamped together while the adhesive sets, and timber battens may be used in order to facilitate the use of large G-clamps along the edges: the thick timber battens should transfer the pressure along the whole width of panels, where even large G-clamps could not reach.

3. When the adhesive has set, cut and then plane away any overlapping material

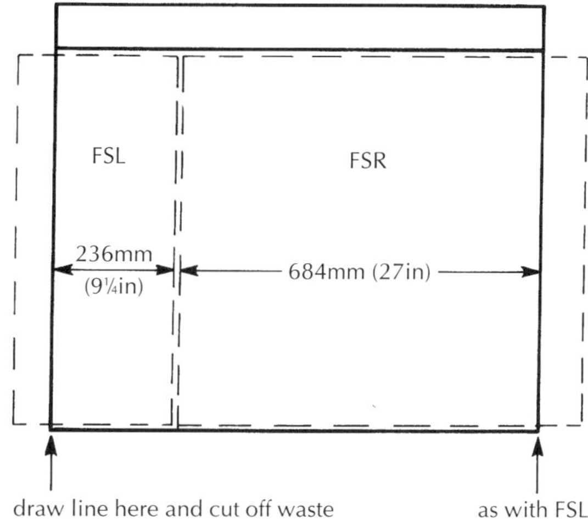

Cutting the FSL and FSR to the correct size.

4. Repeat 2 and 3 with the FSR (larger) panel, keeping the FSL in place and aligning the left-hand edge of the FSR with the right-hand edge of the FSL at the front break line.
5. Cut along the marked lines to remove overlap timber from the FSL and FSR.
6. Mark the envisaged location points of the FSR and FSL for future reference: denote top, base, right and left on the **outside** face.

CONSTRUCTION OF THE FSR AND FSL

1. Draw a line on the front of the FSR, 216mm (8½in) away from its right-hand edge, and parallel to it.
2. Use PVA adhesive to glue the 6mm (¼in) overlap panel to the FSR, with the thinner panel's right-hand edge against this line and the top and bottom edges overlapping the thicker

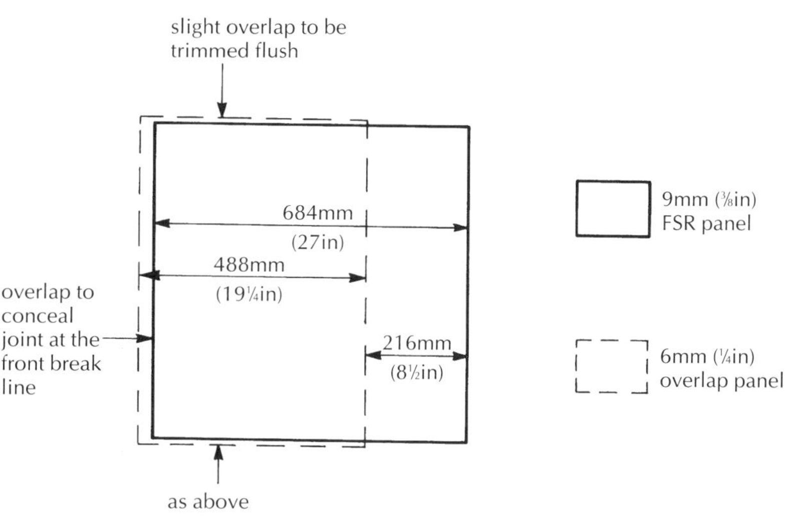

Positioning of the 6mm (¼in) overlap panel for fixing to FSR.

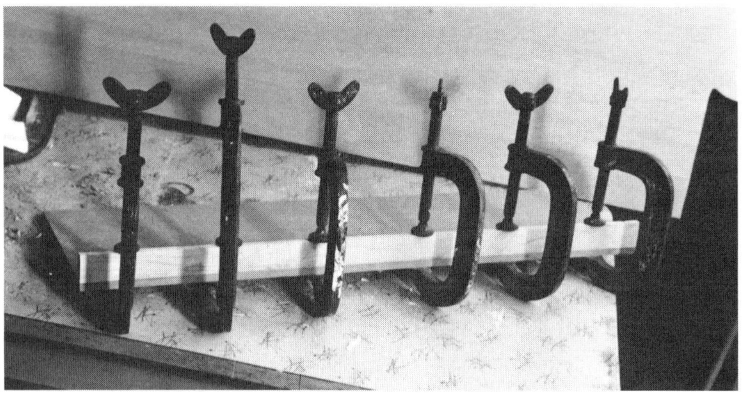

FSL clamped and glued to the edge (hinge-bearing) batten.

from the top and bottom of the overlap panel, so that these edges of both bonded panels are perfectly aligned.

4. Cut two 720mm (28⅜in) lengths of the 32 × 9mm (1¼ × ⅜in) hardwood batten.
5. Using PVA adhesive, glue and clamp the battens to the FSR and FSL as in the photograph above, against the inside faces at the left-hand and right-hand edges respectively (the hinge sides), so that a roughly equal amount projects at each end.
6. When the adhesive is dry, plane off any minor projections so that the joined abutting surfaces are smooth. Then trim off the overlapping batten timber at the tops and bottoms of the panels.

CUTTING THE SIDES OF THE MAIN HOUSE TO ACCOMMODATE THE FSR AND FSL

1. Using a marking gauge, mark a line along both sides of the outside of the house, 32mm (1¼in) away from the front edge and parallel to it, as in the diagram below.
2. Draw lines at right angles to these lines with a try-square; at the top, in line with the bottom of the top section; and at the base, along the top surface of the ground floor. Draw other similar lines on either side of the first and second floors.
3. Cut along the lines to remove the front strips – 32mm (1¼in) wide – of the side panels.

Important: The front part of the two side sections is to be removed, but take care not to cut through the first- and second-floor panels. The cutting must be done in stages to avoid this, making extra cuts with the jigsaw above and below the

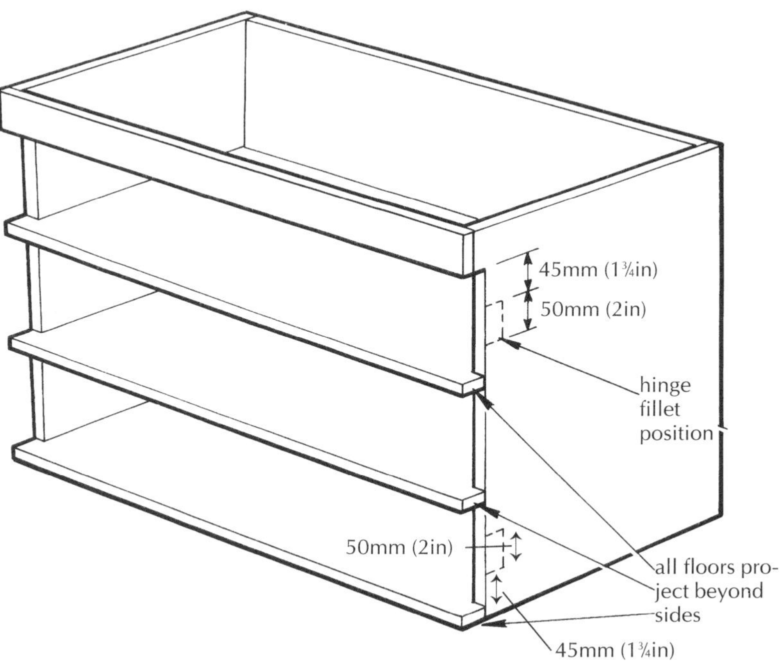

Cutting the sides of the house prior to fitting the FS units.

floors. Ultimately, 32mm (1¼in) of both the upper floors will project beyond the sides, the ground floor projecting slightly more than this.

4. Using the mitre block or precision mitre saw, cut four 50mm (2in) lengths of 12mm (½in) hardwood batten to make hinge fillets. Mark their positions, as in the diagram opposite, cut these out and insert and bond the fillets in place with epoxy resin adhesive (see Chapter 3, The Country Cottage for method). Trim the fillets flush with the sides and the front of the side panels after the adhesive has set.

House with the front sections closed.

(Below) *House with the front sections open.*

HANGING THE FSR AND FSL

1. Fit and rebate the 38mm (1½in) hinges to the edge face of the 32 × 9mm (1¼ × ⅜in) batten on the FSR and FSL units, ensuring that they line up with the position of the hinge fillets on the main house.
2. Hang the doors by marking an estimated screw position on the side of each FS as below, placing the unit in its correct position and continuing this mark along the side of house.
3. Remove the unit and transfer the line to the edge of the hinge fillet, drilling a pilot hole in the centre of this line.

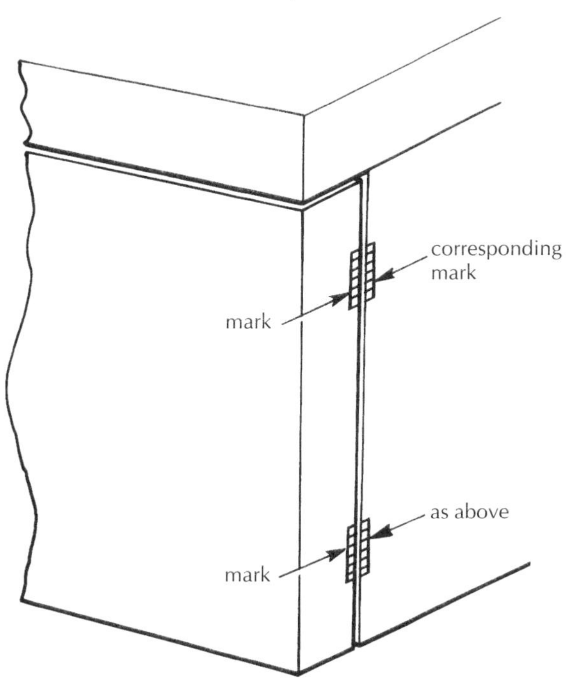

Marking the screw holes for hanging the FS units.

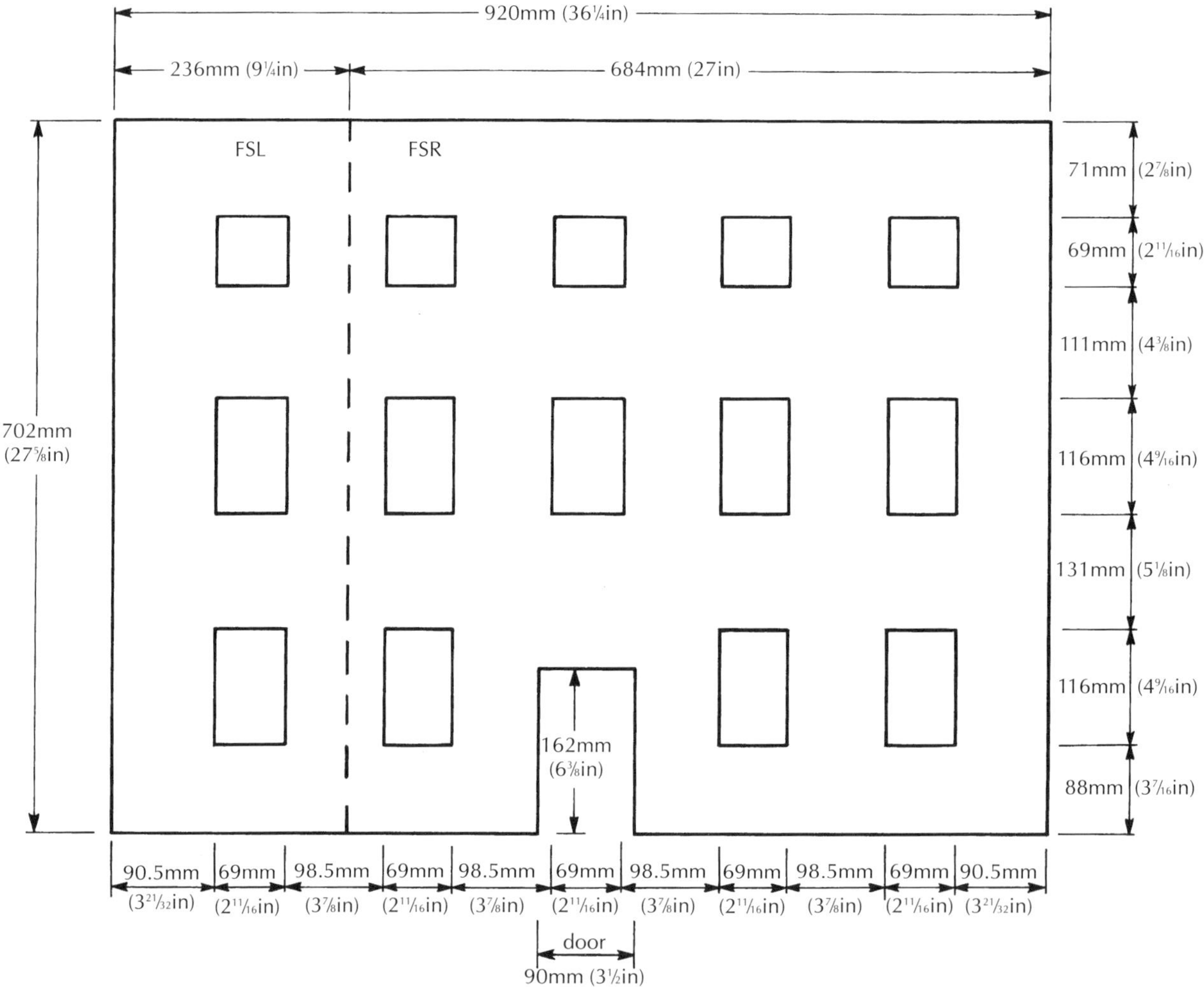

Window and door aperture cutting lines for the FS units.

4. Hang the units, using only one screw at the top and bottom initially, to allow for later correction.
5. Trim the bottom and top of FS panels as necessary to facilitate a smooth, continuous closing movement.
6. Cut windows and door apertures in the panels, as illustrated in the diagram above.

WHEN FS UNITS REFUSE TO CLOSE

If FS units do not close properly, check the following:

1. That the projecting first and second floors are not fouling them. If so, trim away material as required.
2. Some hinges may need to be rebated into the hinge fillets slightly (in addition to the rebating into the FS units). Rebate cautiously, no more than about 1mm (1/16in), as too deep a rebate will also prevent FS units closing properly.

WINDOW UNITS AND FRONT-ENTRANCE PORTICO

CONSTRUCTION OF WINDOWS

Parts involved:
12 × 9mm (½ × ⅜in) glass-bead moulding;
12 × 12 (½ × ½in) picture-frame moulding;
9mm (⅜in) MDF offcuts for making jigs;
25mm (1in) No 4 screws.

The window unit (WU) consists of the three sides of a window frame and its sill. These are constructed as a unit separately, decorated, and then glued to the decorated and glazed front of the house. Because they are constructed separately they must be perfectly square, and also should present a completely flat rear surface so that they will bond successfully to the house front, leaving no gaps. The use of jigs facilitates these two requirements, as well as speeding the work considerably. Offcuts of 9mm (⅜in) MDF are used to make the jigs, each comprising a large back panel with three 20mm (¾in) wide strips mounted upon it, arranged so as to leave a correctly measured internal rectangular area in which the components of the window unit are bounded at their outermost edges.

Window units, large and small.

> ## *JIGS*
>
> A jig is a box in which the components of a unit are assembled while adhesive sets, the idea being that the disparate parts are held in the correct relative positions to one another without the need for repetitive measurement and checking of angles. The finished product is also identical to any other made inside the same jig.

Required:
Nine larger WUs, 93mm (3¹¹⁄₁₆in) (width) × 140mm (5⁹⁄₁₆in) height
Five smaller WUs, 93mm (3¹¹⁄₁₆in) (width) × 93mm (3¹¹⁄₁₆in) (height).

Making the jig for the larger window units

1. Cut a piece of 9mm (⅜in) MDF, 93 × 150mm (3¹¹⁄₁₆ × 6in), ensuring that the corners are right angles. This is the window-unit dummy.
2. Cut pieces of 9mm (⅜in) MDF:
   (i) Back panel: 170 × 120mm (6¾ × 4¾in).
   (ii) A and B (*see* diagram on page 132): 2 @ 115 × 20mm (4½ × ¾in).
   (iii) C: 120 × 20mm (4¾ × ¾in).
3. Using screws, fix strip C to the back panel.
4. Fix strip A as shown in the diagram, ensuring that the angle between A and C is 90°.
5. Place the WU dummy with its long edge against A, and its top corner aligning with that of the jig. Place strip B against the dummy right-hand edge, and fix with screws in this position.
6. Check finally that the dummy fits in the box (part of two sides and top only) correctly, so that all the angles correspond and there are no gaps. Refit B if necessary.

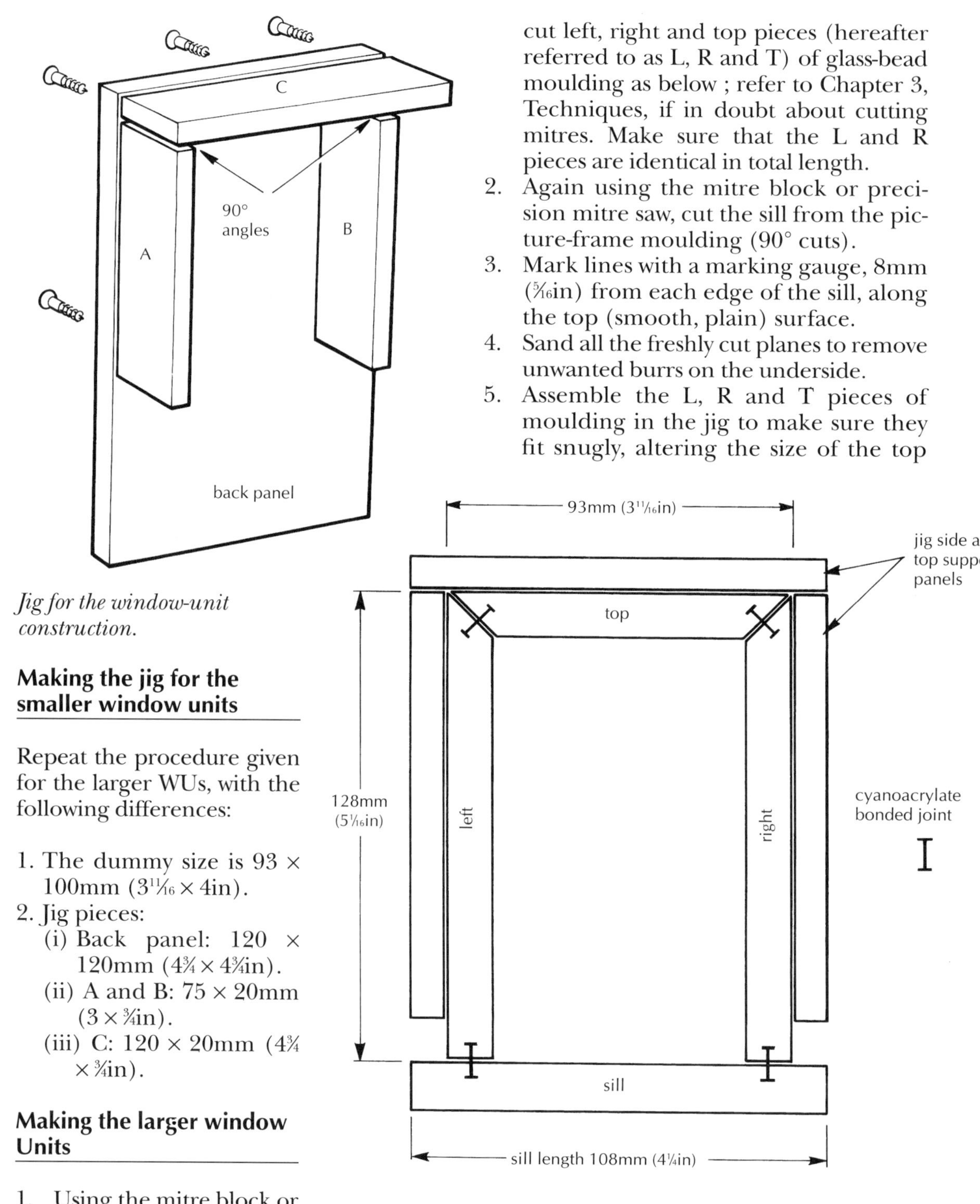

Jig for the window-unit construction.

Making the jig for the smaller window units

Repeat the procedure given for the larger WUs, with the following differences:

1. The dummy size is 93 × 100mm (3¹¹⁄₁₆ × 4in).
2. Jig pieces:
   (i) Back panel: 120 × 120mm (4¾ × 4¾in).
   (ii) A and B: 75 × 20mm (3 × ¾in).
   (iii) C: 120 × 20mm (4¾ × ¾in).

Making the larger window Units

1. Using the mitre block or the precision mitre saw, cut left, right and top pieces (hereafter referred to as L, R and T) of glass-bead moulding as below ; refer to Chapter 3, Techniques, if in doubt about cutting mitres. Make sure that the L and R pieces are identical in total length.
2. Again using the mitre block or precision mitre saw, cut the sill from the picture-frame moulding (90° cuts).
3. Mark lines with a marking gauge, 8mm (⁵⁄₁₆in) from each edge of the sill, along the top (smooth, plain) surface.
4. Sand all the freshly cut planes to remove unwanted burrs on the underside.
5. Assemble the L, R and T pieces of moulding in the jig to make sure they fit snugly, altering the size of the top

Construction of the large window unit within the jig.

piece if necessary. The fit should not be unduly tight or loose.

6. Remove the pieces from the jig.
7. Put two drops of cyanoacrylate adhesive on the mating surface of L, or a small smear of adhesive if the gel-type cyanoacrylate is used. Similarly, put adhesive on both of the mating faces of T and on that of R.
8. Put T into the jig immediately, then L and R, making sure that all pieces meet the back of the jig panel. Push the joints together from the bottom ends of L and R, making sure that all pieces meet back of jig panel and that L and R meet the jig sides.
9. Apply a 12mm (½in) patch of adhesive to two small areas on the rear upper edge of sill, 8mm (5⁄16in) in from each end.
10. Push the sill against the bottom edges of L and R. Hold tightly in this position for a few moments.
11. After approximately five minutes, carefully insert a small screwdriver point between sill and back of jig at one side. Lever upwards until the frame comes free. Do the same at the corresponding point on other side. If any adhesive has spilt onto the MDF, WU may stick slightly, but the bond should be reasonably easy to break.
12. Carefully rotate the WU upwards from the sill end, all the time being aware of the tenuous state of the four joint bonds.
13. Remove the WU from jig.
14. Remove all traces of adhesive from the back of the jig; a sharp chisel is the best tool for this.
15. Repeat for the other windows. If using a precision mitre saw, the adjustable end stop can be utilized to great advantage, and all pieces of the same size cut at once.

Making the smaller window units

Repeat as for the larger units, the only difference being that the L and R mouldings are 81mm (33⁄16in) in length instead of 128mm (51⁄16in).

Small pediment for the central window

The pediment is made from picture-frame moulding.

1. Cut the base strip 121mm (413⁄16in) long, as in the diagram below, cutting each end to a 45° angle.
2. Cut two strips 80mm (33⁄16in) long, and cut one end of each to 60° (this can be estimated if a precision mitre saw is unavailable): these are the left and right strips (L and R).
3. Butting together the 60°-angled ends, position the two strips over the base strip as in the diagram, and draw lines to denote the correct cut-off angles so that L and R will sit on the top surface of the base.

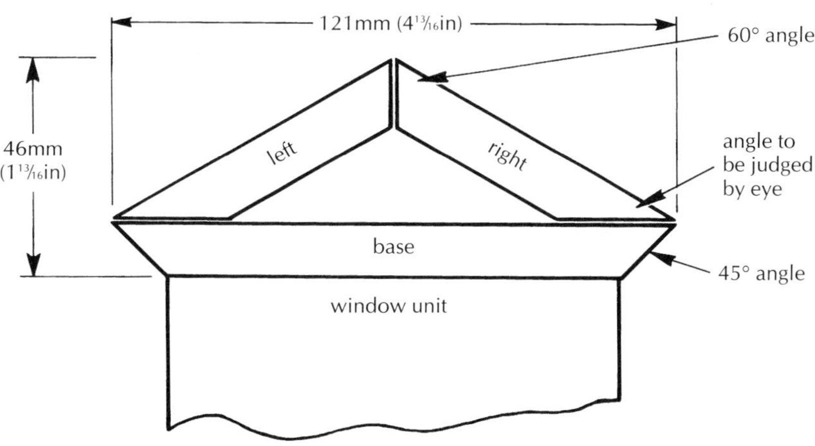

Measurements and angles for the small pediment over the window.

4. Cut along these marked lines.
5. Check that the pieces fit together as in the diagram, sanding or trimming as necessary.
6. Stick the parts together on a flat surface, then fill any apparent gaps with fine surface filler.

Attaching the small pediment to the large WU

1. Measure and mark a central point on the top of the WU moulding.
2. Lay the window unit on a flat surface, then stick the pediment to its top moulding, aligning the centre line with the pediment's apex. Use cyanoacrylate adhesive.

MAKING THE FRONT-PORTICO ENTRANCE UNIT

Parts involved:
Portico back panel (6mm/¼in MDF); portico top panel (9mm/⅜in MDF); picture-frame moulding; 12mm (½in) batten; 12mm (½in) diameter dowel.

1. Mark and cut the portico back panel, as in the diagram top right. The cut-out above the door aperture is a semicircle, 45mm (1¾in) in diameter.
2. Cut two pieces of 12mm-diameter (½in-diameter) dowel, 218mm (8⁹⁄₁₆in) long. Plane along the length of each to form a slightly flattened surface: enough to form approximately an 8mm (⁵⁄₁₆in) width of flattened area.
3. Stick these dowels (the portico columns) as in the diagram, using nitrile adhesive.

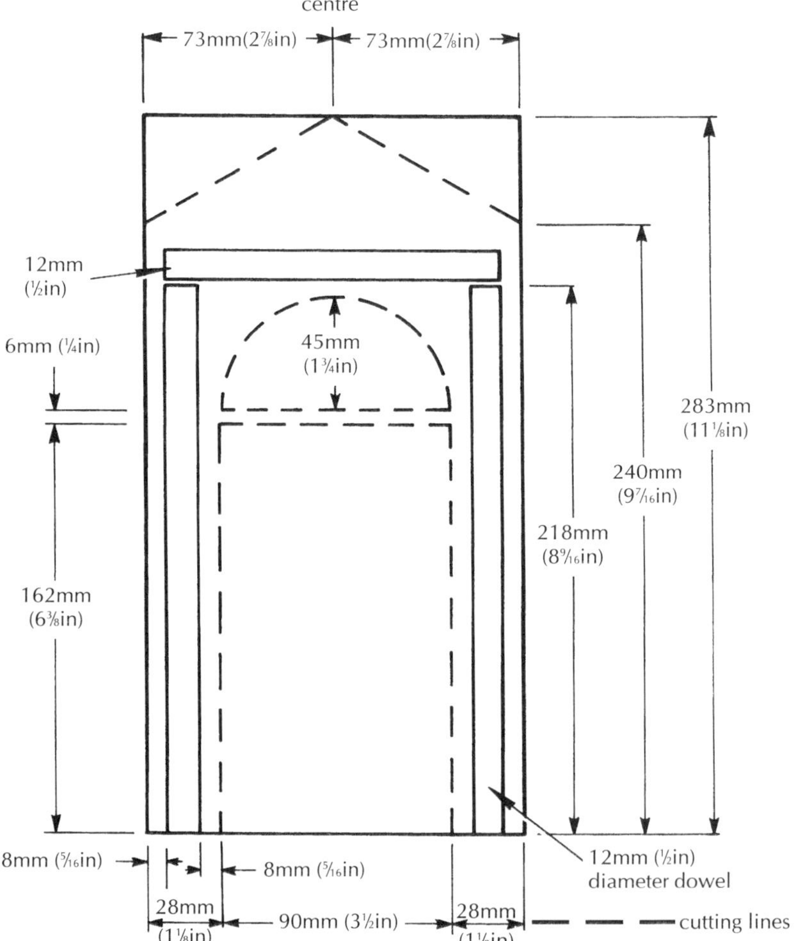

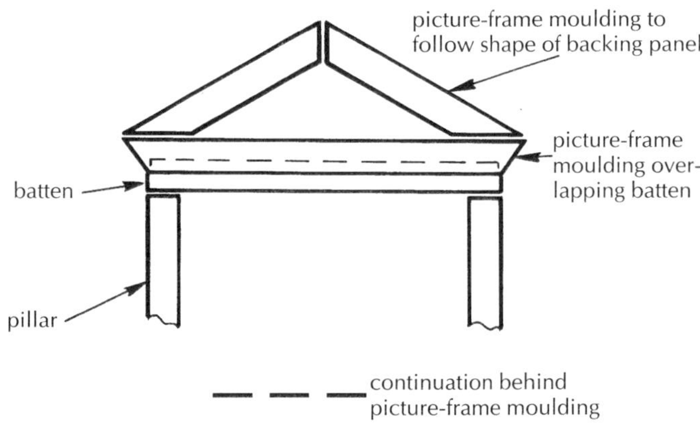

(Top) *Cutting lines for the portico back panel.*

(Above) *Construction of the portico: second stage.*

Front-entrance portico.

4. Cut a piece of 12mm (½in) batten to fit across the top of the dowels, to finish parallel with their outside edges. Stick this to the panel (with nitrile adhesive).
5. Stick the portico top panel (9mm/⅜in) MDF above this batten, so that it overlaps the triangular area above. PVA adhesive should be used, and the panels clamped together until it sets.
6. Trim off overlap of 9mm (⅜in) MDF when adhesive is dry.
7. Frame the front of the portico top panel with picture-frame moulding, judging the angles by eye. Stick the moulding in place with nitrile adhesive. The bottom of the base picture-frame strip should finish in line with the square batten, but the 45° angle should make the overall length of the picture-frame moulding longer. The moulding's lower edge should overhang the square batten.

DECORATING WINDOW UNITS AND FRONT-ENTRANCE PORTICO

1. Fill any obvious gaps and crevices with fine surface filler, then sand the filled areas when they are dry.
2. Prime, then sand all over with very fine paper. Primer nearly always raises the grain of timber, and sanding is usually necessary.
3. Emulsion, or undercoat and gloss paint according to taste. The columns, square batten and picture-frame mouldings should be the same colour as the WUs (white emulsion is used in the prototype), while the triangular panel within the moulding and the panel behind the columns should be emulsion, of the same colour as the exterior walls of house (this was sand-coloured in the prototype).

COMPLETING THE FRONT SECTIONS

DECORATING THE FSL AND FSR

1. Remove the hinges from the FSL and FSR.
2. Hold the front-entrance portico unit in position over the front-door aperture on the FSR, and draw round the semicircular fanlight aperture. Also ensure that the front-door aperture corresponds with that of the entrance portico, marking any overlap on either portico or FSR.
3. Cut out the fanlight aperture from the FSR, also remove any material from either portico or FSR so as to make the front-door aperture sides and top a continuous smooth edge.
4. Sand smooth any rough edges, particularly on window-aperture cut-out corners and cut edges generally.
5. Prime all areas, including the inside edges of window apertures.
6. Sand thoroughly as necessary, then emulsion to the *inside* face of the FSR and FSL according to taste (the prototype was painted in white). Also paint the inside edges of the window, door and fanlight apertures in the chosen colour.

7. Apply emulsion paint the outside face of the FSL and FSR, *not* including the window-aperture inside edges (the prototype was painted a sand colour). It is wise to choose a colour that contrasts well with whatever colour is chosen for the WUs and portico columns.

GLAZING WINDOWS AND FITTING FRAMES

Parts involved:
Clear acetate sheets.

For each window:

1. On the outside face of the FS panel, measure and mark a line 4mm (3/16in) from the outside edges of the aperture.
2. Cut with a sharp knife along these lines to make a fairly deep incision.
3. Remove material from between this cut line and aperture with a chisel, thus rebating a ledge all around the window hole; the depth of this rebate should be approximately 1.5mm (1/16in).
4. Prime and paint this rebated area to match the inside finish of the FS units. A very slight paint overlap onto the panel is permissible, but should not be more than 3mm (1/8in).
5. Cut a piece of clear acetate of a suitable size to fit this enlarged window-aperture space.
6. Use a very small amount of epoxy resin adhesive at the centre of each of the four sides of the rebated surface, then lay the acetate in position. Be careful, as using too much adhesive will cause the paste to be squeezed out and onto the window surface.
7. Before fixing any WUs it is necessary to mark a few inconspicuous lines on the FS units to delineate correct fixing positions with regard to horizontal and vertical alignment. Do this by measuring from the base and the sides of the FS unit. Using these lines to double check the positions of the WUs acts as a safeguard against misalignment, as reliance on the aperture edges alone might lead to individual WUs being out of line with their peers. Occasionally checking the line-up of WUs using a straight-edge or a long ruler can also be helpful.
8. Stick each WU in position using nitrile adhesive, taking care to avoid adhesive squeezing out at the edges; if this does occur, the adhesive can be painted over afterwards. Make sure that the inside edges of the WU align as closely as possible with the apertures, but more importantly, take care that each WU is mounted parallel to the top and bottom edges of the FS units and in line with its peers, as described above.

FITTING THE PORTICO UNIT TO THE FSR

1. As with the windows, rebate around the fanlight aperture and along the complete width of the bar beneath the semicircle.

GLAZING MATERIALS

Acetate is a springy, easily cut material that scratches readily. Store it carefully, and be cautious when using adhesives as strands of these chemicals can be difficult to remove. Thicker, perspex-type material can be used, but is not recommended since this substance is harder to cut, requires a deeper rebate for fixing, tends to attract dust, and has no particular advantages over acetate. Similarly, glass is not ideal for some of the above reasons, and additionally may be hazardous if the house is destined for use as a toy.

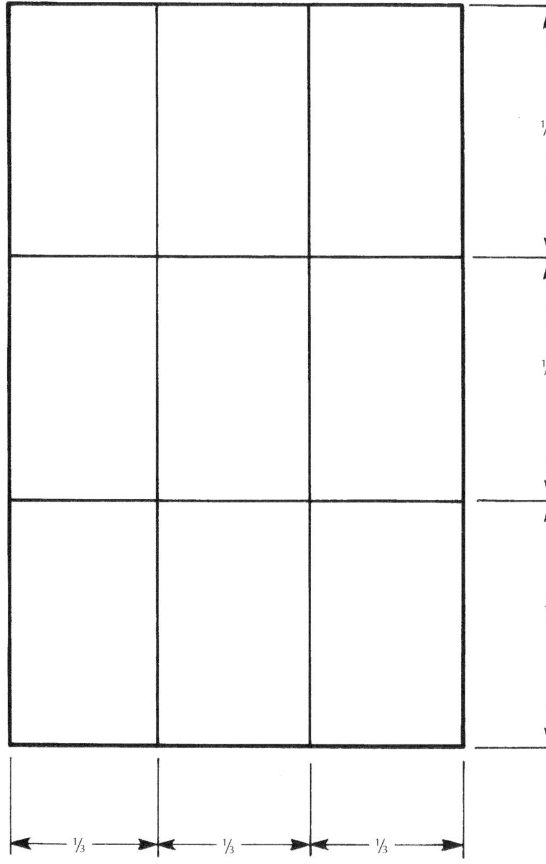

(Left) *Positions of the glazing bars: large windows.*

(Above) *Positions of the glazing bars: small windows.*

2. Cut a suitable piece of acetate to fill the rebated space, and stick it in position.
3. Stick the portico unit in place.
4. Use filler to close gaps on lower side of the upper bar of the front-door aperture.

FITTING THE GLAZING BARS TO THE ACETATE

Parts involved:
Strips of 3mm (1/8in) square-section balsawood.

Prime and emulsion paint a number of lengths of the square-section balsa-wood strip, using the same colour as that used for the WUs. The strips need sanding after the priming coat, as fibre is usually raised.

For each window:

1. Measure and make very small pencil marks on the WU to denote glazing-bar positions, as shown in the diagrams above. Mark only the front of the outermost edge of the frame and sill.
2. Cut two lengths of balsa to a suitable size for fitting on the acetate vertically, within the window-frame unit.
3. Using a minimal amount of cyanoacrylate adhesive at the top and bottom, stick the balsa lengths in position.
4. Similarly, cut small balsa pieces for fitting on the acetate horizontally, between the main uprights.
5. Stick these horizontals in position using a tiny amount of adhesive at each end. Model-makers' tweezers are useful here, as positioning the pieces by hand can be difficult.
6. Using the fine surface filler, make good any resultant gaps or crevices, finally painting filled areas with a fine brush.

FITTING THE GLAZING BARS TO THE FANLIGHT

Parts involved:
Small piece of copper wire or welding rod.

1. Cut a piece of string to the same length as the semicircular outside edge of the fanlight.
2. Divide this length by six, and measure and mark five points along the string accordingly.
3. Place the string around the top of the fanlight and mark these five measured points onto the panel.
4. Bend a small piece of copper wire or welding rod into a semicircle of approximately 9mm (⅜in) diameter. Prime and paint this.
5. Stick the copper wire or rod in position on the acetate (*see* photo of house exterior), using cyanoacrylate adhesive.
6. Stick suitable lengths of painted wire or rod onto the acetate, from the outside edge of the copper wire semicircle to the marked points on the panel.

MAKING AND FITTING QUOINS

Parts involved:
34 × 34mm (1⁵⁄₁₆ × 1⁵⁄₁₆in) L-shaped moulding.

1. Cut approximately 800mm (31½in) of L-shaped moulding, then trim along its length, as in the diagram , so as to reduce the width of one of the sides to 20mm (¾in).
2. Using a mitre block or precision mitre saw, ideally utilizing an adjustable end-stop facility, cut a number of pieces at 90°, each 25mm (1in) in length.
3. Prime and emulsion paint these pieces according to taste (white was used in the prototype). Logically, the stone quoins should be painted to match the (stone) window frames and sills, but some building exteriors do not follow this rule.
4. Stick them in position, using nitrile adhesive, at the corner edges of the FSL and FSR (*see* diagram opposite). Start at the top, if necessary cutting the final (bottom) stone to fit.
5. Sand the fronts of the quoins until they present a continuous level surface. An orbital sander is the idea tool for this, but hand-sanding is equally effective.
6. Re-paint the surfaces exposed during sanding.

MAIN ROOF: CONSTRUCTION AND FITTING

Parts involved:
2 long roof panels; 2 end roof panels; 12mm (½in) batten; 12mm (½in) side triangular moulding, 25mm (1in) No 4 screws.

LONG PANELS

1. Cut panels and use a plane to chamfer the edges as in the diagram opposite, so that the roof panels meet to form a sharp

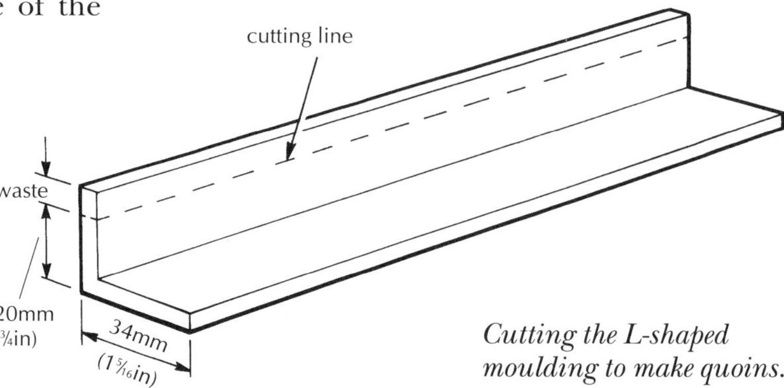

Cutting the L-shaped moulding to make quoins.

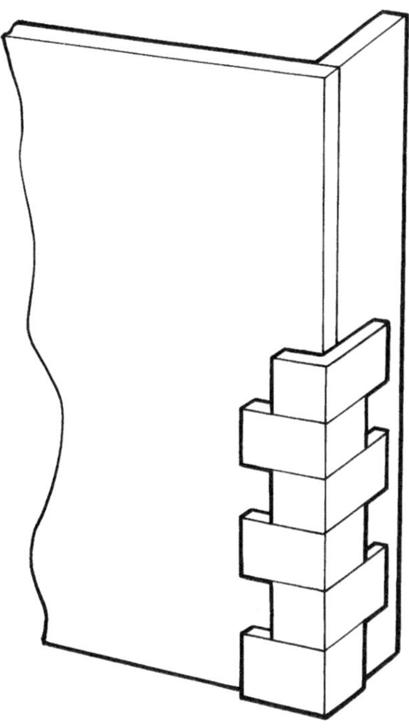

Fitting the quoins to the corner of the FS unit.

edge when in position in the roof cavity. A slight gap is acceptable, as it can be filled at a later stage.

2. Screw a piece of triangular moulding to the underside of both panels as shown in the diagram overleaf, so as to join the two panels at the roof ridge.
3. Place roof panels in their correct positions in the roof cavity, then insert a 300mm (11¾in) length of 12mm (½in) square batten inside the roof space. Place this roughly midway along one side and pressed against the interior face of roof panel and base. Draw a line on the roof base to delineate the position of this fixing batten. Repeat for the other side.
4. Remove the roof and screw the battens in position on roof base.
5. Replace the roof and use four offcuts of 9mm (⅜in) MDF to make small triangular fixing blocks (with sides approximately 70mm/2¾in as shown in the photograph overleaf).
6. One by one, hold the fixing blocks in place and mark their position along the roof base and inside face of the roof panel. Identify each block and its site.
7. Remove the roof and screw the fixing blocks in place on its inside surface. Replace the roof and screw the blocks to the base panel. Screws are inserted

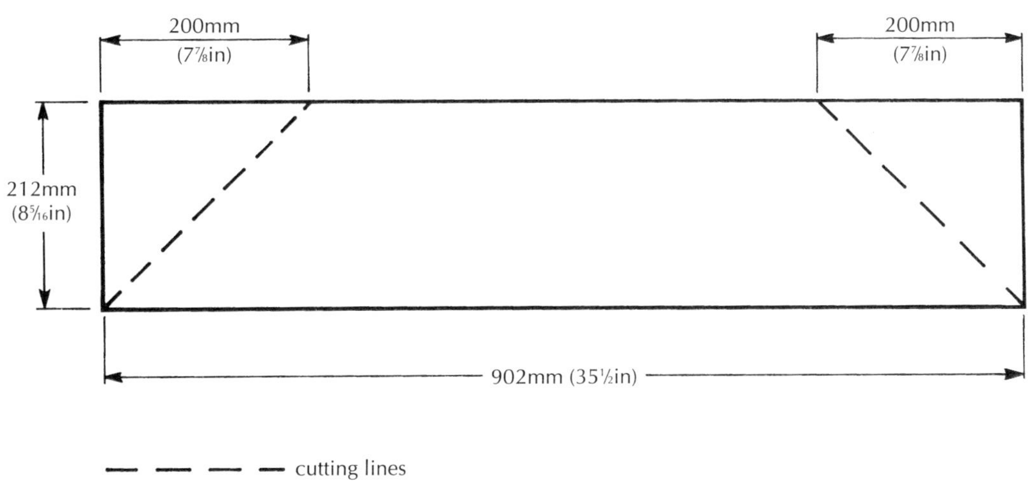

Cutting lines for the long roof panels.

Method of constructing the long roof.

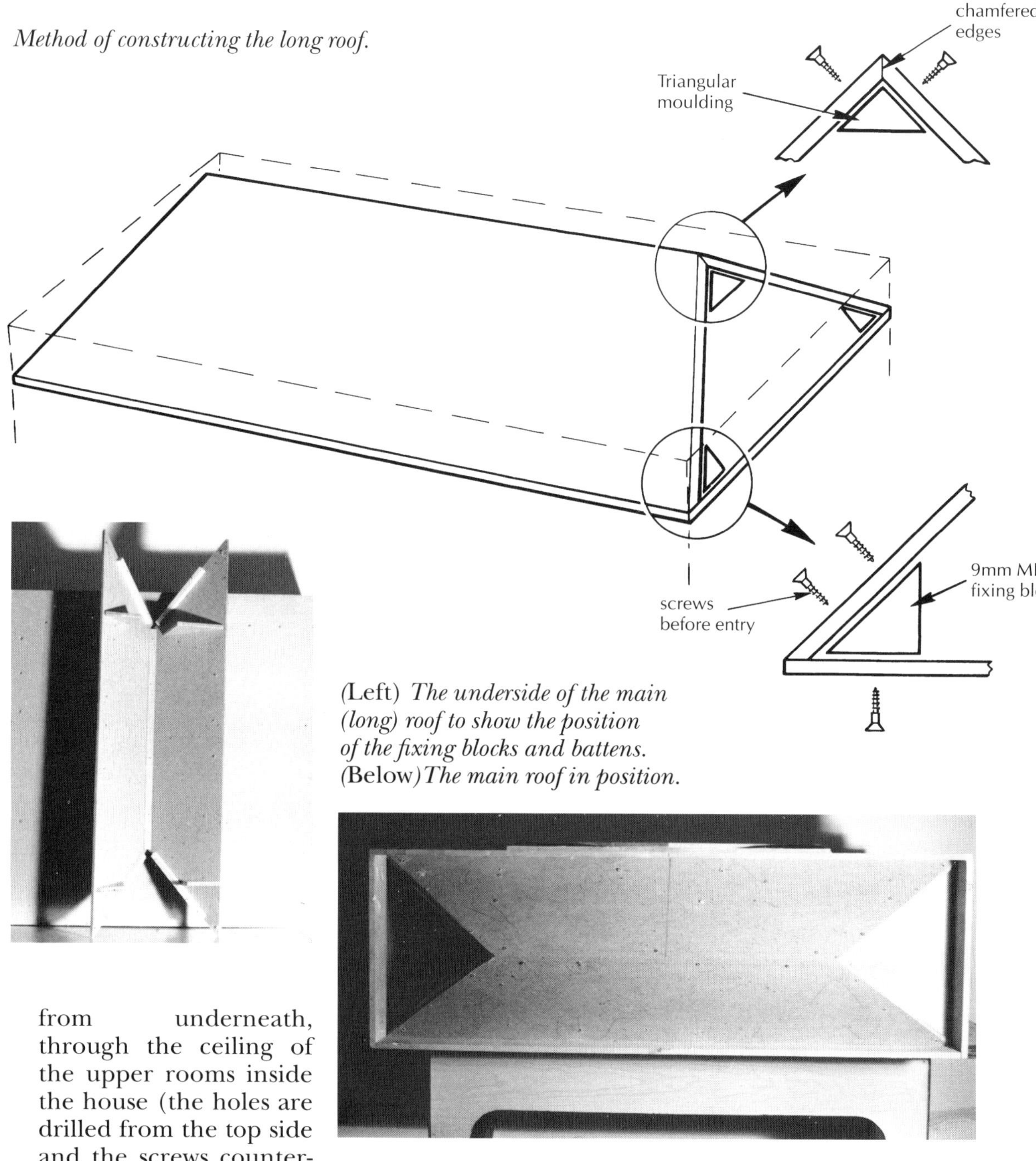

(Left) *The underside of the main (long) roof to show the position of the fixing blocks and battens.* (Below) *The main roof in position.*

from underneath, through the ceiling of the upper rooms inside the house (the holes are drilled from the top side and the screws countersunk).

8. Fix the roof in place with several screws inserted from above and into the batten beneath. Additionally, use a screw at each corner, inserting these directly from above and into the roof base, angling the screw host holes suitably. Take care that the screws are of a suitable length and do not protrude through the roof base and into the room below, even when countersunk.

DRILLING HOLES INSIDE THE HOUSE

Drilling or countersinking holes inside the house can be difficult because a normal-size electric drill will not fit. The solution is to unscrew the drill's chuck and use it separately, revolving it by hand in the confined space. Alternatively, for countersinking, a craft knife works perfectly well.

END PANELS

1. Remove the roof and chamfer the open edges as in the diagram below, so that a reasonably flat surface is presented to the end panels, rather than sharp edges. Do this at each end.
2. Refit the roof and place an end panel in position, against the chamfered edges. Mark the overlap line on the underside of the end panel, then remove the end panel and cut off the waste. Cut at a 90° angle, oversize rather than under.
3. Take pieces of 12mm (½in) batten and fix them with screws to the inside-face edges of the long roof, as in the diagram below.

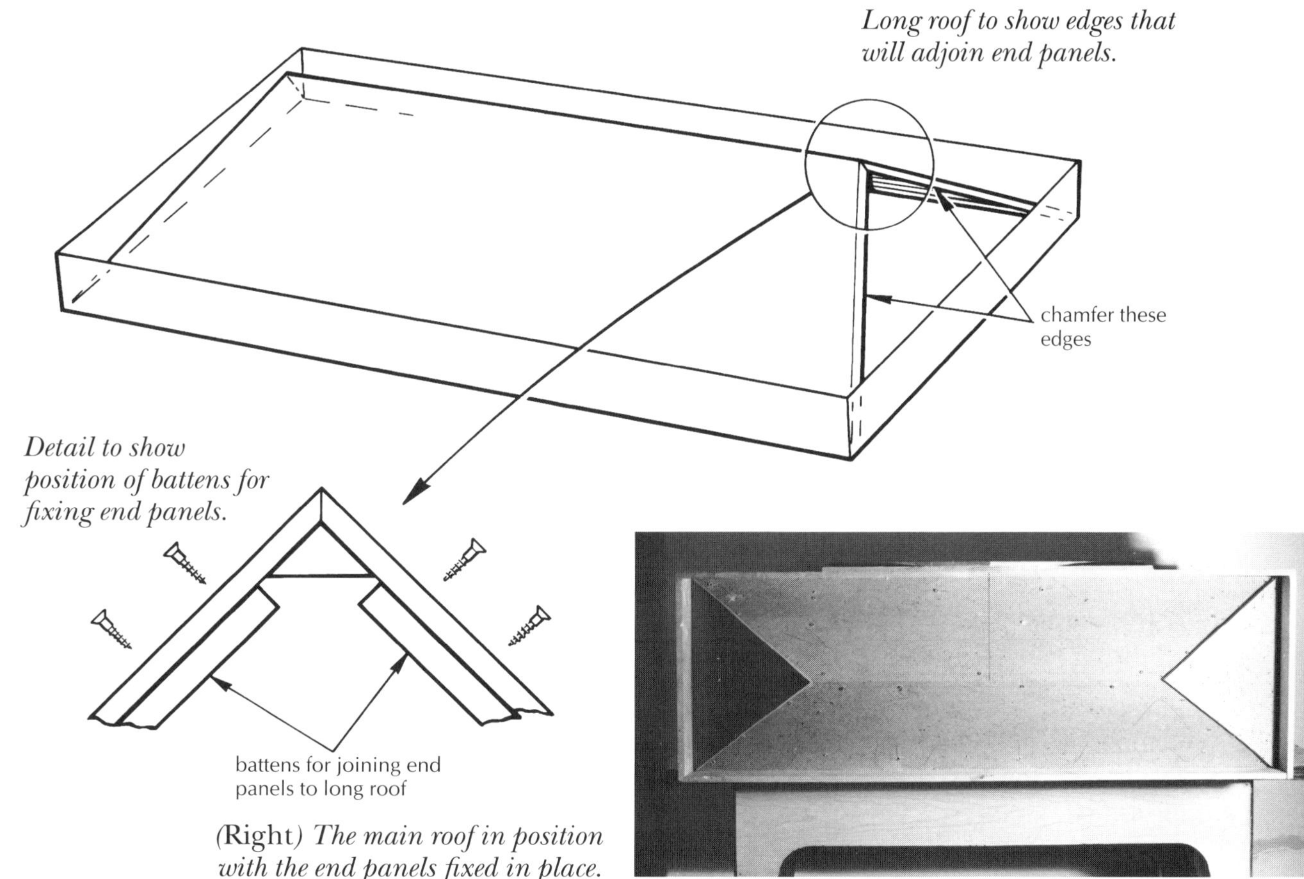

Long roof to show edges that will adjoin end panels.

Detail to show position of battens for fixing end panels.

(Right) *The main roof in position with the end panels fixed in place.*

4. Reposition the end panel and fix it in place with screws into the hardwood batten. Also screw the bottom end to the roof base from above, suitably angling the pilot holes as with the long roof.
5. Repeat for the other end panel.

BONDING THE STRUCTURE PERMANENTLY

1. Dismantle the complete structure, countersinking all the host screw holes, and then reassemble using PVA adhesive to bond all joints.
2. Plane and sand (ideally with an orbital sander) the edges of the end panels, so that these edges follow the angle of the main roof, and so that this slope is maintained along the total length. Where it is impossible to plane, use a chisel to remove waste. Any gaps or crevices that may appear can be filled later.

PEDIMENT AND SUBSIDIARY ROOF

Parts involved:
Triangular-pediment front panel; triangular-pediment backing panel; 2 subsidiary roof panels; triangular moulding; 12mm (½in) batten; 25mm (1in) screws.

1. Using PVA adhesive and G-clamps, bond the pediment backing piece (rectangular) to the front of the top piece, in the position shown below.

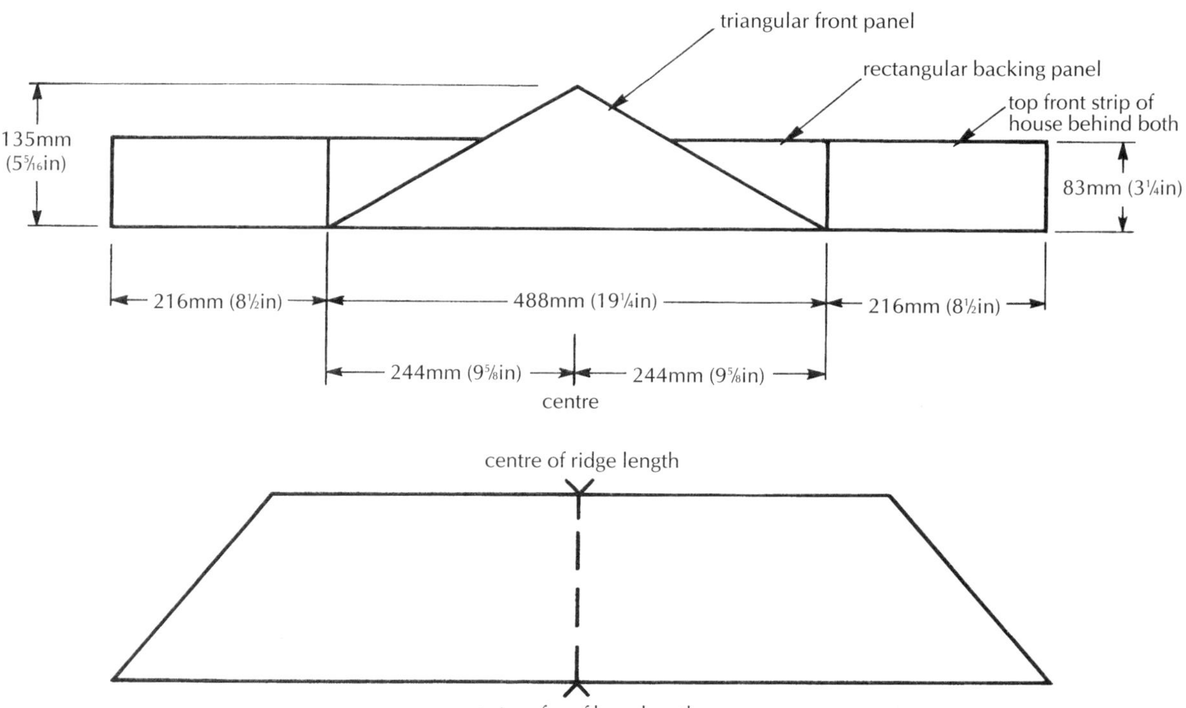

(Top) *Construction of the triangular-pediment front panel and the backing panel.*

(Below) *Marking the centre line of the main roof.*

2. After cutting the triangular-pediment front panel to the requisite shape (as shown in the diagram opposite), stick it to the pediment backing piece in the same way.
3. Draw a line along the front of the main (long) roof to mark the centre, apex to base, as in the diagram opposite.
4. Making sure that the house is on level ground, use a spirit level to ascertain the point at which the pediment roof should meet the main roof, so as to keep the roof's ridge level. Mark where this point intersects the centre line.
5. Cut the two subsidiary panels to shape, as below.
6. Chamfer the long edge of the left one according to the diagram below, fit it in place, then trim the other two edges to fit so as to link the pediment triangle point with the marked point on the central roof line. The small area of chamfering (10mm/⅜in in diagram) has to be very sharply angled, and is best done with a chisel. Remove the panel and repeat the process with the other one.

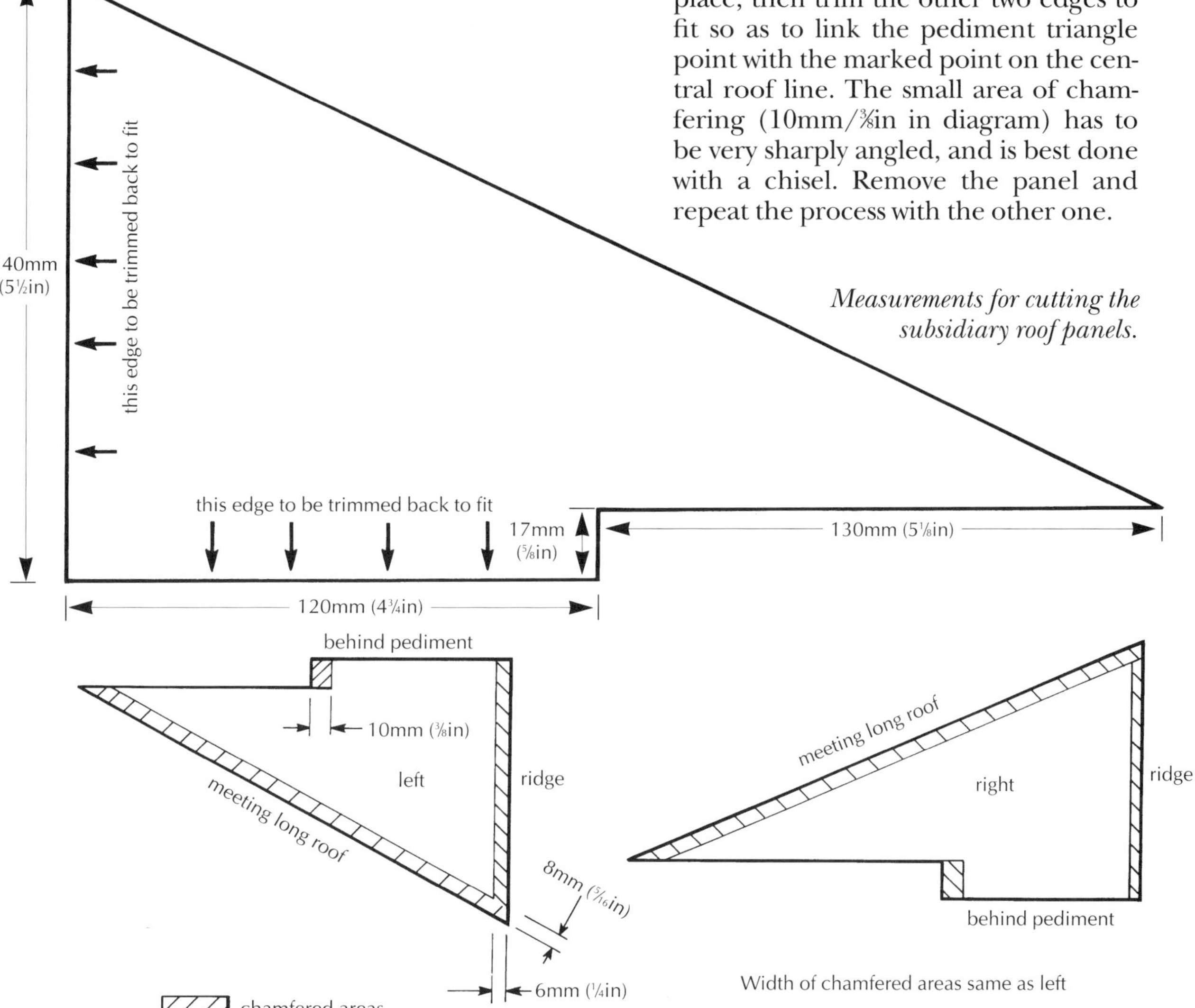

Measurements for cutting the subsidiary roof panels.

Areas to be chamfered on the underside of the subsidiary roof panels.

(Top) *One panel of the subsidiary roof in place.*

(Bottom) *One subsidiary roof fixing block in position on the main roof.*

7. Chamfer the inside face of the ridge sides of both panels so that they meet as the main roof does.
8. Place one panel in its correct position and hold short lengths of 12mm (½in) batten behind it, both where it abuts the main roof and the back of the triangular-pediment panel. Mark the position of these fixing blocks, then remove the panel and fix the blocks in place with screws. Repeat this process for the other subsidiary panel.
9. Join the two roof panels with the triangular batten as in the main roof, then screw these roof panels in place.
10. Dismantle the joints, countersink the screw host holes, and reassemble using PVA adhesive to stick the joints.

THE PEDIMENT ROOF – DEALING WITH GAPS

Constructing the pediment roof is not easy, and gaps are inevitable, especially where roof planes meet. These gaps can easily be filled invisibly later, using ordinary filler followed by fine surface filler. Final painting will unify the structure's appearance and conceal any evidence of filling.

FITTING MOULDING TO THE EXTERIOR

Parts involved:
Picture-frame moulding and decorative moulding.

1. Fit picture-frame moulding as in the diagram opposite, using nitrile adhesive and mitreing the corners (except for the triangular-pediment frontage, where angles are judged by eye). Because the central section of the frontage – the pediment section – is set forward from the rest, it is necessary to cut very small sections of moulding so as to follow the contours of

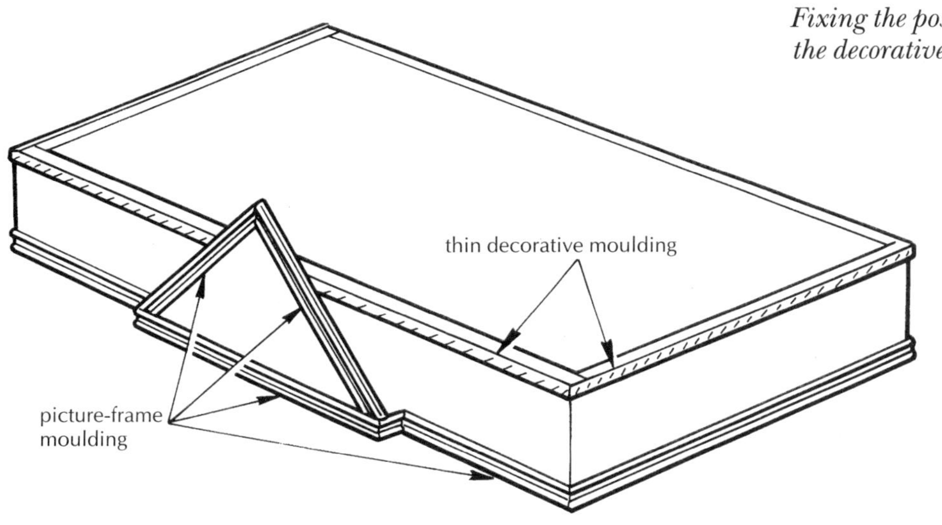

Fixing the positions for the decorative mouldings.

the building correctly. Subsequent holes formed underneath the moulding at these junctions must be filled later.

2. Fit decorative moulding along the top of the parapet front and sides, finishing off as in the diagram. It will be necessary to cut small sections of this moulding, so as to follow the contours of the rectangular backing panel (not shown above).

MAKING AND FITTING CHIMNEYS

Parts involved:
2 chimney panels, 9mm (⅜in) MDF (320 × 50mm/12⅝ × 2in); 2 chimney panels, 9mm (⅜in) MDF (320 × 32mm/12⅝ × 1¼in); 12 × 6mm (½ × ¼in) rectangular cross-section moulding.

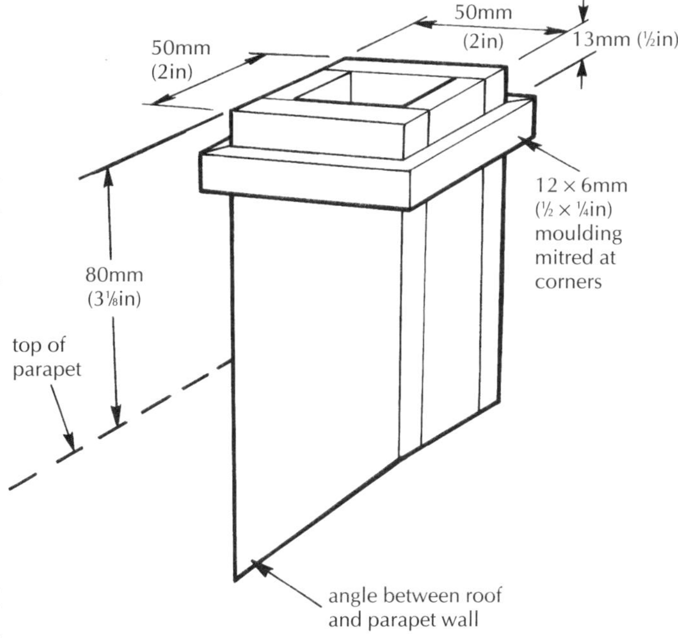

Final measurements for the chimney.

1. Assemble and glue the four pieces of MDF so as to make a long square-sided box, of cross-section 50 × 50mm (2 × 2in). Use PVA adhesive and clamp the joints along their whole length until the glue has set.

2. Use a bevel square to ascertain the angle between the end roof sections and the inside of the parapet panel. Transfer this angle by marking a line along the front of one end of the long chimney box.

3. Using a large handsaw, cut along this line right through the complete box to the other side.
4. Position the angled box so that the cut side is against the end roof panel. Mark the top edge of the parapet wall on the relevant side.
5. Measure and mark a line 80mm ($3\frac{1}{8}$in) above this parapet wall level, and cut right through the box at right angles.
6. Place the chimney midway along the parapet wall (mark the centres of both and align them), then screw and glue the chimney in the usual way, screwing through the parapet wall.
7. As in the diagram on page 145, cut four pieces of 12 × 6mm ($\frac{1}{2}$ × $\frac{1}{4}$in) moulding, mitred at the corners, and stick them on the side of chimney as shown, using nitrile adhesive.
8. Repeat for the other chimney, using the remainder of the chimney box.

DOWELLING: CUTTING THE COST

Large round dowelling is very expensive. A better idea is to use square dowelling and cut it approximately to a round profile, completing the shaping on a lathe. Battens of good timber of this size can often be found in yards for second-hand building materials (usually demolition contractors). The saving when buying second-hand is tremendous, and the quality is as good or better than new – but always remember to check for woodworm and rot before buying.

MAKING AND FITTING FINIALS

Parts involved:
65 × 65mm ($2\frac{1}{2}$ × $2\frac{1}{2}$in) softwood batten (suitable for turning); *or* 55mm ($2\frac{3}{16}$in) diameter softwood dowel (suitable for turning); 55 × 55mm ($2\frac{3}{16}$ × $2\frac{3}{16}$in) square batten.

The finials must be turned on a lathe. A small lathe such as may be powered by an electric drill is all that is necessary, and the skill required to make them is minimal. If no such tool is available, another option may be to hire one. Alternatively, the finials could be made professionally or left out of the design altogether; their addition to the house is by no means crucial to the project as a whole.

If round dowelling is being used, ignore the following section (1–3) which describes the initial shaping of square timber.

1. Cut a 200mm (8in) length of 50 × 50mm (2 × 2in) batten. Use a mitre box or precision mitre saw to ensure right-angle cuts.
2. With a jigsaw, trim off the sharp corners along the length on all four sides. Then plane away the adjacent sharp angles to these, aiming for as close to a round dowel as is reasonably possible.
3. Judge the central point of the circular area at each end, and make deep indentations at these points with a bradawl; these are the centres around which the wood will revolve. It is impossible to identify this central axis accurately, but any discrepancies will be removed later.
4. Fix the timber in the lathe, using the two indentations as the centres for rotation. Sometimes it may be necessary to oil the junction between wood and metal if the fit is tight.

5. Switch on the lathe's motor and gently apply the cutting edge of a large (38mm/1½in) chisel to the revolving timber, resting the main part of the blade against the lathe's chisel guide. Continue carefully until the chisel remains in continuous contact with the wood, indicating that there are no discernible high or low spots.
6. Switch off the motor and check that the timber has become a perfect cylinder of approximately 50mm (2in) diameter.
7. Delineate the top and bottom of a 110mm (4⁵⁄₁₆in) length along the timber, leaving an approximately equal amount of waste at each end.
8. Between these two points, mark the measurements as in the diagram: these define the profile of the finished finial. Continue all these pencil marks around the complete circumference by holding the pencil in one spot and revolving the timber by hand.

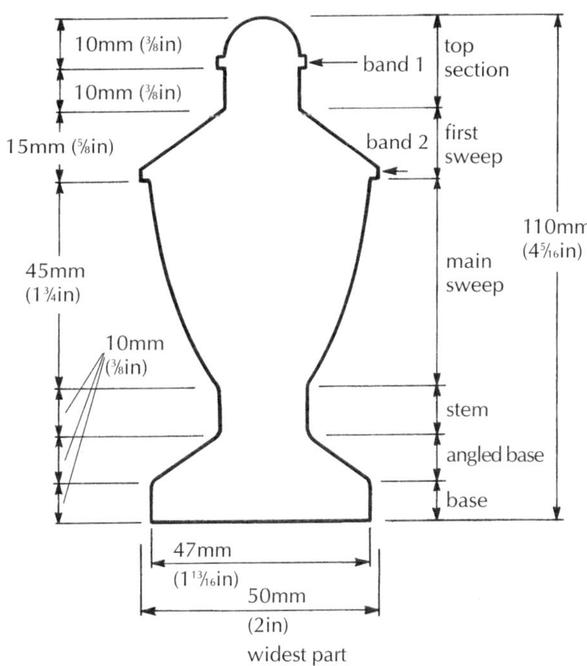

Finial divided into segments, with measurements.

USING A LATHE

- When using a lathe, make sure the chisel is sharp and wear eye protection.
- Be prepared for the chisel to be knocked sharply backwards initially, especially when preparing a timber dowel from an originally rectangular piece.
- It is often a good idea to pass the blade along from left to right, holding it at a slight angle, so that only the right-hand edge does the cutting.
- Never continue to apply blade pressure if the lathe motor slows down appreciably.
- Keep fingers away from the revolving timber.
- Allow for enough extra timber to make mistakes. A certain amount of practice is advisable for anyone unfamiliar with this craft.

9. Switch on the motor and use a 6mm (¼in) chisel to cut the **stem** section as a ring initially; then, with a larger chisel (13mm/ ½in), cut away its top edge to form the lower section of the **main sweep**. Continue to cut the stem until 18mm (¾in) in diameter.
10. Define the top of the **main sweep** with a 19mm (¾in) chisel, cutting in only slightly from the main thickness. This ridge forms the base line for **band 2**.
11. Work from the top to the bottom of the **main sweep** to achieve a gentle curve, finishing off with a smaller chisel as

necessary. The chisels will need to be held at different angles as appropriate.

12. Redefine the **stem**, using a 6mm (¼in) chisel held at right angles to the timber.
13. Using the 19mm (¾in) chisel held at right angles to the timber, trim in from the outer circumference a small amount to define the **base** (approximately 5mm/3⁄16in wide).
14. Cut from **stem** to **base** using a very sharply angled 6mm (¼in) chisel to form the sloping **angled base** plane between the two.
15. As in step 9, cut inwards at the top to form the **top section**. As with the stem, this should eventually be about 18mm (¾in) in diameter.
16. Define **band 1** by using the small (6mm/¼in) chisel held at right angles to either side of its position. The band should be approximately 3mm (⅛in) wide, midway along the **top section**. Either side of this band, the remainder of the **top section** is thus set back slightly.
17. With the small chisel held at a very sharp angle, cut the **first sweep**, which joins the top of **band 2** to the base of the **top section**. Clarify the lines defining **band 2**, so that its width is approximately 3mm (⅛in).
18. Tidy up all planes and neaten edges and angles.
19. Finish with medium-grade sandpaper held against the timber surfaces.

CAUTION!

To sand the timber in the lathe it is advisable to hold the paper by means of pliers or a similar tool so the fingers are not too close to the spinning timber.

20. Remove the timber from the lathe and cut off the waste timber in the mitre box or precision mitre saw, ensuring that the overall length is 110mm (4 5⁄16in).
21. Sand the top of the **top section** so as to form a smooth, rounded edge.
22. Repeat procedure for other four finials.

SUPPORT BASES

1. Cut five support bases from the 55 × 55mm (2 3⁄16 × 2 3⁄16in) batten, 50mm (2in) in length, ensuring right-angled cuts.
2. Stick four of the finials onto these bases, using epoxy resin adhesive. Stick the units onto the inside face of the parapet as diagram at end of chapter. It will be necessary to trim some of the base units to fit against the roof slope beneath.
3. Cut the fifth base so that the angle corresponds with the angle of the roof slope on the subsidiary roof. Transfer this roof angle by means of the bevel square to the base support, and cut the V-shape accordingly.
4. Stick the fifth finial/base-support unit on the subsidiary roof, behind the triangular frontage and in line with the others. Stick the final finial in place.

INTERIOR

FIREPLACES

These are to be positioned in the four larger rooms.

Parts involved:
Picture-frame moulding; 6mm (¼in) diameter dowel; fireplace panels (6mm/¼in MDF).

For each:
1. Cut the fireplace panel as opposite.
2. Cut a 115mm (4½in) length of picture-frame moulding and trim each end to a 45° angle.

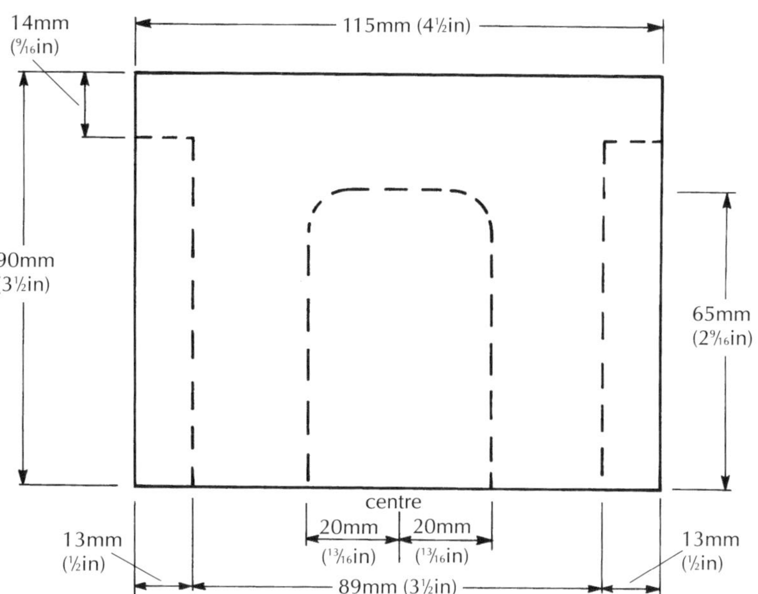

Fireplace back panel: cutting lines.

3. Stick this onto the panel as in the diagram, using nitrile adhesive.
4. Cut four suitable lengths of dowel and trim the tops so that they fit underneath the overlap of the moulding. Stick them in position with nitrile adhesive.
5. Trim the panel to match the angle of the picture-frame moulding.
6. Sand all edges smooth.
7. Fill any cavities, then decorate according to taste.

CHIMNEY BREASTS

Parts involved:
Chimney-breast fronts (6mm/¼in MDF); chimney-breast sides (9mm/⅜in) MDF).

For each:
1. Cut panels to size according to the height of each room.
2. Stick the chimney-breast front onto the chimney-breast sides, with the side edges against the back of the breast panel.
3. Position the fireplace centrally on the front of the chimney breast and mark the cut-out (grate) area. Remove the fireplace and slice away this grate area from the breast, allowing an extra 6mm (¼in) all round.

FITTING CHIMNEY BREASTS/FIREPLACES TO ROOMS

1. Decorate the chimney breast and fireplace according to taste.
2. Stick the fireplace to the chimney breast, using nitrile adhesive.

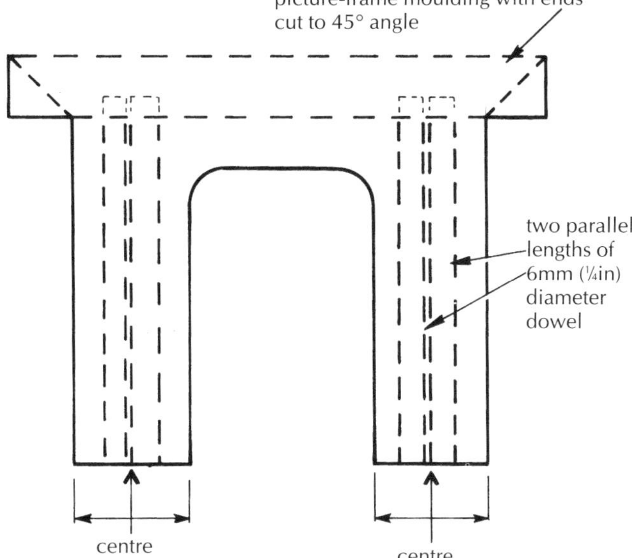

Construction of the fireplace.

3. Stick the chimney breast onto the centre of the largest wall of the room (*see* photographs of the finished house at start of chapter).

DESIGN PROBLEM

As may be noticed, the fireplaces do not line up with the chimneys. This is because the fireplaces could not be viewed to their best advantage if fitted to the side walls, and equally the chimneys would not be seen behind the main roof if fitted in the logical place. The Mary Foster house design ignores this difficulty, and it is the kind of detail which is unlikely to be noticed, or which would be construed as artistic licence. However, the constructor may wish to add chimneys at the back of the house, or to alter the fireplace position.

STAIRS AND BANISTERS

Parts involved:
Stair sides and back panels (6mm/¼in MDF); 19 × 19mm (¾ × ¾in) batten (treads); piano wire (rails); 9mm (⅜in) diameter dowel (handrails).

1. Make the stairs in the usual way (see Chapter 3, Techniques). Two banister and stair assemblies are required.
2. Cut pieces of piano wire, 70mm (2¾in) long. There should be one for each step.
3. Indent a mark with a bradawl centrally on the edge of each step, into the edge of the MDF.
4. Drill 2mm (³⁄₃₂in) holes where marked, to a depth of approximately 4mm (³⁄₁₆in).
5. Cut a 350mm (13¾in) length of dowel: this is for the handrail.
6. Mark a pencil line along one side of the dowel.
7. Mark the exact position of the holes along the side of the stair panel, as in the diagram above.
8. Holding the handrail as in the diagram, continue the pencil lines on the side of the stairs

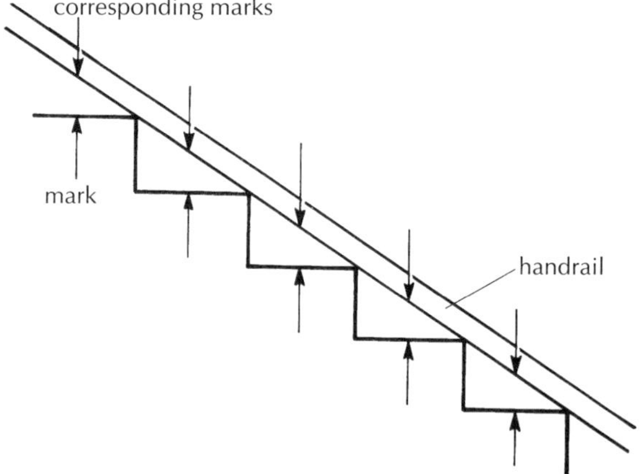

Staircase: method of establishing the correct hole positions.

CUTTING PIANO WIRE

Piano wire is extraordinarily hard and brittle, since its surface is hardened steel. It is possible to cut it using the special side cutter facility incorporated in some pliers; a hacksaw is useless as the blade is not hard enough. An easier way of cutting piano wire is to score the surface with a grinding wheel, after which the piece will easily snap off with pliers. Grinding wheels for cutting metal can be obtained for use with an electric drill. When grinding, always observe the usual safety procedures (eye/hand protection).

along the handrail until these intersect the long marked line on the dowel; these intersections are where the rails will meet the handrail's underside. Mark the dowel top and bottom.

9. After indenting these points with the bradawl, drill 2mm (3/32in) holes at right angles to a depth of only 1mm (1/16in): barely start the hole.
10. Deepen these holes to 4mm (3/16in), this time altering the angle to one that will correspond to the slope at which the rails are to meet the handrail's underside.

ADVICE

This construction can be very tricky, and occasionally it may be necessary to re-drill holes in the handrail's underside to achieve even spacing of rails.

1. It is easiest to start from the bottom, angling the handrail suitably and gently easing each rail into its hole one at a time.
2. If some rails seem too short, they can be pulled slightly upwards out of their stair hole to gain length. Epoxy resin, to be used for bonding the structure together, has gap-filling qualities and will make up for any discrepancies produced.

11. Holding the stairs in a vice, push the banister rails into their holes, then offer the handrail and insert the tops of the rails into the corresponding holes on the underside of the handrail.
12. Judge a length of handrail that is suitable and mark where to cut it off at the top and bottom.
13. Remove the handrail and cut off the excess timber.
14. Sand the top and bottom ends of the rail to take off sharp edges and produce a smooth, rounded surface. Sand off all pencil lines.
15. Holding the stairs in a vice, coat the end of each rail in epoxy resin adhesive and insert them into the stair holes.
16. After putting small amounts of epoxy resin in the reception holes in the underside of the handrail, push the handrail into place.
17. When the adhesive is dry, trim away any excess, especially from the handrail, as if the timber is to be stained and sealed, the epoxy resin will form a barrier to stain penetration. A small chisel is useful for this.
18. Decorate according to taste. The rails must be primed before painting. In the prototype, the handrail was stained and sealed to match the floorboards, the rails painted gloss black, and the stairs gloss white.

BANISTER GUARD RAIL ASSEMBLY

Two guard-rail assemblies are required for this project.

Parts involved:
9mm (3/8in) diameter dowel and piano wire.

For each:

1. Cut two lengths of 9mm-diameter (3/8in-diameter) dowel, one 85mm (3⅜in) and the other 190mm (7½in) long.
2. Cut one end of each piece to a 45° angle and stick them together in a mitre joint, using cyanoacrylate adhesive. Allow the glue to dry. This is the handrail.
3. Trim the handrail to fit the area of floor surrounding the hole for the stairs. The inner face of the handrail should correspond with the edge of the stair aperture. It may be necessary

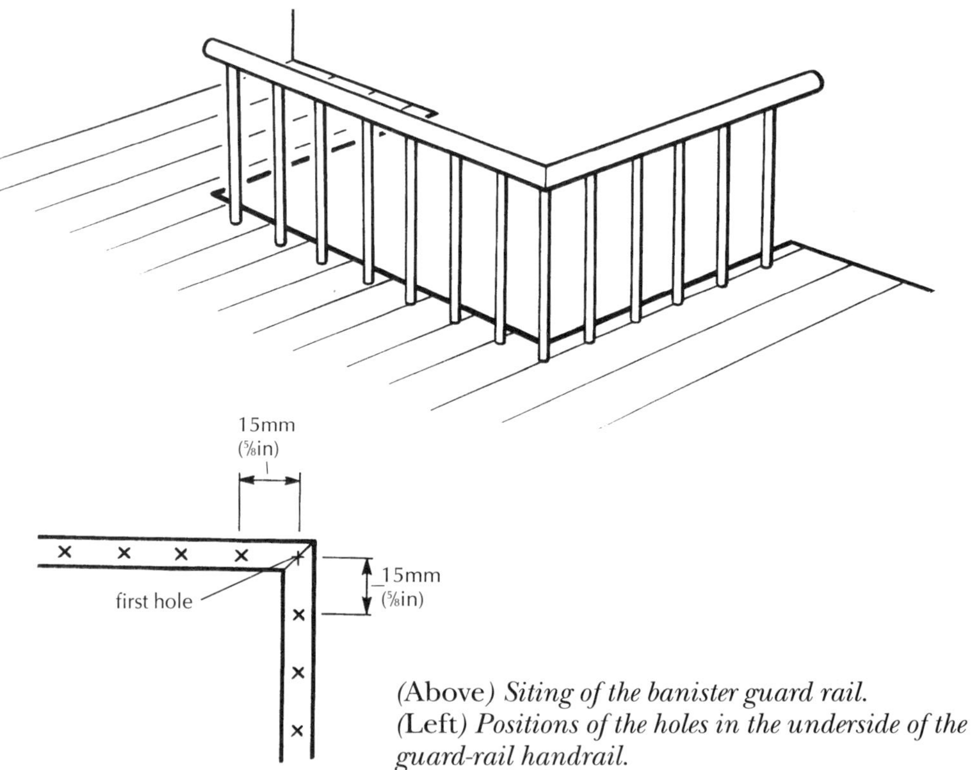

(Above) *Siting of the banister guard rail.*
(Left) *Positions of the holes in the underside of the guard-rail handrail.*

to trim the dowel to fit where it meets the door architrave.

4. Mark a pencil line along the length of the underside of both parts of the handrail.
5. Indent with a bradawl, then drill a 2mm (3/32in) hole, 4mm (3/16in) deep where the two pieces join, as in the diagram above.
6. Measuring from this point, mark, indent and drill other holes at 15mm (5/8in) intervals.
7. Denote the position of the underside holes on the outside face of the handrail with pencil marks.
8. Lay the handrail on the floor of the house, and mark the floor where the pencil marks occur.
9. Drill corresponding shallow holes in the floor of the house, using the drill chuck unscrewed from the drill (as described in the roof section for interior countersinking of screws).
10. As with the stairs, cut 70mm (2¾in) lengths of piano wire and push these into the holes in the floor. Align the handrail holes with the top of the rails and place each in their final position.
11. Dismantle the unit and prime and paint the rails the required colour; sand and stain/seal or paint the handrail; and finally stick the component parts together using epoxy resin adhesive. It may be necessary to wedge the banister assembly in its correct position until the adhesive sets, as it may have a tendency to lean sideways.

SKIRTING BOARDS

Parts involved:
13 × 1mm (½ × 3/64in) strips of timber or skirting board moulding (from a specialist dolls' house shop).

Skirting boards are best decorated in gloss (after priming and undercoating) first, then cut to size for each room, mitreing them at the corners. Finally, fill any cavities with fine filler and touch up with gloss.

FINISHING OFF

THE FRONT DOOR

Parts involved:
Front door panel (9mm/⅜in) MDF.

Trim the front door panel to size, hang it with rebated hinges, and carve it in the same way as the interior doors (*see* diagram). Decorate with a gloss finish according to taste (the prototype was red). A door knocker, as used on the prototype can be obtained from a specialist dolls' house shop. Skirting boards are not vital, but they can cover a variety of faults, and do add considerably to the quality of the finished house. If construction time is short, this is the kind of job that can be delayed until later.

FASTENING OF FRONT-OPENING SECTIONS

A hook and eye was used on the prototype, holding the FSR section to the ground-floor ceiling, and accessible from the front-door opening (for the method, refer to Chapter 4, The Country Cottage). A large magnetic catch may be preferred as a fixing device, sited in the same place.

DECORATING THE TRIANGULAR PEDIMENT AREA

The decorations for this panel comprise:

Central circle – a button or brooch, or a plaster cast made from either.
Outer circle – part of a metal buckle; or could be made from air-hardening clay.
'Stem' on which leaves are placed – string.
Leaves – made from air-hardening clay.
Berries – as above.

Central circle
To reproduce a button or brooch in plaster, first make a rough cube with clay, big enough to press the item into, then press it onto a flat surface so that it will stand firmly. Rub some washing-up liquid or vaseline on to the article to be reproduced, then press it, face down, to only its own depth, into the clay. Leave until the clay is hard, then carefully lift out the item. Mix some dental plaster (or plaster of Paris – available from chemists) with some water to the consistency of thick

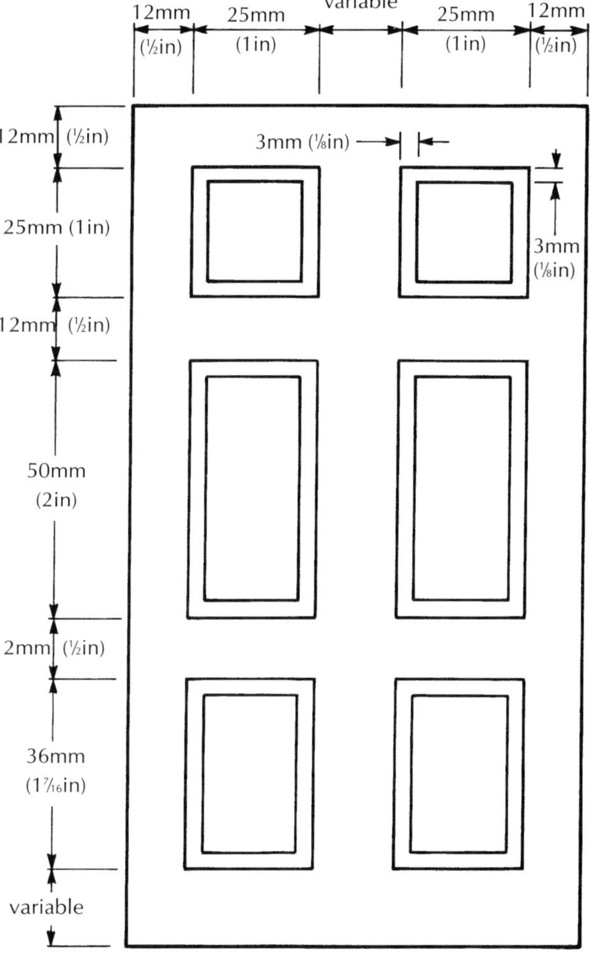

Front door: measurements for carving the panels.

cream. Pour this into the clay mould and leave to set. Remove the plaster reproduction when set and put aside to dry thoroughly. If a button or brooch original is used, it will be necessary to remove any metal parts from the back surface, so that the article will lie flat.

Decorating triangular pediment area.

Outer circle

If a suitable buckle cannot be found, this item can be made from a piece of air-hardening clay rolled into a narrow cylinder and positioned around something circular, such as a jar lid, which is approximately 45mm (1¾in) in diameter. Join the ends and mark leaves on the surface with a bodkin or knitting needle. Leave it to set before fixing.

Bond above two components in place, using nitrile adhesive.

Stem

Dampen a piece of string so that it lies flat, then arrange it as in the drawing opposite and stick it in position, using PVA adhesive.

Leaves

Roll out some clay as thinly as possible, but ensure that it is thick enough to be handled without tearing. From this, cut out the leaves in various sizes. If you find this difficult, leaves intended for decorating cakes or small leaves found in the garden can be laid on the clay as templates. After the clay has dried, arrange the leaves as required, gluing them in place with nitrile adhesive.

Berries

These are simply small balls of clay. Small wooden beads could be used to equally good effect. They are bonded in place with nitrile adhesive.

EXTERIOR PAINTING

After filling and sanding smooth all the cavities and blemishes, prime and finish the sides, back and chimneys with a matt emulsion finish, the same colour as the front (the prototype was sand). The matt roof colour (the prototype was grey) should contrast with the chosen main house colour and ought to correspond with suitable colours of tile. The picture-frame moulding around the triangular pediment and above the FSR and FSL should be picked out in the colour of the WUs, as should the pillars and triangular surround of the entrance portico. Painting the decoration on the triangular pediment in this colour makes it stand out well from the background.

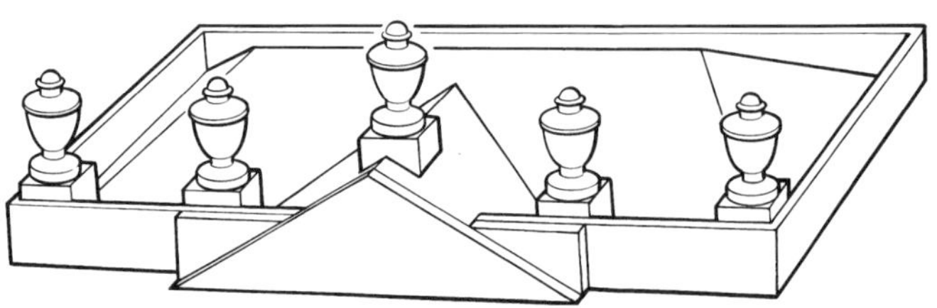

Fixing finials in position.

CHAPTER **seven**

Interiors

This chapter is intended to indicate what is possible, and to give an idea of the kind of products that are generally available for decorating, furnishing and lighting interiors. No specific projects are detailed as in other chapters, but brief descriptions of procedures, materials and some specialist tools for making furniture are given.

SPECIALIST DOLLS' HOUSE SHOPS

The products that the dolls'-house craftsperson is very likely to buy are various raw materials for specific projects: for example, lighting kits and fittings and wallpapers. In addition, retailers stock a wide range of incredibly realistic miniature artefacts made to scale, some of which are listed below.

Such fixtures as baths and washbasins are available from dolls'-house shops in many styles and colours. Taps, and waste-pipes in brass or white metal are also available. Miniature Victorian bathroom suites in fine ceramic decorated with tiny flowers and with matching fittings are available, as is a replica of the authentic tin bath that hung behind the door of a miner's kitchen.

A social historian could reproduce in miniature a Victorian or Edwardian kitchen complete with mangle, washboard, copper and earthenware sink, for all these items can be bought. For the dolls'-house kitchen, white-metal kits can be bought for ranges, stoves, period fireplaces or modern cookers and many other appliances. Instructions for painting and assembly (using epoxy resin or cyanoacrylate adhesive) come with the kit.

In the UK there are some excellent dolls' house magazines on general sale, where such shops advertise; if making a visit to a specialist supplier is not possible, many of them produce catalogues and sell by mail order.

Many articles can be made using a modicum of ingenuity: air-hardening clay, of the type used for flagstones and brickwork for the Tudor house, can be utilized to make larger 'ceramic' articles such as sinks, whereas the heat-hardening type of clay (which is dried in an oven) is more suitable for tiny items, for example plates and chinaware. Pictures can be made from cuttings from magazines, or even from a decorative postage-stamp.

SOME ITEMS AVAILABLE FROM SPECIALIST DOLLS'-HOUSE SHOPS

Ceramic or plastic baths, washbasins and WCs in all styles and colours • Kitchenware: utensils, pots and pans, china etc • Ornaments of all kinds • Mirrors and paintings • White-metal kits for making ranges, stoves or modern cookers • Fireplaces • Doorknobs, door handles, finger plates, door knockers and letter-boxes • Turned wooden items such as banister rails, bedposts and table legs • Moulded wooden skirting boards • Dado rails and cornices • Lighting accessories • Wallpapers • All kinds of ready-made furniture, as well as furniture kits

DECORATION OF INTERIORS

The 1:12 scale should be adhered to throughout, in order to match the scale of the house. This is the standard scale used by collectors worldwide.

WALLS

A wide selection of dolls' house wallpapers with small patterns or Regency stripes is available. If painted walls are preferred (as the houses in this book have been treated), matt emulsion can be used; and, for economy, small sample tins of paint can be bought from some DIY shops.

It is wiser to wallpaper the interior of rooms after construction, even though this calls for patience and tenacity. In some cases it may be possible to paper the walls prior to final construction, but problems can arise where patterns have to be matched, glue may ooze across the paper from joints during final assembly and gaps between walls and ceiling cannot be filled successfully. Use ordinary wallpaper paste, which allows the paper to 'slide' before final positioning, and prime the bare wood or MDF first.

Wallpapering technique

1. Make a paper template for each wall, and use it to cut the wallpaper (allowing extra on each side for the back walls).
2. Apply a thin coat of paste to the walls, then to the back of the wallpaper pieces.
3. Fix paper to the back wall first, lapping 13mm (½in) on either side around the corners onto the side walls.
4. Fix paper to the side walls, butting right up to the corners. Check that ceiling and floor edges are straight, and that patterns are correctly matched.
5. Smooth the paper surface with soft cloth or cotton wool to eliminate air bubbles.
6. Affix (painted) skirting boards if these are required.

Other wall-coverings

Dados (borders to run along the top of the walls) can be made with narrow braiding or lace edging, available from haberdashery (notions) departments or shops which sell fabrics.

Fabrics: These can be used extremely effectively for wall-coverings. A fabric adhesive should be used, preferably one that dries clear. If the fabric is thin, it can be stiffened by using an iron-on backing of the lightest grade, available from most fabric or upholstery shops.

Wainscoting

Wainscoting (wood panelling covering the lower half of a wall) can be replicated using wood veneer, its top edge finished off with a piece of suitably stained timber moulding.

CEILINGS

These can be papered with embossed wallpaper – if the design is small enough – and then painted. A ceiling for a Georgian or Victorian house could have a ceiling rose, moulded cornice and various other decorative ceiling mouldings available from dolls' house shops. The procedure for applying timber ceiling beams for Tudor houses is described in Chapter 5, The Tudor House.

FLOORS

These may be tiled, using air-hardening clay as described for the Tudor house, or carved to represent floorboards as described for all the houses. To save time and effort, wooden plank flooring can be bought and stained a suitable colour.

Vinyl self-adhesive tiles can be used to create a chequerboard pattern by buying, for example, one black and one white tile, cutting each into 25mm (1in) or 13mm (½in) squares and laying them alternately. Dark blue and white would be suitable for a kitchen. The thinnest vinyl tiles should be bought for this purpose.

SUITABLE FABRICS

SOFT FURNISHINGS

Lightweight fabrics are the most suitable, and, for upholstery, material with a slight stretch is easier to work with. Patterns should be very small. A useful test, say, for a floral pattern, is to measure the largest flower. A flower measuring only 13mm (½in) in diameter would be representative of 150mm (6in) in actual size. This may be acceptable – some chintzes have quite large flowers – but it is wise to check.

CARPETS

Furnishing velvet is ideal. Have the pile running towards the front of the house so that the texture shows. As velvet tends to fray easily, use the spray sold for the purpose of preventing fraying, applying it around the raw edges. Fur fabric with a short pile, or sheepskin can be cut to suitable shapes for fireside or bedside rugs. Wool fabric or felt can also be used for carpets.

Stair carpets can be of felt, woollen cloth or velvet. The main problem with stair carpets is making the edges neat, where a hem down both sides would be too bulky. The spray-on solution for preventing fraying is useful here, applied along the edges on the reverse side of the material. Best of all, if a suitable braid can be found, of the correct width, the problem is solved.

CURTAINS (DRAPES)

The material for these needs to be soft, lightweight and natural, such as cotton or silk; it is very difficult to make synthetic fabrics hang gracefully.

A small curtain pole can be made from a cocktail stick, some thin dowelling or a piece of metal rod (obtainable from a model shop). This is suspended from two small 'eyes' or two small nails with their heads projecting to hold the rod. A hem wide enough to thread the rod through is made at the top of the curtains, and a wooden bead can be affixed to each end of the rod. Note that if the window is narrow it could be almost obliterated by the curtains, in which case the curtain pole can be made longer to stretch further across the wall on either side of the window. The curtains can then hang partly across the wall. Make sure that neither curtains nor rod ends are positioned across wall divisions when the house's opening front is closed.

FURNITURE

Furniture of every kind from miniature copies of 'priceless' antiques, to everyday modern items can be bought. The more detailed pieces, especially musical instruments, are exquisite, but expensive.

A dolls' house can be adequately equipped with more simple furniture, easily made. Kitchen and bedroom furniture can be reasonably straightforward: for instance, a wooden refectory table and chairs can be made from offcuts of 6mm (¼in) plywood and timber mouldings that are readily available in softwood or ramin. Modern beds can be made from plywood, and impressive four-posters and half-testers can be produced from similar materials, with curtains, and decorative mouldings added to the headboard. Kitchen cabinets and cupboards present more of a challenge, as does a Welsh dresser. Upholstered furniture can be made from offcuts of plywood or MDF. First of all these are assembled with screws, then taken apart and covered in padding and material, and the unit finally reassembled. Padding for dolls'-house furniture is usually synthetic wadding, called batting, or 6mm (¼in) or 13mm (½in) foam.

Scraps of velvet will make cushions, small lengths of lace make curtains (drapes) for a four-poster or half-tester bed, oddments of silk make bedspreads, while scraps of fine lawn make sheets. Coloured string salvaged from Christmas-present wrappings become tie-backs for curtains.

For finer or more detailed wooden pieces some more specialist equipment is necessary, and hardwood must be used. Examples of suitable hardwoods are mahogany, boxwood, walnut, yew, beech and lime; these can be obtained from timber suppliers as offcuts.

Any piece of furniture can be re-created in miniature, from fine Hepplewhite chairs and gateleg tables with barley-sugar turned legs to bureaux, davenports and desks with opening drawers. For those who are interested in this kind of intricate work, a list is given below of some of the extra tools that are required. Plans for furniture are normally scaled-down drawings of full-size pieces. The shapes of the constituent parts are transferred to the timber using carbon paper.

If the timber is to be stained, this should be done before assembly as PVA adhesive that may ooze from joints will prevent even absorption of the dye. Hardwood furniture is finished off with beeswax polish, buffed to a shine.

TOOLS FOR MAKING FINELY DETAILED FURNITURE

Razor saw: very fine saw for cutting to a high degree of accuracy • Miniature try-square: the kind designed for metal engineering • Miniature mitre box • Small clamps • Scalpel knives • Cutting board or mat • Tiny drills • Needle files • Miniature chisels • Tweezers (various sizes) • Fret saw • Syringe with curved nozzle: for applying drops of adhesive accurately • Useful but not vital: Miniature drill, ideally with lathe attachment

LIGHTING

Nowadays every conceivable type of light fitting is replicated to scale, along with the shades to match. Special lights can be installed in fireplace units so as to give the impression of a flickering fire beneath imitation coals. Gas and oil lamps, candles and chandeliers are all available. Whatever the period of house, from Tudor to modern, lighting that is in keeping with the style can be put in, utilizing accessories such as wall lamps, and table, desk and standard lamps. These accessories are expensive, however, because of the incredible detail involved.

It is, of course, possible to make or adapt other items for shades and lighting units. Those with engineering or ceramic skills will have ideas of their own, as will anyone experienced in needlework. The lighting units themselves and the shades are the most expensive items, so anyone making their own fittings need only buy the transformer, the wire or tape, and the sockets and bulbs.

BASIC PRINCIPLES

1. Lighting kits are available from specialist dolls'-house and model shops, as are the individual items.
2. **A 12V transformer is always used to step down the voltage from the mains supply: never connect dolls'-house lighting circuits direct to the mains plug.**

3. Lights to each room are connected either in series (so that they are all on at the same time) or in parallel (they can be individually switched on and off at switches in each room or at a separate location).
4. The low-voltage power is conducted to wall and ceiling lights and/or socket points via either specially thin conductor wire, or else double copper conductor tape, which has a self-adhesive backing for fixing to wall and ceiling surfaces.
5. Bulbs are replaceable and of a low voltage, and come in candle or spherical shapes. Alternatively, 'grain-of-wheat' type bulbs can be used, and these have wire already attached to them – which poses problems when one needs replacing.
6. A test probe is a useful tool for checking if power is present at any given point in the circuit.
7. 'Plug sockets' can be fitted inside rooms, so that desk lamps and table lamps can be plugged in as required.
8. Free-standing lamps can also be plugged directly into the conductor tape, using special twin-pronged plugs which are made to spike through the copper conductor tapes at any chosen point.
9. The wire is joined by soldering, or, if tape is used, special brass connector nails are made to punch through the overlapped pieces: these ensure continuity of current flow.

Concealing Wire or Tape

The biggest difficulty lies in concealing the wire or tape successfully. In a Tudor house it is less of a problem as there are likely to be ceiling beams behind which the wire or tape can be hidden.

Wallpaper may conceal conductor tape. Alternatively, a narrow groove can be cut in the ceiling and/or wall to accept the wire, and the surface then made good with filler and finally painted or papered.

Sockets should be positioned as unobtrusively as possible, preferably towards the back of the room.

TYPES OF LIGHT AVAILABLE

Tiffany hanging lamp, with shades of assorted colours • Black-metal hanging paraffin lamp, white shade • Two- and three-armed chandeliers, with tulip shades • Single and double wall lights, also with tulip shades • Single and double candle wall lights • Standard light with three tulip shades • Double desk light • Victorian-style brass-metal table oil lamp, with opaque shade and glass funnel • Electrified brass lamps • Street light • Candles (wired as for lamps) • Exterior lamp (square, glazed-box type) • Modern-style, dome-ceiling lights • Oil lamp suspended from ceiling • Flickering fire units for fireplaces

FINALLY

This is only a very brief guide to lighting, intended as a quick reference source. Each electrification project is unique, and decisions as to the number and type of light for each room are essentially personal. Dependent on the chosen position of the different lights is the layout of the wiring, or runs of tape. As a general rule, the wiring runs from walls and/or ceilings towards the back of the house, where it is passed through a hole and transferred downwards to a main flex which connects to the transformer output. Disguising these wires at the back of the house is not as important as those inside, since they are in a far less prominent position.

INDEX